TEJANO ORIGINS IN EIGHTEENTH-CENTURY SAN ANTONIO

T0349907

TEJANO ORIGINS IN EIGHTEENTH-CENTURY SAN ANTONIO

Edited by

Gerald E. Poyo and Gilberto M. Hinojosa

Illustrated by José Cisneros

Published by the University of Texas Press, Austin
for
The University of Texas Institute of Texan Cultures at San Antonio

*For the makers of colonial San Antonio, their historians,
and those who have kept alive the traditions
of Spanish and Mexican Texas*

Copyright © 1991 by The University of Texas Institute of Texan Cultures
at San Antonio

Printed in the United States of America

First paperback printing, 1995

Requests for permission to reproduce material from this work should be sent to
Permissions, University of Texas Press, Box 7819, Austin, Texas 78713-7819.

⊗ The paper used in this publication meets the minimum requirements of American National Standard for Information Sciences—Permanence of Paper for Printed Library Materials, ANSI Z39.48-1984.

Library of Congress Cataloging-in-Publication Data
Tejano origins in eighteenth-century San Antonio / edited by Gerald E. Poyo and
Gilberto M. Hinojosa ; illustrated by José Cisneros. — 1st ed.

    p.   cm.
  Includes bibliographical references and index.
  ISBN 0-292-76566-5 (alk. paper)
  1. San Antonio (Tex.)—History. 2. Spaniards—Texas—San Antonio—History—
18th century. 3. Indians of North America—Texas—San Antonio—History—18th
century. 4. Mexicans—Texas—San Antonio—History—18th century. I. Poyo,
Gerald Eugene, 1950- . II. Hinojosa, Gilberto Miguel, 1942- . III. University
of Texas Institute of Texan Cultures at San Antonio.
F394.S2T43 1991
976.4'3510046872–dc20   90-47345

ACKNOWLEDGMENTS

This book is evidence of the enthusiasm displayed during the last several years by many people interested in better understanding the relevance of the history of Spain and Mexico in the regions that now constitute the United States Southwest. In 1986 The University of Texas Institute of Texan Cultures at San Antonio (ITC) sought funding from the Texas Committee for the Humanities (TCH) for a symposium, exhibit, and book project focusing on community development and identity in a Spanish Borderlands region. A challenge grant from TCH was matched by the Kathryn O'Connor Foundation of Victoria, the City of San Antonio Arts and Cultural Affairs Office, and the Valero Energy Corporation.

These institutions made the project possible, but it was the enthusiastic support from San Antonio's community organizations which made the symposium a great success. The Canary Islands Descendants Association, the Bexareños, the Granaderos de Gálvez, and the Guadalupe Cultural Arts Center

v

all provided support of one kind or another, but, perhaps most significant, their members filled the symposium hall at ITC. They welcomed our speakers, who contributed excellent presentations and cooperated in preparing their papers for inclusion in this volume. Insightful and encouraging comments and criticisms by discussants Oakah T. Jones, Jr., and David Johnson gave direction to the revision process for publication. Although not part of the program, David J. Weber has consistently encouraged us in our work, and we would like to acknowledge his help here.

We also want to express special recognition to John Leal, Bexar County archivist, who over the years has, in his own quiet but consistent way, provided invaluable research guidance; to José Cisneros of El Paso for his drawings of eighteenth-century Béxar in this volume; and to the ITC volunteers who helped on numerous fronts, especially in processing much of the census data used in at least two of the articles.

The Institute of Texan Cultures itself should also be commended for its unflagging support of the project. To our knowledge, no other institution in the state has, in recent years, contributed as many resources to public programming and primary research on Spanish Texas as has the Institute. This volume reflects only a portion of that effort.

CONTENTS

Northeastern New Spain

INTRODUCTION

"The story of Texas can never be complete without the story of her original founders – the Tejanos," declared Andrew A. Tijerina, one of several Mexican-American historians who began tracing their communal roots two decades or so ago.[1] Since that time scholars have written considerably about Tejanos and their heritage. But synthesizing their history is a formidable task, for indeed, a cursory review of the history of Mexican settlers of Spanish-Indian-African ancestry who have resided in Texas since the early eighteenth century reveals a tremendous diversity of experience. Tejano history encompasses a chronological span of some 250 years. It crosses four sovereignties; involves the reorientation of many Coahuilan, Tamaulipan, and New Mexican communities to a Texas identity during the nineteenth century, and includes the birth of new communities established by Mexican immigrants, particularly in the twentieth century. Each of these experiences produced unique communal identities, but at the same time the various communities shared a sense of separateness from the broader society that allows scholars to speak of a Tejano identity. Though identity is a difficult concept to define, its expression ultimately comes from people in their communal settings. The clues about a people's identity are found in the internal economic, social, political, and cultural workings of their communities. Thus, the concepts of community and identity are intimately linked, and it is through the vehicle of community studies that scholars will eventually synthesize Tejano history. Such studies will reveal the diversity of Tejano history and will also point to the areas of commonality that have historically produced a shared sense of Tejano identity.[2]

The Historiography of Neglect

The task of interpreting Tejano history is still in its formative stage, since the field has suffered from a long tradition of scholarly neglect. Only in recent years have scholars begun to examine Tejano community history in some detail. This historic lack of concern for the enduring Tejano civilization is particularly disturbing in light of the prominent role Mexican settlers have played in the state's development since the early eighteenth century.

The pattern of neglect of Tejano communities is evident in Texas historiography as early as the eighteenth century. One of the first histories of Texas, penned in 1783 by Father Juan Agustín Morfi, paid scant attention to the workings of the civil communities. Revealing attitudes prevalent among Europeans of the day, Morfi implied that little could be expected from the inhabitants since they descended "from the lowest classes." He observed that "[the] population [of San Fernando de Béxar, the province's principal settlement] is made up of [Canary] islanders and families from the country [New Spain, who] . . . are indolent and given to vice, and do not deserve the blessings of the land." The work's tone leaves the impression that the province's civil communities were insignificant and that without the missions Hispanic civilization would never have taken root in Texas.[3]

Later Mexican authorities also offered critical judgments about Texas communities. One official, José María Sánchez, who accompanied General Manuel Mier y Terán on a visita in 1828, demonstrated scant sympathy for the hardships inherent in frontier life, particularly the difficulties imposed by Indian hostilities, demographic stagnation, and government-created economic limitations. Instead Sánchez blamed the slow economic progress in Texas on the laziness of the inhabitants, who, he claimed, spent their time on amusements. Not content with this blanket indictment, Sánchez even criticized the settlers for not speaking Spanish properly.[4] Generations of historians relied on these generalizations and accepted the prejudiced judgments of the visiting Spanish and Mexican officials at face value.

This is particularly evident in the treatment of early Texas by Anglo-American historians, who contributed their own biased assumptions. These chroniclers depicted Spanish and Mexican communities as inconsequential and considered their contributions of little enduring value. In 1855 Henderson P. Yoakum described Tejano society as simple and unresourceful, explaining that in 1806 the population of San Antonio de Béxar "was made up of Spaniards, creoles, and a few French, Americans, civilized Indians, and half-breeds . . . [whose] habits were wandering, the most of them being engaged in hunting buffaloes and wild horses." Yoakum had little more to say about San Antonio society except that "the people, having no care of politics, passed their leisure time in playing at games, in dancing, and in conversing, mostly upon one of the subjects of money, women, or horses."[5]

Minimizing the contributions of Spanish and Mexican settlers in Texas served not only to justify the separation of the province from Mexico but also to deny their descendants full membership in post-1836 Texas society. Writing at the start of the twentieth century, Texas historian George P. Garrison failed even to acknowledge the existence of a Tejano society. "The Spanish explorers were daring, energetic, and persistent enough for any undertaking," he observed, "but the conquistador was not backed up by the settler, and the officials could not organize a compact political and social system from native material alone." In sum, Garrison regarded Spain's "grasp" of the area "too weak for permanence."[6] Even as recently as 1983, popular Texas historian T.R. Fehrenbach dismissed the Tejano experience as marginal to Texas history. Despite admitting that "Texas is far less homogeneous than its image," Fehrenbach concludes that "the roots of Modern Texas lie in the British Isles."[7]

Stirrings of Interest in Tejano History

Fortunately not all North American scholars accepted this fundamentally negative view of Hispanic influence on Texas. During the late nineteenth and early twentieth centuries some historians created a formal academic field of study known as the Spanish Borderlands. A host of scholars and history enthusiasts produced works that examined many aspects of Mexican-American society, including economics, politics, and folklore, though communities were not systematically analyzed. Despite some shortcomings, these studies drew academic and public attention to the origins and development of Hispanic society in Texas and created the foundation for a subsequent focus on Tejano communities.

The Spanish Borderlands scholars were the first to counteract the earlier neglect of Spain's role in Texas and the United States. Offering a competing interpretation of Hispanic traditions, they were determined to overturn the anti-Spanish, derogatory images and accounts set by earlier historians. To this end, Hubert Howe Bancroft, Herbert Eugene Bolton, Carlos E. Castañeda, Charles W. Hackett, Odie B. Faulk, and a score of others meticulously described the exploration and settlement of the former Spanish possessions. They produced a substantial and important literature on the northern frontier provinces, including Texas, and revived interest in the area's colonial past. But they were primarily interested in geopolitical questions and in the development of frontier institutions, and their coverage of the communities themselves was inadequate. Further-more, with the notable exception of Castañeda, these scholars did not attempt to link the Spanish era into subsequent periods and processes.[8]

At the same time that these researchers published prodi-giously on the colonial period, a number of scholars from a variety of other disciplines, journalists, and Mexican-American activists began to take a serious interest in the various aspects of the Tejano communities of the nineteenth and twentieth centuries. Among the first was economist Paul S. Taylor, who, during the 1920s and 1930s, focused on Mexican and Mexican-American workers in the United States. Placed in a historical context and based on extensive interviewing, Taylor's analysis of Hispanic laboring communities in Nueces County remains a fundamental source for any consideration of the Tejano ex-perience.[9] Relying heavily on Taylor's work, journalist Carey McWilliams produced, some twenty years later, a widely used and influential overview of Mexican-American history that included the Tejano experience.[10]

Scholars interested in the cultural traditions of turn-of-the-century South Texans also contributed to the growing body of literature on Tejanos. Fascinated by Texas cowboy tradition and folklore, J. Frank Dobie turned to the vaqueros with whom he had grown up and uncovered a wealth of humanistic values and folkways that previous observers had not considered important enough to record. Dobie labored assiduously to cap-ture the Mexican dimension of what appeared to him to be a passing era, and, despite a patronizing view, he inspired other folklorists and anthropologists to look beyond the Anglo-American traditions of the state.[11]

In another field O. Douglas Weeks analyzed political be-havior in counties along the Rio Grande in the early twentieth century. In studying the 1920s Weeks discovered that early Anglo-American leaders in the region adopted the political styles of many Tejano politicos. Armed with this understanding of Mexican influences on politics, subsequent scholars were

better prepared to study South Texas leadership and voting patterns. The result has been the emergence of an image of Tejanos
as active participants in determining their destinies.[12]

Midcentury immigrant communities did not fare as positively under the scrutiny of sociologists. Following strictly the
conventions of their field, these scholars produced "scientific"
studies of Mexican-American communities in South Texas.
While purporting to be objective, most of these sociologists in
fact tacitly accepted the stereotypes of the day. They blamed
conditions in the barrios on the "cultural deficiencies" of new
immigrants rather than on economic conditions and realities.
Furthermore, failing to note the social and political activism
of the neighborhood residents, these sociologists depicted
Tejanos as tradition-bound and passive.[13] Despite a limited,
culturally biased perspective, these scholars sought to capture
the socioeconomic forces within the local community, an approach that others who viewed the Mexican-American experience more positively had not attempted.

Other history enthusiasts, anthropologists, and barrio
activists did not accept the portrayal offered by sociologists of
a passive Mexican-American community. Frederick C. Chabot,
for example, researched the genealogical roots of the "makers"
of San Antonio; local San Antonio community leader and attorney Rubén Rendón Lozano identified many of the Tejanos who
took arms against Mexico during the Texas rebellion; historian
and folklorist Jovita González studied the vibrant community
life and folkways of South Texan Hispanics; and community
activist Alonzo Perales defended Tejano heritage.[14] These observers emphasized Hispanic contributions to the state and to
the larger North American society from Spanish colonial days
to their day.

An Emergent Tejano Community History

The pioneering Spanish Borderlands histories and the early studies of Mexican-American barrios provided a good foundation for a post-World War II explosion in research that led
to the first specific analyses of Tejano communities. Utilizing

new methodologies of the social sciences and influenced by a rich body of historical research on Latin America, scholars produced numerous publications on a variety of issues and topics related to Tejanos.

Though not specifically focused on Tejano history, several works have provided useful methodological and contextual information within which to understand the birth and development of Tejano communities. Perhaps the most useful of these is a recent publication by Thomas D. Hall, which traces the social changes in southwestern societies as they came into contact with differing socioeconomic systems from the 1300s through the 1800s. Hall depicts dynamic and diverse communities, including some in Texas, which, though overwhelmed by outside forces, survived by adapting to changing conditions. Some communities were more successful than others in adapting to change, and those that endured found themselves in a new role as ethnic communities when they became part of the United States.[15]

What became of the Tejano communities after 1836 is the focus of important studies by Arnoldo De León and David Montejano.[16] Approaching the topic from a regional perspective, the two authors focus on diversity within Tejano society, but they also point to the similarities of historical experience that allow scholars to speak of a Tejano identity. Indeed, Anglo-American expansionism of the 1840s converted Mexican settlements from El Paso to Victoria and Laredo to Brownsville into Tejano communities. During the second half of the century, the significantly larger and more heterogeneous population was bound together by their shared historical experience in the Spanish and Mexican past, by their relationship with the northeastern Mexican frontier, by their encounter with United States expansionism, and by their specific relationships as part of Texas.

De León's and Montejano's syntheses grew out of the surge of interest in Tejano history sparked by the civil rights and Chicano movements. During this period scholars in many fields examined records that yielded cultural and socioeconomic data not previously mined. Américo Paredes was among the fore-runners of the new scholarship. Heir of activist academicians like George I. Sánchez, Paredes countered the prevalent image of passive Tejanos by describing how South Texans resisted the efforts of the dominant culture to suppress their way of life and how they formed resilient and enduring communities. Following Paredes's lead, scholars in several disciplines turned their attention to Tejano history and culture. A number of an-thropologists produced work on corridos (ballads), legends, and folkways such as curanderismo (healing). Others, like José Li-món, researched early community organizational efforts such as Laredo's 1911 Congreso Mexicanista, through which Tejanos sought to protect their legal and cultural rights. Limón's work encouraged others to study mutualista societies, the G.I. Forum, the League of United Latin American Citizens (LULAC), the community protest movements of the 1930s that recruited the assistance of the Mexican consuls, La Raza Unida Party, and Mexican-American labor.[17]

De León's study formulated explicitly what many of these studies demonstrated implicitly, that "although Tejanos lived in a markedly different world after 1836, things were not catastrophic." While he acknowledged that "white intrusion had disturbed their old communities," De León observed that Te-janos "retained their 'Mexicanness', " maintained old traditions and beliefs, promoted their ways, and survived quite well de-spite a very hostile environment. At the same time De León argued that Tejanos defied easy categorization: "the variety of work [Tejanos] performed, the diversity of positions they oc-cupied, the difference in achievement, the degree that set apart the literate from the illiterate, the politicized from the unin-terested one, the pious and the nominal Catholics, the believers in curanderos and the skeptics, and other contrasts argue well for an image of a heterogeneous community."[18] Despite all these differences, De León clearly linked these communities together under a specific Tejano identity.

The diversity of experience again emerged as a central theme for Tejanos in Montejano's recent study. This wide-ranging synthesis described how urban and rural Tejano communities fared after the imposition of Anglo-American political and economic rule. Montejano traced capitalist development in South Texas since 1836 and showed its impact on relationships between Anglos and Mexicans. In doing this he offered important clues as to what forces created a shared Tejano identity among diverse Mexican communities. A common Mexican heritage in an Anglo-dominated society, similar hardships stemming from discrimination and exploitation, and ethnic solidarity founded on a struggle to attain equal rights all contributed to a heightened sense of Tejano identity, despite very real differences among and within communities in class, race, and local traditions.

While De León's and Montejano's broad syntheses demonstrate that Tejano diversity and shared identity have existed side-by-side, specific studies of communities reveal the same phenomenon. Perhaps the most important work of a specific Tejano community is Mario T. García's description of the Mexican barrio of El Paso from 1880 through 1920. Focusing on the community's economic, social, cultural, and political composition, García detailed the forces at work in the birth and development of a post-1836 Tejano community. Mexican immigrants to El Paso represented different economic classes, expressed varying political ideals, brought many cultural traditions, and were even of different racial backgrounds. Nevertheless, through various integrative political and socioeconomic processes, the Mexican barrio pulled together and formed a coherent and distinct society within El Paso.[19]

García's study describes a community that emerged out of an immigrant experience, but Tejano historiography must also take into account communities that made the transition from being part of the dominant society in the Spanish and Mexican periods to becoming ethnic communities within the United States. While the desirability of such a goal may seem self-evident, in fact only in recent years have scholars of Mexican-American history paid much attention to the Spanish- and Mexican-period origins of the Hispanic communities of the Southwest. For Chicano historians writing in the 1960s and 1970s about their recent history, the large body of Spanish Borderlands literature seemed irrelevant at best because, as Juan Gómez-Quiñones noted, "The history of the Southwest is beclouded by assumptions of Spanish this and Spanish that" and "is devoid of human content." "The literature," he continued, "has information based on legal documents concerning administrative practice, architecture, laws (ideally operating) and economic trade, but there is relatively little as to the people, their values and relations as they developed over time. . . . Settlement was carried on, in the majority, by indio-mestizo-mulatto settlers. Nonetheless, upon reviewing the literature, an individual of Mexican descent can speculate, understandably, about the probability of a Machiavellian conspiracy to deny the historical presence of ancestral kin."[20]

In recent years, however, this separation (both in methodology and historiographic tradition) between Spanish- and Mexican-period studies and Mexican-American studies has diminished, and an integration is emerging. Scholars of the early period are now utilizing methodologies of social and economic history, long used by Chicano historians, to reveal the continuities of communities across sovereignties. Historians have begun to focus on the origins of Tejano society and are discovering that, despite real differences between pre- and post-1836 communities, similar patterns exist in such processes as immigration, community formation, adaptation to change, racial composition, and class structures. It is now clear that, although the early communities were affected by changes in sovereignty, they did not discard their traditions.

Gilberto M. Hinojosa's study of Laredo was an important step in demonstrating this continuity. He provided an overview of one community's struggle to respond to changing geopolitical conditions from the mid-eighteenth century under Spanish rule to the late nineteenth as part of the United States. Hinojosa analyzed the role of class and race in a changing society and described the impact of war and shifts of sovereignty on the local economy and social structure. "Despite the confluence and partial success of the [external] forces pitted against Laredo," the author noted, "Laredoans defended themselves and introduced stability and order that allowed them to hold their place in the chaparral."[21]

Specific aspects of the political and socioeconomic processes of change described by Hinojosa for Laredo have been examined more extensively in the case of Spanish and Mexican San Antonio. Demographic research by Alicia V. Tjarks and Oakah L. Jones, Jr.; studies of ranching by Sandra Myers, Robert Thonhoff, Robert Weddle, and Jack Jackson; work on Indian-Spanish relations by Elizabeth A.H. John; research on mission communities by Mardith Schuetz; and land-tenure research by Félix D. Almaráz, Jr., provide a wealth of new data on colonial Texas and San Antonio. The best synthesis to date of economic and social development of Béxar during the eighteenth century is a dissertation by Jesús F. de la Teja. [22]

While these scholars examined the Spanish era, several others have concentrated on San Antonio's Tejano community of the Mexican period (1821-1836). In a 1970 pioneering study of Mexican Texas, Fane Downs observed that "Texas historians of the 1820-1845 period have limited their work as it relates to Mexicans and Mexico to the 'official' or 'nuisance' levels: legions are the histories of foreign relations, the Revolution, and border skirmishes. But absent are works about the Bexareños and other native Texans of the era." Andrew Tijerina also studied the Tejanos during the Mexican period but focused on the links between the Spanish and Mexican periods. A more recent study by Jesús F. de la Teja and John Wheat, reprinted in this volume, provides the best brief overview of the Tejano community during the 1820s and 1830s. Their treatment vividly depicts life in the heart of Mexican Texas. When placed within David J. Weber's recent comprehensive treatment of the northern provinces under Mexican sovereignty, these studies that depict tumultuous changes and transformations experienced by the Tejano community in the 1830s and 1840s become meaningful. [23]

Origins of
the Tejano Community of San Antonio

Despite this considerable research on Spanish and Mexican Texas and San Antonio, existing studies have not delved explicitly into the processes during the colonial period that gave the community a distinct Tejano identity. Without an understanding of these colonial-period socioeconomic, cultural, and political developments, nineteenth- and twentieth-century Tejanos appear devoid of roots. The papers in this volume were written and assembled to uncover Tejano origins in the eighteenth century. Most of the essays were presented originally at a symposium at The University of Texas Institute of Texan Cultures at San Antonio; all contribute to an understanding of how San Antonio's earliest settlers built a community with a specific Tejano identity.

The Spanish settlement of San Antonio de Béxar began as several distinct communities. To ensure a stronger presence in the northeastern corner of its North American colony, between 1718 and 1731 the Spanish Crown approved the foundation of five missions and a presidio on the banks of the San Antonio River. Administered by Franciscan friars, the missions constituted independent pueblos, or towns, for Texas Indians. The military garrison established along with the missions was composed of northern Mexicans who settled and defended the frontier. Furthermore, to encourage population growth and economic development, the Crown also decreed the creation of a formal town, San Fernando de Béxar, and provided the financial assistance to settle fifty-five immigrants from the Canary Islands. Despite their physical proximity to one another and their shared allegiance to the Spanish Crown, the three principal population groups did not, as a practical matter, share similar culture, interests, or goals in 1731. Consequently, in the early years members of these institutions competed and fought one another for land, water, political authority, and Indian labor.

But, as the century progressed, economic forces, social interaction, merged political interests, and an emergent shared cultural identity drew the once-separate communities into a single body. This collection of papers demonstrates how that convergence occurred. The first contribution by Jesús F. de la Teja and John Wheat appeared originally in the *Southwestern Historical Quarterly*. This description of Béxar in the 1820s and 1830s provides a good context for considering trends in the eighteenth century from which the community emerged. De la Teja and Wheat depict the fullness of the Spanish-Mexican period of the Tejano experience.

A second contribution by de la Teja sets the stage for the development of San Antonio by tracing its early establishment and growth as a mission-presidio complex. De la Teja underscores the original contributions by the Mexican soldier-settlers, generally ignored by past historians. Reversing this neglect, he portrays the local military as responsible for the creation of the permanent community of San Antonio.

A contribution by Gerald E. Poyo traces the process by which the Canary Islands settlers who arrived in 1731 integrated with the presidio community during the century. Despite efforts by these Spanish immigrants to establish their monopoly over local socioeconomic resources, the realities of frontier life made cooperation and interdependence necessary, resulting in the emergence of a distinct Tejano community.

The next essay is Gilberto M. Hinojosa's interpretative work on the attitudes of the Franciscan missionaries and the role of their Indian communities within the larger settlement. According to the author, the missionaries strove to establish permanent Indian pueblos along the San Antonio River, but demographic trends, frontier realities, and political forces combined to integrate the Indian-religious establishments into the larger community, although not in a way commonly perceived.

Another paper by Poyo treats the theme of immigration and integration in late eighteenth-century Béxar. Through an analysis of immigrant heads of households in the 1793 census and an examination of the status of the numerous immigrants to Béxar from the East Texas community of Los Adaes, Poyo reveals the important role newcomers played in Bexareño society and points to how some achieved considerable status in the local community. Hinojosa and Anne A. Fox then examine the Indian presence in San Fernando de Béxar. They examine the integration of Indians into the town and their overall cultural impact on the community. Using census materials and archaeological evidence, the authors argue that although the significant Indian presence in Béxar did not have an important sociopolitical impact, its cultural influence was considerable.

An essay by Elizabeth A.H. John then analyzes the relationships between the independent (or nonmission) Indians and the San Antonio community. While not linked to the settlement, the various Norteños (Nations of the North, including various Indian groups) presented an economic and political force to be reckoned with, and contacts with these outside groups unavoidably affected townspeople, friars and mission Indians, and soldiers. Through trade, social exchange, and raids, Comanches, Apaches, and other Indian groups shaped Béxar's development during the century. John depicts the contacts with these "outsiders" both generally and with very specific examples.

Finally, the editors offer a concluding summary of the emergence of a clearly defined Tejano community and identity in Béxar during the century. They point to the economic, social, political, and cultural dimensions of this process and reveal how a better understanding of these processes can contribute to the comprehensive history of Tejano communities.

Map of San Antonio, Texas, and Vicinity, 1764

Courtesy British Library

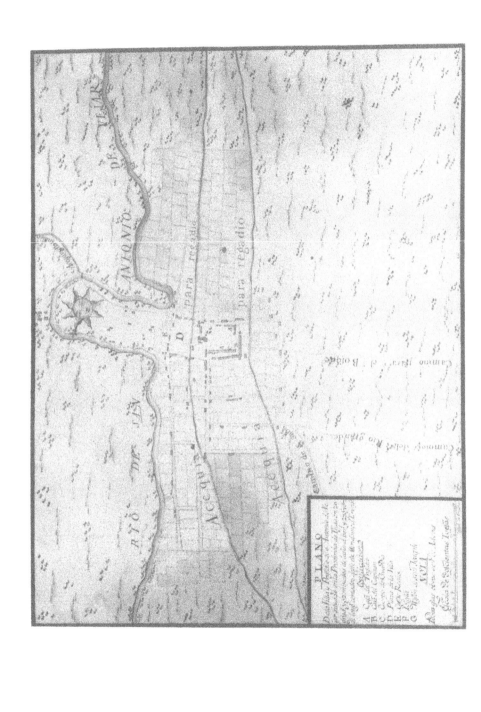

I
Béxar:
Profile of a Tejano Community, 1820-1832
Jesús F. de la Teja and John Wheat

Introduction

Mexicans settled Texas a full century before the first Anglo-American colonists arrived. Anglo-American settlement began with the Mexican period of Texas history (1821-1836), a period in which Mexican Texans—Tejanos—witnessed many significant changes in their region. By 1832, three years before the revolutionary struggle in Texas began, these changes had both fueled the Tejanos' aspirations and frustrated their attempts to realize them. A major statement in 1832 by Tejano leaders, reviewing their experience under the Mexican republic, was a critical event in the history of Mexican Texas. Yet historians have largely neglected the Tejano experience and focused instead on the story of Anglo-American colonization and revolution.[1] In part this neglect stems from the traditional Anglo bias in Texas historical writing, coupled with a language barrier that has prevented many historians from using essential Mexican sources. Nevertheless, a full appreciation of Texas history requires an understanding of the world of the native Mexican communities of Texas, their people and institutions, their patterns of community life, and their view of the broader world.

Origins of San Antonio de Béxar

Chief among these communities was the capital, San Antonio de Béxar, commonly known during this period as Béxar. Established by the Spanish Crown for military and political purposes and facing a hostile and alien world, Béxar developed in isolation from the mainstream of Mexican life. Indeed, Jean Louis Berlandier, the French naturalist and a member of the Mexican Boundary Commission, wrote of Béxar in 1828:

> Trade with the Anglo-Americans, and the blending in to some degree of their customs, make the inhabitants of Texas a little different from the Mexicans of the interior, whom those in Texas call foreigners and whom they scarcely like because of the superiority which they recognize in them. In their gatherings, the women prefer to dress in the fashion of Louisiana, and by so doing they participate both in the customs of the neighboring nation and of their own.[2]

San Antonio de Béxar comprised three different communities in 1820: the religious-Indian settlements of the five Franciscan missions, the military presidio of San Antonio, and the civil settlement of San Fernando de Béxar. The missions were, over time, secularized and incorporated into the civil administrative system. Along the entire frontier missions faced a scarcity of missionaries and a lack of support from the new national government. In Béxar conversions virtually ceased after the secularization of the missions in 1793-1794. By 1820 the former missions had been satellite civilian communities, Indians had become a minority, and townspeople held large amounts of mission land.[3] Final secularization occurred in 1824, spurred by the efforts of Béxar's political leadership. Although the missions continued to elect their officials, they were under the authority of the town.[4]

The presidio, which was established in 1718 along with Mission San Antonio de Valero, formed the core of the area's settlement. In 1801 a company of light cavalry was also stationed in Béxar. By 1820 this unit and the original presidial company made up a garrison of 170 men. The 1820s was a decade of poverty and decline for Béxar's military as it was for the presidial system throughout northern Mexico. The political struggles of central Mexico and the economic disarray following independence meant long periods without pay or supplies for frontier troops.[5] Soldiers were forced to farm, hunt, round up livestock, and rely on charity to keep themselves and their families alive. Some resorted to theft and the unlicensed slaughter of cattle. Conditions were so poor in late 1822 that Governor José Félix Trespalacios convinced the ayuntamiento (town council) to establish a bank of issue in Béxar to cover the salaries of the soldiers until Mexico City sent their wages. In 1825 the citizens, claiming to be superior fighters, threatened to usurp the role of the military in fighting the Indians. Extensive charity had to be provided in 1832 for the desperate soldiers. At the urging of the jefe político (political chief), a citizens' board collected corn, beans, flour, sugar, salt, and even young bulls for them. Because they were a major market for the agricultural production of the area, hard times for the soldiers brought economic distress to the rest of the community.[6]

The town of San Fernando de Béxar, founded in 1731 with families from the Canary Islands, had evolved into four neighborhoods or wards, called barrios: Sur, where most of the long-established families lived; the more prosperous and dynamic Norte; Valero, a military neighborhood, situated across the San Antonio River from these two; and, last, Laredo, on the western edge of town, a section for which little information is thus far available. This overwhelmingly agricultural community, most of whose inhabitants lived in mud and stick shacks (jacales), was governed by an elite composed of descendants of the original Canary Islanders and presidiales. Controlling the best farmland nearest to the settled areas, these men had sufficient wealth (reflected in their large stone houses near the main plaza), education, and social prestige to control the ayuntamiento as well.[7]

Residents of Béxar

Béxar's demographic characteristics in 1820 reflected its status as the oldest, largest, and most successful community in the sparsely settled province. Among its almost 2,000 inhabitants, females slightly outnumbered males (1,021 to 973), while 47 percent of the population was under age twenty. By 1830 San Antonio had experienced a mild but balanced population decline: among the 1,750 individuals reported, females still outnumbered males, married couples constituted the most common form of household, and widows remained a significant part of the population. One possible explanation for this population decline is a move by many people into the countryside, for during the late 1820s many ranches that had been inactive during the previous decade of political turmoil and Indian hostilities were reopened.[8]

A look at the census figures raises several questions concerning the situation of women on the frontier. Women who termed themselves widows headed 30 percent of all households. It is possible, however, that some of these were abandoned women or unwed mothers. Other households were composed of clusters of women, young and old, who probably gathered for welfare and protection. Some of these women were married without resident husbands; others were single or widowed. The tendency, in San Antonio and elsewhere, seems to have been for these women to remain on the frontier, possibly in hope of remarriage, but more likely because they lacked sufficient means to resettle in the interior. Under such conditions, women assumed a variety of socioeconomic roles, including those of storekeeper and ranch or farm manager.[9]

Although there has been recent debate over the validity of using the racial categories or late colonial censuses as a reflection of contemporary society, thus suggesting caution in generalizing about the ethnic composition of the population, some observations are nevertheless possible. As in Laredo and much of the frontier, a large portion of Béxar's population claimed Spanish descent. In San Antonio in 1820, españoles accounted for 55 percent of the municipality's residents. Indians, on the other hand, made up only 15 percent of the total. Of the mixed bloods, mestizos formed the largest percentage, while mulattoes represented a small but important group. Béxar, like many other parts of northern Mexico, was clearly the scene of widespread miscegenation and also of the reduction of the hispanicized Indian and casta (mixed) populations through racial passing.[10]

By 1832 Béxar's demographic position reflected its diminishing importance. Within the whole of Coahuila y Texas, San Antonio was the thirteenth city in size, with a reported population of 1,634. The municipality of San Felipe de Austin, which had not existed twelve years previously, was already three-and-one-half times as large as that of Béxar and was the third-largest reporting center in the state. Goliad and Nacogdoches also grew significantly during this period, making Béxar's demographic stagnation all the more striking.[11] Thus, while other areas of Texas entered a boom period, San Antonio remained a frontier outpost, isolated from the progress in the rest of the state.

Political Affairs in Béxar

During the early 1820s, however, Béxar had enjoyed a predominant role in the political affairs of Texas, as befitted the oldest and largest population center. For much of the colonial period San Antonio was the capital of the province as well as the only entrepôt for supplies headed for Nacogdoches and La Bahía. In 1811-1813 Béxar had been a center of revolutionary activity and the site of a battle between royalist and insurrectionist forces. After Mexico's independence from Spain Bexareños represented the province of Texas at the national congresses and, with the downfall of Emperor Agustín de Iturbide in 1823, took it upon themselves to establish a provisional governing committee (junta) for the province. When Tejanos formed a provincial deputation some months later, Bexareños made up most of the membership.[12]

This brief period of autonomy for Texas gave way in 1824 to union with Coahuila and a reduction in Béxar's influence in the affairs of the newly formed state. In the state constituent assembly, created in 1824, Texas had but one deputy. When the constitution of Coahuila y Texas was adopted in 1827, the department of Texas was granted two representatives to the state legislature. As the population of the area grew, Texas was divided, in 1831, into two districts and, in 1834, into three separate departments.[13] Bexareños came to exercise control over a progressively smaller area, the one with the fewest Anglo-American inhabitants.

Until 1820, when La Bahía was allowed to establish an ayuntamiento, Béxar was the only Spanish community in Texas with a town council. Nacogdoches subsequently established one in 1825, and the Austin colony held its first municipal election in 1828.[14] The ayuntamiento was the arena in which the local elite consolidated its full leadership role, for electoral laws limited the franchise to only a small portion of the adult male population. The Béxar ayuntamiento of 1820 consisted of an alcalde, functioning both as mayor and judge of first instance; four regidores, or aldermen, who served as public inspectors and revenue collectors; and a síndico procurador, functioning as the city's attorney. The members of the ayuntamiento were aided by other prominent citizens, since no lawyers, scribes, or other officials of municipal bureaucracy were available. The size of the ayuntamiento fluctuated dramatically during the decade after 1820, expanding or contracting according to changes in national and state law.[15]

Financial Matters in Béxar

The principal concern of Béxar's city fathers was raising enough revenue to meet community needs. Béxar's sources of income were limited to rents from city-owned farmland, fines, proceeds from the sale of livestock with unknown brands, and taxes on unbranded livestock that was rounded up and on animals that were slaughtered within the city.[16] In the course of the decade the ayuntamiento seized every opportunity to expand the revenue base. Taking advantage of the political uncertainties of the early 1820s, the city completely reformed its finances and empowered itself to tax the export and import of horses, mules, wagon and mule loads, dances and serenades, and shops and market stalls. By January 1826 further revenues came from a tax on irrigation water used on farmlands of the former missions. In 1830 the city began collecting rent on gaming and food stalls set up in the plazas during Christmas holidays.[17] Ultimately, however, the revenue-raising powers of the municipal government continued to be controlled by state and national authorities, and funds remained inadequate for the city's needs.

Béxar's dependence on the garrison for its livelihood is nowhere more clearly indicated than in the attempt to establish the National Bank of Texas. With the troops unpaid for months, Governor Trespalacios formulated a plan establishing a bank of issue to pay the soldiers in paper money until their salaries (paid in silver) arrived. Holders could redeem the scrip then, or, if they wished, they could pay their taxes and buy land using the paper currency. The bank issued notes in November and December of 1822, at which time a payroll arrived for Texas troops and bank operations were suspended. Negotiations with the federal government for the redemption of 2,000 paper pesos held by the city dragged on until 1829, and the silver was not received until a year later.[18]

Public Order and Judicial System

Isolation also forced Bexareños to rely on their own limited resources for the administration of law and order, and they found it difficult to enforce dictates issued from remote centers of power. For several years after independence Tejanos adhered to traditional legal procedures held over from the colonial period. Not until 1826-1827 did the state set up a formal system of courts, but enforcement of its provisions proved impossible. Béxar continued to administer local justice without trained lawyers, as it had since colonial days. Legal review and final adjudication of serious cases were matters for distant higher courts, and the resulting delays and complications plagued the justice system throughout the period.[19]

The ayuntamiento assumed direct responsibility for maintaining public order. The city fathers themselves policed the city, acted as public inspectors, ordered arrests, and ran the city jail. Each barrio was headed by a regidor, who chose a barrio commissioner to assist him in reporting violations, resolving disputes, and making arrests. Later ordinances expanded these efforts, requiring the alcalde or the regidor on duty to lead eight armed citizens on nightly rounds between 9 p.m. and 3 a.m. Outside the city law enforcement likely fell to the mission alcaldes and designated commissioners. In the fields beyond the settlements, rural judges (jueces de campo), chosen by the farmers and ranchers, preserved order and enforced agricultural regulations.[20]

The formal police apparatus could accomplish little without the aid and cooperation of the community. The law required, and city leaders expected, that citizens report violations and turn in offenders engaged in contraband trade, theft, or the pollution of streets and canals. Jail receipts show that community elites sometimes turned in their own household servants as punishment for thefts or other offenses.[21] The large military community, which was supposed to police itself, often ran afoul of civilian authorities. Chronic poverty often led soldiers to criminal activity and left them unprepared to meet their military responsibilities, which resulted in a significant strain in civilian-military relations.[22]

Civil and criminal cases streamed steadily through the alcalde's court. In both types of cases the alcalde relied on a citizen fact-finding process formalized by state decree in 1827. In this system worthy citizens, called hombres buenos or con-jueces (assistant judges), were chosen by the accused and the plaintiff to represent their cases. Responsible for examining witnesses, gathering pertinent information, and making recommendations to the court on how to proceed, the citizen con-jueces functioned as grand juries, investigators, and counsels. Given the amount of legal detail and sheer paperwork, and the lack of trained lawyers, it is little wonder that by 1829 community leaders were expressing the need for an additional alcalde to help handle the judicial burden.[23]

An 1824 trial for the murder of a woman's husband by her reputed lover illustrates the delays created by requiring serious cases to be sent to distant courts for review. After taking a host of depositions in August, the alcalde forwarded the proceedings to the governor in Saltillo because there was no local authority competent to conclude them. Since the new state of Coahuila y Texas still lacked a tribunal of justice, the governor returned the proceedings to Béxar, where the new alcalde had to forward them for review at the higher court (audiencia) of Guadalajara. That court ruled that Béxar's investigation had been deficient and returned the proceedings for further action. Apparently little more was done, however, perhaps because by that time – December of 1825 – the prisoner had escaped (no great feat) and fled to Louisiana. This complicated case resurfaced in 1828, when the fugitive's father-in-law asked for his pardon and return from exile. Unable to locate the records on the case, the alcalde took more depositions. Finally, when one of the victim's own relatives urged that the fugitive be set free, the court concluded four years of proceedings by dropping the charges.[24]

Béxar's frontier position and need for manpower probably mitigated the sentences handed out to offenders. Although robbery was the most common crime on the books and was perceived as a serious threat to community stability, trial records show that sentences generally were not severe. One month in jail was a frequent penalty; six months was imposed for more serious cases; rarely was a longer sentence applied. Major and minor violations often drew fines ranging from four reales to two pesos, or the equivalent of a day's income for an artisan or four days' income for a field hand. Municipal ordinances set heavier fines for illegal fires and public intoxication, the former as a threat to life and property, the latter as an offense to public order and moral propriety. A state decree set still heavier fines of up to 500 pesos for judges who failed their public duty.[25] Since most prisoners were subsistence farmers and manual laborers who lacked the money to pay fines, they were often sentenced to perform public work, such as cleaning streets and canals and constructing or repairing bridges and public buildings. The prisoners also spent many of their days working on the houses or property of the city's elite. Private labor by each convict generated two reales a day, which the city could apply to prisoner upkeep.[26]

Sanitation, Health, and Welfare

In addition to fighting crime, the ayuntamiento promoted public sanitation and community health. Repeated directives against dumping trash or washing clothes in the irrigation ditches (acequias), littering the streets, uncontrolled animals, and the sale of spoiled or unclean foodstuffs all attest to the city's awareness of the close connection between filth and disease. The city subjected violators to fines or to cleaning and construction work.[27]

In its efforts against filth and disease the community could rarely rely on professional medical services. For most of the period 1820-1832 no hospital or doctor existed in Béxar. The army assigned a physician to Béxar in 1820, but his fees and medicines proved too costly for most citizens. After his departure in 1822 the records mention only an occasional soldier or civilian attempting some form of medical treatment as the need arose, especially during epidemics.[28] For the majority of everyday ailments Bexareños probably relied on curanderismo, or folk medicine. Still practiced today in the Spanish Southwest, curanderismo combined European traditions, Amerindian practices, and a knowledge of the medicinal value of herbs to offer cures for a whole range of natural disorders, as well as for those thought to be induced by evil or sorcery.[29]

Recurrent epidemics of yellow fever, smallpox, and, later, cholera galvanized the Tejano settlements into systematic com-

munity-wide efforts. Perhaps because of the efficacy of measures adopted in Béxar or because of its relative isolation, San
Antonio was spared the full force of the epidemics that ravaged
Goliad and other centers to the east during this period.[30]
Bexareños looked to the state government in Coahuila for instructions and medical supplies during these epidemic emergencies. The instructions came, but often the community had
to improvise its own medications when supplies failed to arrive.
In the smallpox epidemic of 1831 Béxar citizens not only found
local substitutes for the medical supplies that never arrived
from Coahuila, but also managed to inoculate children throughout the city with a vaccine extracted from an infected cow
udder. That epidemic led to the establishment of Béxar's first
community health commission (junta de sanidad), as had been
called for in the municipal ordinances of 1829.[31]

The city played a limited role in providing for the welfare
of its needy citizens. Béxar, like other cities of Spanish America,
cared for its homeless and destitute through private charity,
often in association with the Church. Although municipal ordinances reiterated the city's responsibilities in helping orphans,
widows, the poor, the aged, and the infirm, no formal delivery
apparatus existed. Private charity carried most of the burden
of providing for the needy or unprotected, who were simply
taken into the homes of those who could afford to receive them.
The city's main burden was the care of prisoners, who were
most likely from the poorest levels of society.[32]

Local revenues were inadequate not only for meeting the
common welfare needs of poorer citizens and for carrying out
the basic functions of municipal government, but even more
so for funding the emergency programs needed from time to
time. When the local corn supply gave out in 1823, the ayuntamiento was forced to borrow heavily from the fund for Indian
gifts in order to buy supplies in Coahuila. In 1825 the city petitioned the state legislature for funds to repair its own jail and
council chamber. For common emergencies the ayuntamiento
and jefe político acted as coordinators for fund drives. In 1831

they managed to raise a respectable 316 pesos in anticipation of the smallpox epidemic that had already hit Goliad. When the epidemic struck, private citizens provided more supplies for treatment and relief of the sick. In 1832, at the urging of the jefe político, a citizens' board collected supplies for relief of the destitute troops.[33]

The disastrous flood of July 1819 strained the community's resources beyond capacity. Flood waters swept away fifty-five dwellings, hitting especially hard in the Barrio del Norte, and claimed nineteen lives, most of them women and children. Unable to deal with a disaster of such proportions, the authorities of Béxar appealed to the citizens of Coahuila for relief. Though the aid was generous, it was a long time in coming. Local authorities were still distributing relief funds on Christmas Eve of 1821. In the meantime, many of the homeless found shelter with other families in the city.[34]

Education and Public Information

Education was also severely affected by the scarcity of public funds. Although Mexican authorities at all levels recognized the need for education, bankrupt treasuries and widespread poverty kept a coherent school system from emerging. The constitution of Coahuila y Texas, for instance, called for the establishment of "a suitable number of primary schools" in all the towns of the state. Throughout the northern frontier schools sprang up in response to new aspirations for progress and autonomy, but many soon closed because they lacked funds for attracting qualified teachers. In San Antonio Béxar's leaders continually voiced their commitment to public schooling during the decade, while practical considerations made a school a luxury they often could not afford.[35]

Throughout the 1820s San Antonio managed to have a functioning school only sporadically. When one did exist, the burden of maintaining the school and teacher fell mainly on the community. In the early years of the decade the school depended solely on contributions from the parents of school-age children in Béxar. By 1827, after efforts had failed to have the state assume some of the education costs, the city decided to devote the revenues collected on the slaughter of cattle, goats, and sheep to the maintenance of a school. Since these funds were not very plentiful, however, parents continued to carry most of the load. In order for this system to work, the wealthier parents had to make up for the small contributions of the poorer. Having the options of sending their children to school away from Béxar or of providing for their education in their homes, the wealthy of Bexar had little incentive to take up a disproportionate share of the cost.[36]

Under such fiscal constraints, keeping a school operating properly was virtually impossible. Teachers were apt to leave or to abandon teaching if their wages fell too far in arrears (a frequent occurrence).[37] When open, the school operated on the Lancasterian system, which was popular in Mexico at the time because it allowed teachers to handle large classes by using advanced students as tutors. The curriculum was basic: the fundamentals of arithmetic, reading, and writing; the Catholic catechism; some lessons in civics; and, for the more advanced, some knowledge of grammar. Although absenteeism was a chronic problem, approximately one hundred students attended the Béxar school in 1832. The teacher that year reported that forty-four students were learning to read and that fifty-six could read books. Twenty-nine were beginning to write, fifteen could write adequately, and twelve could write well. Progress in arithmetic, however, lagged: eleven students were able to add fractions, and only three could divide them.[38]

Such school supplies as slates, paper, catechisms, and books were always dear because they had to be ordered from Mexico City or New Orleans. The state ordered the ayuntamiento to provide supplies free to many of the needy children who could not afford to buy them. In these circumstances, the donation of copies of *The Life of Saint Peter,* the gift of one hundred pesos in memory of a deceased wife, or the exchange of one of the school's Spanish-English dictionaries for a proper Spanish one, represented monumental strides.[39]

The desire to obtain knowledge went beyond efforts at establishing a school, though the scantness of the record on the reading material available in Béxar makes analysis difficult. On the frontier practical knowledge was of primary consideration. In addition to the ayuntamiento's file on remedies for epidemic diseases, printed by the state and national governments for sale by such isolated communities as Béxar, instructional materials on the development of agriculture and industry were sent to Béxar in 1830 by the governor of Coahuila y Texas. Books on the wool and silkworm industries and on agriculture also apparently made the rounds.[40]

Practical knowledge also included keeping up to date on political developments. Contact with the outside world consisted of the movement of merchants and soldiers through Béxar and included a regular weekly mail service within and outside Texas. The available pamphlets, broadsides, pronouncements, newspapers, and other printed documents in the Béxar Archives show that Bexareños had the opportunity to be well informed on political developments throughout Mexico.[41] Governor Trespalacios even brought a printing press to Béxar in April 1823 with the hope of better integrating Texas into the nation, but the *Correo de Texas*, the newspaper Trespalacios hoped to found, apparently never saw print. After a few months in San Antonio the press was sold to the provincial deputation at Monterrey, and all that remains of its work in Béxar are a bill for the printing of some government decrees and some examples of published documents.[42]

Celebrations and Entertainment

Béxar also participated in the greater Mexican society through the celebration of various secular and religious feasts. For the entire Béxar community these holidays were a source of diversion and conviviality in an otherwise harsh and dangerous world. Public feasts and ceremonies also helped to focus community feelings on the symbols of religion and patriotism and on the leadership of the elite. On holidays, mass was sung, the ayuntamiento held no meetings, prisoners were spared from public work, and all other work ceased.[43]

The city's elite were responsible for organizing public feasts. In the early 1820s the city still followed the Spanish custom of designating prominent citizens to assume responsibility for the expenses and preparations of religious celebrations. Sometimes those honored had to request relief from this obligation because they lacked the necessary money. Preparations for celebrating the day of Mexican Independence, September 16, were different. Overall control rested with a patriotic committee (junta patriótica), which appointed subcommittees to organize the festivities and collect donations.[44]

Fortunately we can get some idea of how these Independence Day celebrations were prepared and carried out from the records of the one held in 1829. On the eve of the holiday the citizens gathered for a procession through the streets, announcing the coming festivities with the pealing of bells, gun salutes, and the playing of music. Early the next morning the authorities and citizens attended mass and a Te Deum, followed by another procession in the afternoon and then a speech on the meaning of the day.[45] The biggest celebration came that evening:

> On the night of the 16th a great ball will be held at the town hall, for which a committee will be made responsible. . . . The committee will also be responsible for holding a minor dance at another place for the entertainment of the public.[46]

Finally, on the morning of the 17th, the townspeople would again gather at the church, where a mass for the dead would be sung.[47]

Clearly the establishment of a republican form of government had not greatly altered social relations as they were manifested in public ceremony. Separate dances segregated the elite from the rest of the community, and the formalism of the processions and speeches and the release of prisoners held on minor charges reinforced the elite's leadership of the community. To celebrate the victory of Mexican troops over the Spanish at Tampico in 1829, no fewer than five dances and balls were held, including two public dances on September 27. The list of contributors to the festival fund reveals total pledges of more than 326 pesos.[48]

Celebrations were not the only opportunities for dancing in Béxar. Several contemporary reports of San Antonio emphasize the Bexareños' love of dancing and gambling.[49] Though the moralistic tone of some of these accounts betrays their writers' biases, the revenue documents from Béxar indicate that these Tejanos did greatly enjoy dancing. The fact that the ayuntamiento in 1823 decided to tax dances and serenades (gallos) suggests the popularity of these forms of entertainment, a popularity stemming from the limited number of alternative forms of diversion available. In 1827, for example, the city collected thirty-six pesos from licensing dances at the rate of four reales a dance. Thus, at least seventy-two dances were held in private residences that year, in addition to the untaxed public or official balls. In other words, Bexareños could attend more than one dance a week. Dances were held only on weekends or on the evenings before feast days.[50]

The other major diversion, gambling, was also widespread. It involved cockfights, horse races, and card games throughout the year, and other games of chance during the Christmas festival. The custom in Béxar was to hold feasts from the first week of December through the beginning of the new year. During this time the plazas were turned over to vendors and game operators, who paid rental fees to the municipality for their stalls or concessions.[51]

Solemnizing these religious and secular celebrations was apparently the major role of the Church, except for dispensing the sacraments. Refugio de la Garza, the parish priest of Béxar throughout the Mexican period, had a worldly bent. He was deeply involved in politics and was one of the wealthiest men in the community. While representing Texas at the national Congress in 1822, he lobbied for the final secularization of the Texas missions; he was later to have considerable holdings of former mission lands. He was also one of the largest owners of livestock in Béxar. An inspection of parish finances and re-cords in early 1825 showed carelessness and negligence in the running of the parish and considerable impropriety in the han-dling of its funds by lay administrators. As one historian has noted, Father de la Garza "and his equally worldly assistant, José Darío Zambrano, both sadly neglected their spiritual du-ties – saying Mass only occasionally, never preaching, and sel-dom, if ever, visiting the sick or comforting the afflicted."[52]

Béxar's Economy

While the Church might have neglected the spiritual life of the community, the San Antonio River valley was blessed by nature with a mild climate, fertile soil, and abundant water. Its economic horizon, however, was seriously limited by phys-ical isolation, sparse population, Indian hostilities, and chronic lack of specie. Poverty and exposure to frontier dangers were constant themes of Béxar memorials and petitions throughout the 1820s. Tejano leaders understood that in order for the region to prosper it must be more densely populated, linked with other centers in the region, and freed from heavy government con-trols of its economy.

By the 1820s San Antonio had developed only a modest agrarian economy that centered on subsistence farming, with few profits and little surplus for export. Most cultivators worked small, family-owned plots, while many others worked as tenant farmers or day laborers. The wealthier farmed enough land to provide a small surplus for the local market, which consisted largely of the impoverished military sector. These wealthier landowners gradually increased their holdings during this period, especially in the lands of the former missions. Many Bexareños also participated to some degree in the cattle indus-try, already a century old. Ranching at this time consisted less of cattle raising than of cattle chasing, since large herds of branded and unbranded cattle and horses, dispersed by storms, Indian raids, and other agents, ran wild through the brush country around Béxar. The elite landowners supplied beef to the local market and occasionally exported cows or horses to Coahuila or Louisiana. The livestock export business, however, was saddled with government restrictions and beset by Indian raids and a shortage of capital and manpower.[53]

The skilled trade and commercial sectors of the Béxar economy grew more in size than in importance in the decade after 1820. The twenty-five artisans and nine merchants in 1820 had increased to forty-five artisans and seventeen merchants ten years later. Though both sectors nearly doubled during this period, their economic significance was less impressive. The artisans still had little work, which suggests that their listed skills were not necessarily the reason for their presence in Béxar.[54] Nor had the manufacture of such basic items as blankets, hats, and shoes yet developed to any extent in Texas.[55] The need to import these and other necessities gave some impetus to Béxar merchants. While a few of them owned stores, others merely engaged in the occasional import and sale of Mexican and foreign goods. The nascent merchant sector included a handful of foreigners but consisted mostly of the native Tejanos who held the land, livestock, political power, and social prestige.[56] Consequently, merchants' inventories for the period list not only food staples and basic manufactures, but also the wines, liquors, and fine fabrics that only the more prosperous could afford.[57] Freighting also played a role in this sector, though its full significance will require further study. Oxcarts and mule teams from Béxar plied trade routes east to La Bahía (Goliad) and Nacogdoches and south to Laredo, Monclova, and Saltillo. Though undertaken on an occasional basis only, freighting required a city license and thus provided another source of much-needed municipal revenue.[58]

Mexican trade laws for frontier Texas perpetuated the old Spanish colonial aim of protecting the native economy from smuggling and foreign intrusion. Among their strict controls on the importation of merchandise, the laws gave special emphasis to tobacco, a major source of tax revenue for the national treasury. Foreign tobacco was kept out in order to protect Mexican tobacco, over which the government held a monopoly.[59] To enforce these controls, the Mexican government attempted to restrict the importation of goods to a single port of entry (Galveston) and required a passport or customs permit for transport and travel.[60]

Tejanos continually sidestepped these laws, however, and a growing contraband trade involved many Béxar citizens. The chronic protests of exasperated military and treasury officials, the high level of illicit trade that persisted in the area throughout this period, and the relative wealth of some citizens would suggest that Bexareños were in the thick of the smuggling business.[61] The Béxar ayuntamiento admitted as much in 1820, in instructions to its provincial deputy. The ayuntamiento offered, however, the following justification:

> We repeat the request for the opening of the said port [of Matagorda] in order to destroy, at its roots, the odious contraband trade across the frontier of which some of the citizens of this place are accused. Yet, if some practice it, it is not from ambition to accumulate riches, but because of the miseries they suffer and the ease with which they can relieve their sufferings. And, if this is the only relief these inhabitants receive, there is no reason for depriving them of it by seizing upon the contraband goods which they accumulate.[62]

The persistence of contraband trade in Texas reflected the desire of Tejano merchants to free up the flow of goods throughout northern Mexico. While land, cattle, and family might bring them power and social prestige, commerce held the key to prosperity. Tejanos envisioned themselves as the center of an extensive commercial system linking Béxar with Louisiana, Coahuila, Chihuahua, and New Mexico.[63] Aspiring to be the agents as well as the beneficiaries of Texas' economic development, Béxar's leaders pushed for increased colonization, the opening of Gulf ports, and exemption from taxes, embargoes, and other burdens.

The promotion of agriculture, trade, and industry depended on a sufficient population and labor force. Texas was supposed to be colonized by other Mexicans, but the region never could draw enough settlers from the interior. Anglos and other foreigners, on the other hand, were pouring into Texas in ever-greater numbers under the liberal provisions of the March 24, 1824, colonization law. With their industry, skills, and families, the new settlers seemed to guarantee achievement of the long-sought goal of regional development. Consequently, Tejano leaders pinned their hopes on Anglo colonization and made every effort to protect foreign immigration from the Mexican government's attempts to restrict it. They faced their greatest challenge in the law of April 6, 1830, which sought to halt further North American immigration. Tejano spokesmen came to the defense of Anglo-American interests, even where this involved an accommodation to the practice of slavery, by now outlawed in Mexico.[64]

The promotion of trade also depended on adequate port facilities. The port of San Bernardo on Matagorda Bay was the closest Gulf Coast landing for Béxar's seaborne trade. Nevertheless, the Mexican government closed that port in 1827 and decreed that all shipments must enter Texas at Stephen F. Austin's newly requested port at Galveston. Béxar merchants, protesting the extra distance and bad roads to which the Galveston route would subject them, responded by continuing to use San Bernardo illegally. Although the hard times facing Béxar led the authorities to tolerate this defiance for a while, the commandant general reiterated the ban in October 1827 in order to curtail rampant smuggling. When the military turned a deaf ear to their renewed protests, the Tejanos took their case to the national Congress, where they finally achieved their goal. In October 1828 the government of Coahuila y Texas was authorized to reopen San Bernardo and establish a customs house at La Bahía.[65]

Tejano leaders complained repeatedly to the central government that their hard and dangerous existence on Mexico's northern frontier entitled them to certain privileges and exemptions. Though they never overcame the poverty and neglect that plagued the region, Tejanos won some occasional concessions. Their most important victory was a September 1823 decree that all effects of any category, national or foreign, introduced into Texas for the direct consumption of its inhabitants were to be free of duty for seven years. In 1827 the state legislature also decreed that in Texas such staples as corn, beans, and chilies were to be free from the alcabala, or excise tax. In 1831 the legislature declared a six-year exemption from all duties for growers of cotton and livestock in Monclova and Béxar, as well as a twelve-year exemption for sugarcane and grapes and their products.[66]

Béxar gave eloquent voice to its needs in a petition to the national government in 1829, as the seven-year grace period on imports was about to expire. Bexareños argued that the same conditions that had justified the original concession still applied. In mother-child imagery they emphasized that, since the social body of the department was still in its infancy, Texas was not robust enough to sustain itself and therefore needed the care and nurturing of the mother. In more practical terms they pointed out that new import duties would require salaries and enforcement machinery that would themselves cost money and would force the price of goods upward, thus reducing the ability of merchants to sell and of consumers to buy. Eventually public revenues would decline, and any new duties imposed to offset this decline would only encourage still more contraband. Therefore, Bexareños argued, Texas needed an exemption for at least twelve more years. Apparently Mexico City agreed to a short extension.[67]

Tejano Grievances

The achievement of occasional victories and concessions, coupled with the great promise of immigration for future development, raised Tejano expectations to new levels. Béxar leaders understood that their local progress depended on the development of the entire region. Most significantly, in the early 1830s they still considered themselves to be the principal spokesmen for all of Texas. For those in other settlements as

well as for themselves, Bexareños yearned for greater participation in national life and greater control over local destinies.
Tejano leaders sought both political and economic integration
in order to increase their roles in domestic and international
trade and in the representation of their interests in the legislature. They sought to improve municipal and departmental
government through adequate staffing and administrative reforms. Their continual, though frustrated, efforts at public education reflected their hope of overcoming Béxar's cultural isolation as well.[68]

The Tejanos' high expectations foundered on the realities
of life in Texas. Bexareños lived in geographical, economic, and
social isolation. Unlike Santa Fe, for instance, which opened
direct economic links to the United States and consequently
overcame much of its physical isolation, Béxar had yet to establish economic ties or to improve communications with other
regions. Both Santa Fe and Béxar failed to attract substantial
numbers of immigrants, who tended to settle in new communities. In Texas Béxar stood in painful contrast to the thriving
Anglo settlements growing up to the east. Political initiative
shifted away from Béxar to the more dynamic Anglo-dominated
areas. In the distant state government Bexareños suffered
chronic neglect, while the new colonies grew in both influence
and representation.[69]

Lacking sufficient local self-government, Tejanos were
never able to solve their greatest problems. Sources of revenue
were largely controlled by state and national authorities, and
the sources available to the ayuntamiento never generated the
funds needed for carrying out municipal programs in education, public works, and welfare. Béxar also failed to achieve
the local administrative development it so badly needed; thus,
the community was forced to struggle on without trained
judges, notaries, or a municipal bureaucracy. The money-poor
and underpopulated community was still unable to sustain vital
professional services in law, medicine, and education. During
this period Béxar's economy could never provide enough work
for its modest number of skilled artisans nor did it even develop
basic manufactures.

The accumulation of Tejano grievances – administrative, political, military, and economic – culminated in 1832 in a bold declaration from the Béxar ayuntamiento to the state legislature. In its review of the Tejano experience under the Mexican republic, this Béxar Memorial surveyed the desolate condition of Texas settlements and reiterated the constant themes of hardship and danger. For the first time in public, however, the Bexareños blamed most of the troubles in Texas on its union with Coahuila. They scorned the state legislature for its continual neglect of the Texas judicial system, military defense, and public education. The law of April 6, 1830, struck even deeper at Tejano interests: by barring industrious and law-abiding North American settlers but failing to stop illegal adventurers and vagabonds, the new law seriously hindered the development of Texas.[70]

The ayuntamiento concluded its declaration with a series of urgent demands including the passage of a new colonization law favorable to both Mexicans and North Americans, the establishment of an effective civil militia for frontier defense, the creation of an adequate judicial system, state support for public education, a ten-year extension of the exemption from import duties on items for local consumption, and increased Texas representation in the legislature. The Bexareños warned the legislature to act quickly before these conditions led to the total ruin of Texas and closed with the ominous suggestion that the desperate inhabitants might be forced to take matters into their own hands.[71]

The frank declarations of the ayuntamiento were significant for several reasons. Motivated by the Tejanos' new level of expectation and frustration regarding the role of Texas in the Mexican republic, the memorial signaled a departure from the more conservative behavior of the Béxar leadership in the 1820s. The fact that the grievances were penned at the direct urging of Austin and other Anglo leaders reflected the consonance of Tejano concerns with those of the Anglos at this stage of the Texas drama. The tenor of the memorial evinced a strong desire for local autonomy, with the implied goal of eventual independent statehood. Finally, the Béxar Memorial represented the high-water mark in Texas' attempt to remain loyal to the Mexican nation.

Conclusion

After 1832 relations between the Mexican government and the Anglo-American colonists deteriorated in an atmosphere of alleged despotism, mutual suspicion, and deepening hostility. The Tejanos of Béxar were caught in the middle of a crisis that they had not created and could not control. The rush of events of the mid-1830s further isolated the Bexareños from Mexico and Anglo Texas alike. Finally the great hopes that Bexareños had nurtured for so long went up in the smoke of the Texas Revolution. Though many Tejanos ultimately sided with the revolutionaries against Santa Anna, the independence movement not only wrested fortune from their hands but also left them outsiders in their own land. Thus the Tejanos of San Antonio de Béxar were forced to seek their destiny on the margin of a new Texas society.

*

Tejano community life was vibrant and expanding during the 1820s and 1830s. A real sense of Tejano regional identity had emerged by this time – an identity that was forged during the previous century by various peoples with differing cultural backgrounds. The remainder of this volume focuses on these groups and the multidimensional process by which they contributed to the formation of a Tejano community in San Antonio de Béxar.

– EDITORS

II
Forgotten Founders:
The Military Settlers of Eighteenth-Century
San Antonio de Béxar

Jesús F. de la Teja

Introduction

H istorians have generally looked upon the foundation of
the formal villa of San Fernando de Béxar on March 9,
1731, by a group of Canary Islands immigrants as the beginning
of San Antonio. But shrouded in the mists of meager documentary evidence that has largely escaped the attention of scholars
is Béxar's earliest history. Indeed, the more familiar story of
the Canary Islanders, or Isleños, could not be told if a determined and resourceful group of military settlers had not established a small but thriving community despite dangers and
isolation. Without the protection and instruction of these Mexican frontiersmen, the band of Old World immigrants who
came to the Texas wilderness would not have survived long.

The Isleños' arrival in Béxar marked the end of an initial
flourishing based on military settlement by frontiersmen from
Coahuila and Nuevo León. The emerging community's simple
and united society, which was centered on the presidio, gave
way to social and political cleavages between existing and new

settlers. Yet the Crown's creation of a villa (town) and grant of privileges to the new arrivals did not alter the endurance of the settlement's frontier character. Béxar's garrison continued to protect civilians from Indian attack, served as a market for local goods, and provided impetus for population growth. Without the fort, the town's existence would have been tenuous at best. Scholars must therefore look to the early military settlement and its population in order to trace the development of community in San Antonio de Béxar.

Béxar's Settlement

Settling an intermediate location between the Tejas missions of East Texas and the Rio Grande was essential to the successful occupation of the province, a task Crown authorities considered critical to protect New Spain's rich northern mining districts from French encroachment. On the edge of Mexico's advancing frontier, Texas and Béxar began as imperial outposts, first against a rival European power and later against Apaches and Comanches. They continued in this role throughout the eighteenth century and well into the nineteenth.

Interest in the San Antonio region arose early. A plan drawn up in 1689 by Coahuila governor Alonso de León called for a presidio on the Guadalupe River to discourage French advances. Explorer Domingo Terán de los Rios in 1691 considered the upper San Antonio River valley, with its abundant water supply, woods, and agricultural land, the ideal site for missions and towns.[1] The same vicinity made a deep impression on Fray Antonio San Buenaventura Olivares, who, according to historian Carlos Castañeda, "had nursed a hidden desire to found a mission at the headwaters of the San Antonio River," ever since his visit to the region in 1709.[2] Fray Olivares advocated Spanish settlement of the area, "for an entire province will fit in the said river [valley]."[3]

The viceroy's orders to Martín de Alarcón, named governor of Texas in 1714, reflected these recommendations. In addition to establishing missions between the San Antonio and

Colorado rivers, the viceroy envisioned the founding of two towns or cities. One town was to be established on the San Antonio River by at least thirty families, who would receive all the rights and privileges granted by royal laws.[4] And to partially offset the obvious hazards associated with occupying hostile Indian country, each settler was to receive a salary of 450 pesos, livestock, and other supplies.[5]

Despite the incentives, recruitment proved troublesome because of the small number of available settlers in the sparsely populated provinces of Coahuila and Nuevo León.[6] Nevertheless, a small expedition that included artisans and a group of women and children arrived at San Antonio in late April 1718. On May 1 Alarcón designated a spot on the west bank of the river for Mission San Antonio de Valero. Approximately three-quarters of a league from the mission near San Pedro Springs he selected a site for the "Villa de Béxar" and performed the act of possession on May 5.[7]

New Spain's Northern Advance and Béxar's Founders

People accustomed to frontier life built, protected, and fostered what became Texas' most successful colonial settlement. These people included soldiers, friars, and settlers who worked together at San Antonio (as they had on countless occasions throughout the Mexican north) to defend Spain's claims to the region through the incorporation of Indians and land into the colonial system.

The settlers from Coahuila who moved north to found the settlement of San Antonio followed a pattern that was well established by the early eighteenth century. Throughout the colonial period pioneers from the most recently settled areas usually spearheaded the further extension of the frontier. Sinaloans settled Sonora, and these two provinces furnished the people for California's settlement. Nueva Vizcayans settled New Mexico and southern Coahuila. With the exception of a few Canary Islanders, pioneers from Coahuila, Saltillo, and Nuevo

León settled Béxar. As the prominent Spanish Borderlands historian Oakah Jones observes: "In all cases, therefore, most of the colonists either had passed through the frontier experience themselves recently or were still in that stage."[8]

Béxar's frontiersmen brought elements of northern Mexico's distinctive society to Texas. The inhabitants of the northern regions made their living primarily in mining and ranching. The sparse population and long distances between urban centers mitigated against a manufacturing economy. Indeed, local investments centered on mines, mule trains, and land. Commerce involved the export of raw materials (wood, hides, livestock, and a little cotton) to the central provinces of New Spain in return for manufactured goods and tropical agricultural products.[9] The vast, open rangelands of South-Central Texas fit snugly this land-oriented economy.

Alarcón's expeditionaries founded Béxar not only in their capacity as military personnel but also as settlers. Since the colonial Mexican presidial companies were not regular army units, they relied on inhabitants of the frontier who willingly defended presidio outposts in return for the opportunity to participate in the establishment of a permanent settlement. Soldiers took families to their new posts and together provided a small but viable market for merchants, artisans, ranchers, and farmers who congregated around the presidios. After retiring from service soldiers often obtained land grants near their frontier posts, swelling the civilian population. Friendly Indians also frequently sought security and integrated into the presidio communities.[10]

Though isolated and harsh, life in the northern presidios offered large numbers of frontiersmen opportunities for social and economic advancement. Usually of mixed-blood heritage, frontier soldiers could hope to rise through the ranks to become noncommissioned and commissioned officers and even acquire the title of "don." Such mobility was less feasible for persons of mixed-blood backgrounds in the more-established areas of New Spain. If young soldiers remained in a particular company for some time, they could expect to marry into a family of the neighboring civilian settlement, acquire land and livestock, and even become socially influential in the community.[11]

Béxar's Population in the 1720s

The Béxar presidio provided the most important demographic foundation for the permanent settlement of Texas. While the presidio's original population is not known, it grew steadily throughout the 1720s. Alarcón's expedition had seventy-two persons, including thirty-four soldiers (seven with their families) and several muleteers, but the number that settled permanently in Béxar is unclear. In all probability, not all remained, since conditions on the frontier were very difficult. In fact, during 1724 Governor Fernando Pérez de Almazán reported on the shortage of recruits and the difficulties of attracting settlers. "It is necessary to seek [recruits] outside this province because here there is no population whatever," Almazán complained. He suggested that some inducements be given to potential recruits "besides their salaries, because of the resignation with which they all come to this country."[12]

On the other hand, Béxar benefited from the political instability on the border with French Louisiana. When the French invaded Spanish East Texas in 1719, many settlers retreated to San Antonio. Subsequent efforts by the Marqués de San Miguel de Aguayo, governor of Coahuila and Texas, to reestablish Spanish authority in that area in 1721 likewise brought increased numbers to San Antonio.[13] When the Marqués left Texas in 1722 he increased Béxar's garrison to fifty-four men, of whom approximately twenty were members of Alarcón's original military contingent.[14] Four years later, in 1726, Governor Pérez de Almazán calculated a total of two hundred inhabitants distributed among fifty-four presidial families plus four civilian residents.[15]

Consistent with the soldier-settler philosophy of frontier development implemented in the Mexican north, the Presidio de San Antonio de Béxar also had a civilian character almost from the start. To ensure the establishment of a permanent civilian settlement, Alarcón's original instructions called for granting the first pobladores (settlers) all the privileges and concessions allowed by the law, including "the lands, pastures, water, and proportionate woods, with the sole reservation that there be left vacant enough lands for one hundred families who will be introduced in time."[16] Furthermore, the act of possession in May 1718 gave the new settlement a civilian title, "Villa de Béxar."[17]

The civilian contingent of four residents cited by Pérez de Almazán in 1726 grew considerably during the next five years, increasing to an estimated twenty to twenty-five male heads of household. This growth is explained by two factors. First, as a result of a frontier inspection that found things quiet at Béxar, the government reduced the garrison by ten soldiers. At least some of the retired soldiers remained and joined the civilian community. Second, the families that came to Texas with the soldiers in the 1720s probably included individuals who did not join the presidio but instead established their own civilian households.

The arrival of these families ensured that Béxar, like other parts of New Spain's nonmining north, would develop as a balanced and stable community with real possibilities of growth. Many of the soldiers' families arriving in Béxar included children of marrying age.[18] Two of Cristóbal Carvajal's daughters, for example, married soldiers in Béxar between 1721 and 1723.[19] Over all, eight daughters of the first Bexareños (who arrived in 1718) married soldiers in the period 1720-1724. Another four marriages involved widowed women and local soldiers. There were, by 1730, approximately forty married couples in the settlement, at least half of whom were wed at San Antonio.[20]

In Béxar, as in the north of New Spain generally, commonality of purpose, isolation, and a small population resulted in relatively unrestricted racial boundaries. On the frontier, and in San Antonio, many passed as "Spanish" despite their dark skin. The ethnically mixed were the rule rather than the exception.[21] Despite the desire of Fray Antonio de Olivares of

San Antonio de Valero mission that "pure-blooded" Spanish families settle the area, virtually all of Alarcón's recruits were "mulattoes, lobos, coyotes, and mestizos." There, according to the priest, were "people of the lowest order, whose customs are worse than those of the Indians."[22] Nevertheless, San Antonio's missionaries generally collaborated with obscuring their racial "shortcomings." In registering the civilian population for baptisms, marriages, and deaths, the friars did not indicate an individual's ethnic status unless he or she was considered Spanish. For instance, only one interracial marriage is registered in San Antonio during this time–between a Spanish settler and the commander's Indian servant.[23] And, as in another case, even when the groom is identified as the son of a Spaniard and an Indian, he is listed in the marriage register as Spanish, not mestizo.[24] Such obfuscation permitted descendants of racially mixed individuals to "pass" as Spanish, the preferred social status in the larger colonial society.

Life in Early San Antonio

Throughout the 1720s life in Béxar revolved around the presidio and its obligations. The soldiers' military functions were numerous. They protected supply convoys and travelers between the presidio at Rio Grande and East Texas; two or three soldiers stood guard at Missions Valero and San José, a second mission founded in 1720, and acted as overseers and teachers to the Indians; they protected the horse herd from continual Indian thefts; and, of course, they stood guard duty and scouted.

As a military outpost Béxar faced the test of Indian hostility almost at once. In 1720 Lipan Apaches attacked supply trains and killed soldiers, civilians, and mission Indians in their efforts to obtain horses. Three years later Apaches made a direct assault on the presidial horse herd, absconding with eighty animals. After the raid Captain Nicolás Flores led a force of thirty soldiers and an equal number of mission Indians over three hundred miles in pursuit of the raiders. Flores achieved a decisive victory, capturing hostages and a large Apache horse herd, but this failed to stop depredations. Despite his military successes, Flores could not obtain permission for a major campaign two years later, and Bexareños had to content themselves with short pursuits of raiders after each attack.[25] By 1727 the garrison had become proficient in pursuing raiders, as witnessed by Brigadier Rivera during an inspection of San Antonio. He observed that "these Indians have learned by experience what the soldiers can do in the exercise of their duty when the occasion arises[;] they observe a certain restraint which minimizes the need for vigilance." While "it is a habit of the Indians to steal, and they do not fail to indulge in thefts, robbing the soldiers of their horses when not watchful," Rivera continued, "they are generally chastised by the troops for their daring." [26] As a result of his observations during this visit to Béxar, Rivera recommended a reduction of the presidial company by ten men. In fact, the lull in Apache activity was not solely attributable to the military effectiveness of the soldiers, and Béxar's security was seriously endangered by the reduced presidio contingent.

The military system also served to supply the settlement with food and manufactured goods. Until 1728 the governor controlled the settlement's provisioning, providing seed, farm implements, oxen, and even some Indian labor. Through his connection with Mexico City merchants, the governor arranged for the collection of the garrison's payroll and its use to purchase provisions, armaments, clothes, and even luxury items. After Rivera's inspection in 1727, Béxar's captain became solely responsible for supplies but under a similar arrangement.[27]

At the same time, the settlement worked to become self-sufficient. Soldiers and Indians opened acequias (irrigation ditches) for the presidio-villa and mission at the time of the settlement's founding. They also cleared land and planted maize and huertas (vegetable gardens). Pobladores opened another acequia when the presidio was relocated in 1722 as a result of its exposure to Indian attack. The acequia was described as "capable of irrigating the two leagues of fertile land found within the angle formed by the San Pedro and San Antonio, taking the water from the former for the benefit of the presidial troops and settlers that might join them."[28] The new acequia allowed settlers to utilize lands south of the presidio for crops and gardens.

The community's social structure was simple, even after the increase in the civilian population toward the end of the 1720s. Béxar's social hierarchy consisted of a usually "well-bred" governor (when he was present), the captain, the troops and their families, and the civilian settlers. Soldiers and former soldiers alike worked the presidio's irrigated fields, which belonged to all. They also possessed at least rudimentary blacksmithing, carpentry, and other skills which were used in the presidio and community.[29] Friars from Missions Valero and San José tended to the settlement's spiritual needs. While some soldiers had homesteads some distance away, most of the population lived around the military plaza. Civilians and military lived side by side, and those soldiers with families did not live in the barracks but in their own dwellings.[30]

As would be expected in a young frontier community, Béxar's physical appearance was not impressive in the 1720s. Most structures consisted of simple jacales, constructed of upright wooden poles plastered with mud or clay, that were easy to build and abandon. While suitable to this frontier situation, the thatch-roofed jacales caught fire easily. Late in 1721, for instance, sixteen jacales and a similarly built granary burned, affording the governor an opportunity to move the settlement to a more favorable location.[31] After 1722 jacales and adobe buildings began to give way to some stone structures.[32] The actual presidio was also modest. In fact, during his inspection of the presidio in 1727, Brigadier Rivera found no formal presidio fortification at all; instead, he noted a few stone houses "constructed by Don Fernando Pérez de Almazán in the year 1726." The presidio also included "an as yet unfinished chapel" and a barracks "in which the soldiers live . . . made of the same material [i.e., sticks and mud] as those of the Presidio de Texas."[33] Isolated and concerned with matters of survival, the pobladores did not build more than they absolutely needed nor sought title to the plots they worked, a decision they would soon regret.

The Old Settlers Become New Residents

By 1731 San Antonio de Béxar had consolidated its position as a permanent settlement. A community routine and tradition was clearly emerging, but the town's trajectory was altered by the arrival of a new group of settlers from the Canary Islands. The community changed in many ways, but the immediate impact on the soldier-settlers was the loss of their lands.

The Isleños arrived at the critical spring planting season, preventing presidio Captain Pérez de Almazán from sufficiently reflecting upon his instructions for settling the new arrivals. One immediate problem was that the land designated in his instructions for the Isleños' town site and farmlands had no irrigation facilities. Concluding that it would be too expensive and time-consuming to open up a new irrigation ditch, the captain distributed the irrigated fields south of the presidio among the recent immigrants.[34]

Furthermore, Pérez de Almazán apparently believed that his orders required him to maintain the presidio as a separate jurisdiction from the new villa to be established by the Isleños. He excluded the garrison's civilian population from any participation in the new town's creation and distributed town lots only to Islanders.[35] The captain also named an all-Islander town council, thus excluding non-Islanders from participation in local government. Until now the presidio commander exercised civil jurisdiction as chief magistrate (justicia mayor), hearing all civil and criminal cases in the region. When the town magistrate elections began under the Canary Islanders, the commander's jurisdiction was considerably reduced.[36] Furthermore, apparently without much thought to the consequences, Pérez de Almazán gave the immigrants general privileges as original settlers (primeros pobladores) to an area occupied by the military settlers for over a decade.

In several short months the military settlers were dispossessed, but they did not remain passive. While some sought permission to leave the province altogether, noting that "having observed the Islander families' behavior, it has not appeared good to them, and they do not wish to be neighbors with [Canary Islanders]," most were determined to stay and demand their rights.[37] Demonstrating their unity and sense of community, they protested their treatment as a group, submitted formal petitions for land to replace what they had lost, and demanded participation in the municipal government.

Initially the results were mixed. By 1734 only three non-Islander residents, former soldiers Alberto López and José Martínez and the blacksmith Juan Banul, had received town lot grants. Another four individuals received lots from Governor Manuel de Sandoval shortly after he took up his post in 1732. None received water rights with their grants, but this was the least of their problems, for Sandoval's farmland grants to six of these settlers met with so much opposition from the Isleños that, despite viceregal support, none of the grants were actually sustained locally.[38]

Despite the reverses, some pobladores managed to gain access to irrigated farmland in the Islanders' labor, or farmlands. As some Isleños found less profit in farming than in other activities, including military service, they found buyers among the military settlers. Retired soldiers Francisco Hernández, Gerónimo Flores, and Pedro Ocón y Trillo, as well as Captain Toribio de Urrutia, all bought farmland from Isleños in 1739-1741.[39] The ability of these men to pay for land they had once freely used attests to their influence and strength in the community and dispels the myth of monolithic Islander control over the settlement and its resources.

The military settlers also succeeded in breaking the Isleños' monopoly over local administration. During San Fernando's first decade they petitioned Mexico City on more than one occasion to be made participants in the town's council. The settlers demanded that one of the two alcaldes (magistrates) be a non-Islander and that half of the regidores (aldermen) be appointed from their group as the original incumbents died.[40] These petitions received a favorable response from viceregal officials in the capital, but the Islanders objected. Not until 1741 did the Isleño council give in to pressure from the majority population and begin selecting an alcalde from among the military settlers. Death, departure, incapacity, and intermarriage also forced the dwindling Isleño male population to grant the pobladores posts as regidores. In 1745 three military settlers served as regidores on the town council.[41]

Conclusion

In the summer of 1730, before the Islanders even left Veracruz on their long trip to San Antonio, the viceroy (on the advice of Brigadier Rivera) recommended to the king that he discontinue the recruitment of Canary Islanders for settlement in Texas. The prohibitive costs of transportation and equipment made the program impractical, but in addition it soon became apparent that such immigrants were ill-prepared for settlement on that far-off frontier. Soon after their arrival in Béxar, for example, Captain Pérez de Almazán observed that the Islanders did not know how to tend to their livestock or even fire weapons, making them useless for watch duty.[42] Obviously Mexican families accustomed to frontier life were preferable and could be recruited far less expensively.

No further recruitment efforts were launched, however, even among Mexican families. After the Isleño experiment, migration to Texas once again depended on the voluntary movement of frontiersmen. The presidio continued to act as a magnet for population as new soldiers brought their families to San Antonio or settled down with one of the local daughters. In time, most families in Béxar, presidiales and Isleños alike, could trace their San Antonio roots to these settlers of the 1720s. Such terms as primeros and principales pobladores came to mean both the early military settlers and the Isleños they mixed with to form one of the most successful Spanish colonial communities in the American Southwest.

III

The Canary Islands Immigrants of San Antonio: From Ethnic Exclusivity to Community in Eighteenth-Century Béxar

Gerald E. Poyo

Introduction

On March 9, 1731, a band of fifty-five exhausted immigrants from the Canary Islands arrived in the Presidio de San Antonio de Béxar to begin a new life. At the presidio they encountered a community of Mexican soldier-settlers and their families who had founded the garrison in 1718 to protect the Franciscan mission of San Antonio de Valero and to serve as a supply station for Spanish settlements in East Texas. As new arrivals the Canary Islanders, or Isleños, faced the same dilemma that immigrants have encountered throughout the ages: the contradictory problem of seeking accommodation while struggling to maintain their Old World identity and some link to their past. Initially the maintenance of identity and familiar values was paramount to the immigrants and was reflected in their less-than-compromising attitude toward the already-established settlers in Béxar, but as the newcomers set forth to build their own community, they soon found that life on the frontier required interdependence and cooperation. This reality quickly caused interactions between the two groups that, in time, produced a distinct Tejano community that both groups claimed as their own. Group distinctions became submerged in this new regional identity.[1]

Isleño Attempts to Create an Exclusive Community

Foremost in the minds of the Isleños in 1731 was economic security in this distant region that on the surface did not seem to offer much opportunity. In fact, they had anticipated the difficulties of frontier life and had secured from the Crown certain privileges in return for their agreement to settle in Texas. Besides the largely honorary title of hidalgos, which gave them status locally, the Isleños received political and economic advantages. Their most important privilege was full control of the town's cabildo, or city council. Ten Isleños received life appointments to govern the new villa, San Fernando de Béxar. Six regidores (councilmen), an alguacil (sheriff), an escribano (notary), a mayordomo (commissioner of lands), and a procurador (city attorney) annually selected the two alcaldes ordinarios (regular magistrates) who ruled on the legalities of community life.[2]

Furthermore, the Canary Islanders arrived in Béxar with social attitudes that justified pressing their Crown-bestowed advantages to their fullest extent. From the first encounters with New World peoples, Europeans considered themselves inherently superior. In Spain's American empire peninsulares (Spanish-born individuals) had always placed themselves at the top of a highly stratified, racially determined social structure, even above the white criollos (Spaniards born in America) who could not guarantee their "purity of blood."[3] Thus it is not surprising that the Isleños who arrived in Béxar in 1731 brought like attitudes and looked down on the predominantly mixed-blood presidio population that had originally settled the region. In their view, their status as Europeans gave them an inherent right to dominate political, social, and economic life in Béxar.

Initially the only non-Isleño in a position of authority in the cabildo was the presidio captain, who acted as the justicia mayor (chief magistrate). The precise powers of the chief magistrate in the local council are not clear since daily administrative and legal activities seemed to have been handled by the regular magistrates, but the office did serve to moderate Isleño authority somewhat.[4] Yet even this restraint on Isleño power diminished in 1740 when the cabildo blocked the appointment of Captain Toribio de Urrutia as chief magistrate to succeed his late father. Urrutia complained to Mexico City that it was customary for the captain to act as justice, and, in any case, he noted, only as magistrate could he "exercise control over some contemptuous measures taken by the council of the Islanders."[5] Although the viceroy ruled in Urrutia's favor, the captain's influence was seemingly never sufficient to overcome the powers of a determined Isleño council.

The Isleños naturally used their political advantage to advance their economic position within the settlement. Shortly after arriving, the Canary Islanders received from Captain Juan Pérez de Almazán farmlands and irrigation works to the south of the presidio, which the soldier-settlers had toiled on for many years.[6] In addition, the new arrivals claimed rights to virtually all the nonmission lands west of the San Antonio River and sought to monopolize water from the river itself and the San Pedro Creek.[7]

Since the presidio settlers had never received official land titles or water rights in the community, they were virtually defenseless from a legal standpoint. Nevertheless, they petitioned the viceroy in Mexico City to grant them equal access to land and water in the new town. A favorable ruling in 1733 ordered the governor to distribute the resources equally within the community, but the Isleños objected and were able to delay any implementation indefinitely by initiating in the cabildo a lengthy and cumbersome appeal process. Their control of the city council allowed them to circumvent viceregal rulings, displaying how local officials often imposed their desires in such matters even in the face of contradictory decrees from the colony's highest authority.[8]

The local political struggle over land heated up in early 1734 when Governor Manuel de Sandoval formally measured and legally recorded Isleño lands. This had not been attended to when the Isleños first arrived because of the urgency to establish the town and plant the initial crops. The governor granted thirty-two suertes of irrigable farmland south of the villa (extending from the San Antonio River to the San Pedro Creek) to fifteen Isleño families and four single men.[9] But, much to the cabildo's distress, the governor also ordered the distribution of similar grants to eight soldiers.[10] The city council objected strenuously and argued that the available water was insufficient for all. More to the point, the council argued that "it is not necessary that all who settle in cities, villas, or other places be given land and water for farming because if all are farmers there would not be anybody to purchase the products."[11] Already in competition with the missions for the local market, the Isleños feared that additional farms would make matters untenable, especially since the constant harrassment from Indians prevented settlers from leaving the immediate vicinity of the town to pursue other economic endeavors. The cabildo blocked the land grants to soldiers, which it justified by claiming that authorities in Mexico City simply did not understand frontier conditions.[12]

Actually, control of irrigation was more important than absolute control of land. Soldiers did receive small plots for homes, orchards, and gardens, but irrigation for farming was limited to the original grants. In May 1738, for example, Domingo Flores de Abrego, one "of the earliest settlers of this place, having served as a soldier for twenty years and as a resident for five years," requested a solar, or house lot, on the south side of the presidio plaza. While the governor approved the grant, the land did not include irrigation rights "because at the present time there is none [irrigation ditch], except that at San Pedro Springs, and the use and ownership of said water is rested in the Canary Island settlers and founders of San Fernando." The same document included the promise that Flores would have unrestricted right to "draw whatever water is needed for the land from the conduit that will be made from the San Antonio River for the benefit of all now residing in the said city."[13] Although several grants through the mid-1740s specifically upheld the soldiers' irrigation rights from the San Antonio River, the cabildo did not move to construct the necessary canal.[14] In the meantime, the villa's acequia madre, which ran from the headwaters of the San Pedro Springs through the town to the farmlands below, irrigated only the original Isleño lands.

After 1741, grants for solares rarely mentioned water at all, suggesting that they did not include rights to irrigation. Why governors failed to enforce the viceregal decisions to grant irrigable lands to all residents of Béxar is not clear. Governor Franquis de Lugo, a Canary Islander himself, tended to favor his compatriots over the local soldier-settlers and ignored the issue, but his successors were perhaps motivated by expediency.[15] For indeed, the cabildo enjoyed sufficient power to cause considerable problems for any governor. Perhaps it was easier to allow the cabildo to handle local community matters, particularly since the governors were usually based in Los Adaes where they were occupied with the French and matters of imperial concern.

By the end of their first decade in Béxar, the Isleños had successfully established themselves as the local political and socioeconomic elite. They achieved their initial goal of attaining political dominance and relative economic security in their new home. An added benefit was social status. Increasingly, full membership in the villa required an Isleño political or economic connection, and, as time passed, any blood relation with a Canary Islander, however vague, could be used to advance one's stature in the community.

Isleño monopoly could not last, however, because even as they struggled to consolidate their position, their initially exclusivist vision was modified by the political and socioeconomic realities of daily life on the frontier. Interactions and conflicts within the Isleño community, as well as between them and the others, brought change and new perceptions resulting in their integration with the larger community before the end of the century. This process had various dimensions, but its fundamental character involved the deterioration of institutional segregation between the villa, presidio, and missions, and the emergence of an integrated though socially stratified community based less on ethnicity than on socioeconomically determined status. If community integration in Béxar was perfectly natural and perhaps inevitable as interactions took their course, integration was also conflictive because establishing new relations required basic changes in values and ideas on the part of all. These adaptations came more easily to some than to others.

Social Integration

Individual social and economic relationships between people of the missions, presidio, and villa eventually created a unified community in Béxar. Despite the desire by Isleños to maintain and perpetuate their distinctive identity, they faced situations that left little choice but to interact with the presidio community. This interaction by its very nature changed the Spanish immigrants.

Intermarriage played a central role in the integrative process. Although almost all Isleño heads of household arrived married or were soon married to members of their own group after settling in Béxar, matrimony between Isleños and the Mexican residents occurred quickly and frequently. Already by 1733, María de los Santos, daughter of Isleño Antonio de los Santos, the cabildo's third-ranking regidor, had wed Lieutenant Matheo Pérez of the presidial company.[16] Between 1742 and 1760 San Fernando celebrated at least thirty-two marriages involving Isleños. In only five unions did Isleños marry their compatriots.[17]

The Alvarez Travieso and Arocha families illustrate well the process that reduced ethnic distinctions in Béxar. Vicente Alvarez Travieso (the sheriff) and José Francisco de Arocha (the notary) were among the strongest proponents of maintaining the integrity of a separate Isleño community. Despite this fact, their children contributed to unifing the settlement by marrying Mexicans. Two of Alvarez Travieso's sons married daughters of prominent presidio families originally from Coahuila. Of his six daughters, one married an Isleño, two married European-born Spaniards, and three married former presidio soldiers. At the same time, two of Arocha's daughters married sons of Isleño unions, while one married a retired soldier originally from Aguascalientes. Of Arocha's seven sons for which information exists, all married the daughters of presidial families.[18]

The first generation of Arocha and Alvarez Travieso children born in San Antonio, then, contributed to blurring the social distinctions between Isleños and Mexican presidio families. While racial distinctions remained an important determinant of status within the community, racial passing was common. The originally rejected mixed-blood soldier-settlers became part of Isleño family networks, and thus their "suspect" bloodlines became less of a problem socially. In fact, even before the Isleños arrived many of the mestizo soldiers had already achieved "Spanish" status in baptismal and marriage documents. Later census materials show that mixed bloods other than mestizos (mostly mulattoes) often outnumbered mestizos. Since New Spain's society emerged from the mixing of Indians and Spaniards, one would expect to find a higher degree of mestizos relative to others. But, in fact, it seems that most mestizos, at least in Béxar, managed to attain classification as Spaniards. A Spaniard, then, was anybody with European features, relatively white skin, or economic or military status regardless of physical appearance. At the same time, mixed bloods with Black-Indian combinations without wealth usually had difficulty "passing," accounting for the relatively high number of mulattoes, lobos (mixture of Black and Indian), and other racial categories in the records when compared with mestizos.[19] Thus, as a general rule, while racial distinctions between Spaniards and mestizos became blurred, the distinctions between Spaniards and mestizos on the one hand and other mixed bloods (such as mulattoes and lobos) on the other remained clearer. A scarcity of Spaniards rather than a lack of racial concern explains the concurrent phenomena of exogamy and racial bias in Béxar.

Other social relationships also began to tie the communities together fairly early. In March 1734, for example, Martín Lorenzo de Armas and his wife, María Rodríguez, both Isleños, chose as godparents for their child Fermín de Ybiricú and Gertrudes Flores, both of the presidio community. That October notary José Francisco de Arocha's son became the godson of Francisco Cos and María Luisa Ramón, also of the local community. The following year Arocha stood as godfather to the daughter of Diego Hernández and Juana de Sosa, a presidio couple. The exact factors motivating these kinds of voluntary compadrazgo ties are difficult to determine, but it was probably not inconsequential to Lorenzo de Armas that Ybiricú, for example, was referred to as "don," had commercial ties with Saltillo merchants, had herds of mares at Presidio La Bahía, and collected property rents at Presidio San Juan Bautista.[20] At the same time, Diego Hernández, one of the first settlers of the presidio, probably thought that a relationship with Arocha, the town notary and influential politician, would be beneficial.[21]

Social integration also had a spatial dimension. In the early years of the settlement Isleños lived around the Plaza de las Islas, while the military families lived either in the presidio or adjacent to it, north of the Plaza de Armas. As the community grew, however, the geographic separation of the two communities disappeared. During the century the children and grandchildren of the Isleños and soldiers, as well as some immigrants, initially received solares for homes north of the plazas. But as demographic pressures grew, lands for homes began to be granted west of the San Pedro Creek and in the horseshoe bend of the San Antonio River directly east of the town, known as the potrero. Land-granting patterns began to reflect the town's social and economic structure. The prominent descendants of the earliest Isleño and Mexican settlers generally sought land north of the villa, while citizens and new immigrants with less status usually ended up west of the creek. By the early nineteenth century most of Béxar's elite lived around the plazas and the barrio to the north, and the original spatial segregation between Isleños and the military families disappeared.[22]

Economic Integration

In addition to the social relationships that changed basic attitudes and identities, divergent economic interests and expanded opportunities over time eventually led to a convergence in economic activities among settlers of the region. Initially the Isleños envisioned themselves as an agricultural elite who would provide products to a subject Mexican community. By the end of the century a socially and culturally integrated community had forged an economic system in which virtually everyone farmed and ranched. This system, in addition, implied a cultural convergence based on shared identities as both farmers and ranchers.

From the moment they arrived some Isleños looked beyond their own community for economic opportunity. Antonio Rodríguez Mederos, the cabildo's first mayordomo and procurador, is an early example of a Canary Islander who promoted the integrative process by seeking his livelihood outside the agricultural sector. He initially shared the prevalent exclusivist attitude of most Isleños, but he was sufficiently shrewd to foresee personal economic gains in the unfolding of community integration. Rodríguez's involvement with the broader community began soon after his arrival in Béxar when he established ties with the missionaries. An experienced acequiero in the Canary Islands, Rodríguez supplemented his cane- and corn-growing activities in the 1730s by directing the construction of the Mission Concepción irrigation canal. He later aided in other mission construction projects.[23] Moreover, he became involved in land speculation and home construction, which seems to have become his primary source of livelihood. By 1750 he had been involved in a dozen or so land transactions and had built some fourteen houses in the villa. Both his customers and employees were Isleños and soldier-settlers alike. Rodríguez had a particularly close working relationship with the prominent presidio family, the Carvajals, who hauled rocks and worked as masons on his building projects.[24] Rodríguez established good economic relations with the broader community and lobbied in the cabildo to give the soldiers greater access to economic resources.

But even without Rodríguez's apparently conscious efforts to promote economic integration, normal interactions increasingly tied the groups together. Among the early examples of economic cooperation were the business relations of Isleños Juan Curbelo and Martín Lorenzo de Armas with José Antonio Rodríguez, a retired soldier originally from Coahuila. The three ran a pack train between Saltillo and Béxar and provisioned the presidio. Rodríguez owned the fifteen-mule train but was aided by Curbelo and Armas. As a result, Rodríguez enjoyed the confidence of the Isleños and became one of the most prominent members of the presidio community. In fact, his son and daughter married Alvarez Travieso offspring.[25]

Just as normal interactions led some Isleños to leave farming for other activities, some soldiers obtained irrigable farmlands through the same process. Juan Leal Alvarez, for example, decided that opportunities in Béxar were too limited and left for Coahuila in 1741. Before departing, however, he sold his two suertes, or plots, of irrigable land to the presidio captain, Toribio de Urrutia, for 350 pesos. In one of his speculative ventures, Rodríguez Mederos purchased this land from Urrutia in 1749 and resold it to soldier-settler Miguel de Castro two weeks later. Rodríguez had previously sold his own suertes and water rights to yet another soldier, Francisco Hernández, in 1739. In still another transaction retired soldiers Pedro Ocón y Trillo and Gerónimo Flores purchased suertes from Isleños Manuel de Nis (Rodríguez Mederos's father-in-law) and Joseph Padrón respectively. Padrón joined the presidio and obviously decided to abandon farming permanently.[26] These private transactions gave the purchasers from the presidio an economic legitimacy that made them, in effect, if not in name, full vecinos, or citizens, of San Fernando.

Despite these cooperative economic relationships and transactions, some Isleños resisted efforts to undermine their de facto group dominance in the community. The struggle over irrigable farms in the settlement during most of the century is illustrative. Although the cabildo had, for the most part, succeeded in dominating land and water resources, members of the old presidio families continually sought to recover their rights to farmlands in the villa, even after their first successful petition to the viceroy was ignored by the cabildo. In 1745 the soldiers managed to obtain a reaffirmation of the earlier vice-regal ruling giving them rights to land and irrigation. No action followed, and during the 1750s several soldiers reminded the governor of their rights and presented him with a copy of the official decree. But, as they noted, "not known are the motives or particular ends that assisted him in not carrying out the cited superior dispatch, thus opposing the will of His Majesty and the superior command and leaving us totally helpless, deprived of the benefit of being able to advance and cultivate the lands."[27]

Eventually other factors in the community combined with this persistence by the soldiers to open new farmlands for cultivation. By the 1750s a shortage of land for homes in the villa served as the impetus for change. Initially lands had been granted in the area between the central plazas and the propios, or common lands, to the north of the villa. After this land was distributed only plots west of the creek were available, which were undesirable for many because of their exposed position to Indian attack. Faced with this situation, Governor Jacinto de Barrio ordered that the villa's propios be opened as needed for distribution as solares. In December 1760, for example, a new arrival to Béxar, who had served at the presidios of Santa Rosa, Río Grande, San Xavier, and San Sabá, asked for a solar "on land that is part of the land of the original settlers." The cabildo granted the fifty vara "to the four winds" lot "since we have the superior order of Governor Jacinto del Barrio to grant land from the land of the original settlers." The cabildo maintained a right to tax the property, however.[28]

A subsequent governor, Angel Martos y Navarrete, further advanced the interests of non-Isleños. In 1762, soon after taking office, Martos initiated a general visita, or inspection, of the province and upon arriving in San Fernando received a grievance from soldier-settlers complaining again that the viceregal decree of 1745 had never been implemented. Determined to take action, the governor appointed Gerónimo Flores, from the presidio community, to survey the vacant land north of the villa and assess the possibilities of building a new acequia from the San Antonio River, to which the soldiers had clear rights. Flores reported that the new irrigation ditch would cost in the vicinity of 3,000 pesos, in addition to community labor.[29]

Nothing occurred for a decade, but the governor had reaffirmed the soldiers' right to irrigable land. A second acequia was finally constructed during 1777-1778, and, for the first time in Béxar since the early 1730s, farms with irrigation rights were distributed. Twenty of the twenty-five individuals who received the lands were of the military families. Although some were married or otherwise related to Isleños, it is evident that they obtained their lands as members of the originally excluded Mexican group and not as Isleño in-laws. The remaining five grants went to second-generation Isleños who presumably had not inherited farmlands south of the city. After almost fifty years the soldier-settlers had received their rights to land and water in the villa of San Fernando.[30]

A similar process of economic integration took place within Béxar's ranching economy, perhaps the most powerful force in creating a unified cultural identity in San Antonio. Although the Isleños had initially sought security by attempting to monopolize farmlands in Béxar, they soon recognized the importance of ranching. The soldiers they had displaced from farming very successfully followed the example of the thriving missions and established their own ranches. Furthermore, Isleños soon recognized that farming in Texas was neither easy nor very profitable. Indeed, Béxar's farmers faced a variety of obstacles. They lacked markets for their products and often had to compete with the missions or with the presidio itself in providing foodstuffs to the soldiers. Moreover, the scarcity of laborers and limitations imposed by Indian raiding impeded rapid agricultural expansion, as did the high cost of building irrigation systems and the lack of adequate technology on the frontier. Ranching, on the other hand, had lucrative markets in Louisiana, needed relatively few hands, could often evade the Indians, and required little capital.[31] Information on the early acquisitions of land for private ranching is sketchy, but beginning in the 1730s a few residents of the presidio community received extensive grants in the area of La Bahía, as well as south of Béxar along the San Antonio River. Military families, such as the Hernández and Menchaca, initiated ranching operations during the 1750s after a peace treaty with the Indians made individual and family enterprises feasible. Shortly thereafter several Isleños entered the business and by the 1760s and 1770s had ranch operations along the river. This developing ranching economy not only provided the Isleño and presidio communities with similar economic interests but also created a unifying cultural experience that promoted a common Tejano identity.[32]

Political Integration

These social and economic interactions also contributed to the development of a political integration exemplified by the changing membership of the cabildo. Initially Isleños controlled the council exclusively and made decisions that favored their ethnic community to the detriment of the others. But by the 1760s and 1770s political alignments in a more fluid cabildo reflected social and economic interests that went beyond the earlier narrow control by the Canary Islanders.

At first, political factions in the cabildo developed around personalities. Juan Leal Goraz and Juan Curbelo emerged to lead the immigrant group during the trek north from Mexico City in 1730. Once in Béxar, the presidio captain appointed them to the most prominent positions in the cabildo, senior councilman and second-ranking councilman respectively. The new cabildo immediately split between the two, but Curbelo emerged to dominate the body with the help of his two influential sons-in-law, José Francisco de Arocha (the notary) and Vicente Alvarez Travieso (the sheriff).[33]

The initially personalistic character of politics in the cabildo soon became more complex as the two groups debated the extent to which they should interact with the neighboring settlers. The governor's attempt to distribute irrigable lands to eight soldiers in January 1734 initiated a sometimes bitter political struggle that quickly divided the community. Curbelo and his sons-in-law vigorously opposed the grants, arguing that resources were insufficient for Isleño needs. But Leal and his son Juan Leal Alvarez (sixth-ranking councilman) saw no reason to deny the grants. Whatever their motivations, the stance taken by the Leals shattered the unified Isleño commitment to building an exclusive and closed community.[34]

At least one other council member, Antonio Rodríguez Mederos (the attorney), agreed with Leal. His motives seem clearer for, as we have seen, Rodríguez benefited from his interactions with the broader community. After Leal's death in 1740 Rodríguez Mederos managed to obtain appointment as senior councilman, and he allowed the military community to participate in the town's affairs. In 1745, for example, he gave the soldiers the opportunity to present formally through the council their grievances to the viceroy. He also supported their participation as council members. Arocha and Alvarez Travieso continued to resist efforts to dilute traditional Isleño rights and prerogatives, however, and a bitter power struggle ensued. They fought with Rodríguez Mederos, charging him with a variety of improprieties, including selling council positions to members of the presidio community. Rodríguez denied the accusations, but his detractors succeeded in removing him from office in 1749.[35] Despite regaining their previous influence on the council, Arocha and Alvarez Travieso could not reverse the trend toward inclusion. The participation of soldiers in the cabildo became routine during the next decade.[36]

This greater involvement of the Mexican community can be attributed, in part, to the fact that by the 1750s several of the life appointees to council seats had died. Once vacated, the positions became elective on an annual basis, creating numerous openings. Furthermore, viceregal rulings ordered the cabildo to include the soldiers. But perhaps the most important forces driving political integration were the social and economic interactions that blurred ethnic, racial, and occupational distinctions. As Isleños married into and established business relations with military families, they became more accepting of broader political participation in the cabildo.

By 1766 officeholders in the cabildo represented both groups. In that year perhaps the most influential cabildo official was Vicente Alvarez Travieso, the sheriff. The council included his son Juan Andrés Travieso (second-ranking councilman) and his son-in-law Jacinto Delgado (fourth-ranking councilman) of another prominent Isleño family. Delgado's uncle, Domingo, served as first alcalde, or magistrate, and another in-law, Joaquín Menchaca, brother of the presidio captain, was second magistrate. The only other person of Isleño extraction on the council that year was Juan Granados (fifth-ranking councilman). The rest of the council had military backgrounds. In addition to Menchaca, Marcos de Castro (third-ranking councilman) and Francisco Hernández (sixth-ranking councilman), both related by marriage to Granados, were from founding families of the presidio in 1718. Two others with military backgrounds who gained election in 1766 were Ignacio Calvillo (city attorney and commissioner of lands) and Juan José Montes de Oca (senior councilman), both married to Arochas.[37] This council reflected the growing integration of the Isleño and presidio settlers. Clearly, participation in the body involved some combination of family connections and socioeconomic status in the community beyond racial and ethnic considerations. Influential citizens of any social group now had the possibility of holding office in the cabildo.

The public controversies between the Arocha and Alvarez Travieso families exemplify the role of socioeconomic factors in defining political participation and competition in Béxar. Despite the close political alliance between the two families earlier in the century, by the early 1770s some of their members engaged in political competition. In 1774 the cabildo in which Vicente Alvarez Travieso was still sheriff opposed the governor's appointment of Simón de Arocha (José Francisco's son) as lieutenant governor of the province.[38] Most ranchers probably felt that such an appointment gave Arocha unfair political and economic advantage in local affairs. Later in the decade Alvarez Travieso and his son-in-law Francisco Javier Rodríguez openly accused the governor of favoring the Arochas over other ranching families.[39] A few years after that Rodríguez and others filed still another grievance in which they accused the Arochas of manipulating cabildo elections to their advantage.[40] The conflicts between the two families illustrate how their commitment to Isleño ethnic solidarity weakened as the century progressed. As socioeconomic interactions blurred the initially strict divisions between Isleños and soldiers, political realignments occurred among the Arochas and Alvarez Traviesos. Islander solidarity bowed to concerns about advancing family economic interests within a broadly integrated community.

Expressions of Community in Béxar

By the 1770s, and perhaps before, Béxar's Isleño and presidio populations had begun to view themselves as composing one community, with similar interests and goals. This was reflected most poignantly in their common dependence on the cattle industry, the most lucrative and best-suited economic endeavor for the region. Citizens of Béxar of all backgrounds learned the techniques of ranching, utilized its vocabulary, adapted the appropriate dress, became exceptional riders, and shared the understanding that the welfare of San Fernando depended not only on the maintenance but also on the expansion of their ranching economy. Whenever Bexareños perceived a threat to their livelihood, they closed ranks politically to defend their community and shared destiny. Individuals and groups in San Fernando continued to compete for relative political and economic advantage throughout the century, but this rivalry was cordial when compared to the conflicts provoked by mission and Crown officials who advanced their interests at the expense of the local community.

Indeed, by the mid-1750s the initially antagonistic Isleño and presidio communities found themselves in a natural political alliance against the expanding missions. In 1756 Isleños (Francisco Delgado, Vicente Alvarez Travieso, Joseph Curbelo, and Joseph Padrón) joined with leaders of the military community (Luís Antonio Menchaca, Martín Flores, and Andrés Ramón) to oppose a request by the friars to reduce the size of the military garrison. They all agreed that the villa would slowly die without a robust garrison to defend the region and to provide employment and a much-needed market.[41] At the same time, they suspected the missionaries of attempting to weaken the settlement in order to expand mission property. Isleños and soldiers alike understood that their differences were of little consequence compared to the political threat posed by the missions. During the next thirty years the pervasive preoccupation with their mission neighbors united Béxar's citizens, who cooperated, thus furthering their common identity.[42]

Similar conflicts with the Spanish government reenforced this unity in Béxar. Throughout the final half of the eighteenth century, Spain implemented a series of measures known as the Bourbon reforms, which were calculated to streamline colonial bureaucracy, increase economic efficiency, and enhance colonial profitability. In Texas during the 1770s these reforms took the form of a stronger official Crown presence, administrative reorganization, and regulation of the cattle industry. As part of a general reorganization of the northern frontier provinces of New Spain, the Crown ordered the abandonment of the East Texas presidio of Los Adaes and declared San Fernando de Béxar the capital. The governor henceforth resided in Béxar. Furthermore, a new breed of governor appeared in Texas, personified by Juan María Vicencio Barón de Ripperdá (1770-1778) and Domingo Cabello y Robles (1778-1786). Schooled in reform and Crown authority, they immediately clashed with Béxar's independent-minded citizens. Faced with new demands made by the Crown and its representatives, the cabildo fought to maintain its autonomy. During the final third of the century Isleños and soldiers joined together to defend their traditions against what they considered to be the heavy-handed intrusions of unsympathetic Crown bureaucrats in their local affairs.[43]

Conclusion

The political, socioeconomic, and cultural convergence of Isleños and members of the presidio community is critical to understanding the history of eighteenth-century Béxar. Their early relations were characterized by a lack of cooperation and conflict, but during the century these differences were overcome by the blurring of ethnic lines, resulting in a society divided mainly by economic interests. Although political battles among Bexareños did not end, their conflicts transcended ethnically based Isleño versus soldier interests and became individual, family, or economic-group competition. A new spirit of community resulting from internal socioeconomic developments and outside pressures united the inhabitants of Béxar and perhaps of the entire province. Indeed, during the first two decades of the nineteenth century this shared identity, which gave the community its form, became even more entrenched and eventually contributed to the complex struggle on Texas soil for Mexican independence.

IV

The Religious-Indian Communities:
The Goals of the Friars
Gilberto M. Hinojosa

Introduction:
The Missions on the San Antonio River

The Franciscans who accompanied the Spanish entradas into Texas in the late seventeenth century were carrying out their order's longtime commitment to bring the gospel to the Indians. On the frontier this task involved the establishment of missions, institutions designed to "civilize"– that is, to settle and Hispanicize – the seminomadic northern tribes as the first step to Christianizing them.[1] The friars directed their initial efforts in Texas to converting the Hasinai in the Neches River area, but evangelization of these natives proved fruitless, and the missionaries withdrew to the headwaters of the San Antonio River to await the opportune moment to resume their work in the East Texas field. On the San Antonio the padres established missions that were initially designed as autonomous towns but which in time merged with the larger civilian and military community of Béxar.[2]

The five area missions became the nucleus of religious activities in the new province of Texas. The first of these institutions, San Antonio de Valero, opened its doors in 1718. Originally this mission and the accompanying garrison, the Presidio de San Antonio de Béxar, were to serve as halfway stations between the Rio Grande settlements in the province of Coahuila and the missions and forts on the edge of the empire; but placed amidst several sizable Indian nations, the new religious establishment inspired other evangelization efforts in the area. "As we envision it," Fray Antonio Margil de Jesús wrote the governor in December of 1719, "this area of San Antonio and its environs . . . will become the heart from which we will spread in all directions."[3] A few months later Padre Margil founded Mission San José y San Miguel de Aguayo some three leagues downriver from Valero, and by year's end the two institutions housed over 500 Coahuiltecan Indians. By the early 1730s three other missions, La Purísima Concepción de Acuña, San Juan de Capistrano, and San Francisco de la Espada, were in full operation. Two decades later the friars were serving more than 800 natives.[4]

The missionaries found the San Antonio area ideal for settlement. "The climate is healthful, with rainy, cold, and hot seasons resembling those of Old Spain," one missionary reported, confident that the missions would soon be producing large surpluses of wheat, wine, and olive oil. While the river valley never produced those Old World crops in abundance and some not at all, the stream remained "as bountiful as its namesake, St. Anthony of Padua, was prodigal in answering prayers," providing all five missions with large quantities of water for irrigation.[5] From this secure base Franciscans from the Apostolic Colleges at Querétaro and Zacatecas manned and supplied their remaining East Texas operations as well as Mission Espíritu Santo and (later) Nuestra Señora del Rosario on the coast. The prosperous San Antonio missions also became the springboard for expansion to the San Xavier River and to San Sabá in the middle 1700s. Though these riskier ventures failed, the Central Texas establishments continued to bloom until the end of the century.[6]

These missions in the upper San Antonio River valley did not evolve in isolation. A nearby garrison, the Presidio de San Antonio de Béxar, aided the friars in recruiting Indians and provided defense for the mission pueblos. The padres, in turn, supplied the presidio and otherwise assisted the garrison, serving the Crown with arms as a vehicle for the expansion of empire as well as in their efforts to settle the nomads.[7] The missions also depended on the civilian settlers for craftsmen and ideally were preparing the natives for participation in the mainstream of colonial life.[8] However, despite this interaction and shared imperial objectives, the missions, like the town and the presidio, were primarily designed to meet the needs of their own members and inevitably came into conflict with the other two agencies of settlement and expansion.[9]

The drive for autonomy was rooted in all three institutions, but particularly in the missions. Although the five San Antonio religious establishments were founded and operated separately as independent corporations and were governed by two distinct Franciscan administrative units, all the missions shared various features that unified them, gave them a special identity, and distinguished them as a group from the presidio and the town. These characteristics included their common goals of "civilizing" and Christianizing the Indians; their use of the same techniques that originated in the early colonial period; their similar development as the colony expanded northward; and their parallel demographic and physical growth in the San Antonio River valley. Also enhancing the solidarity and uniqueness of the missions was the support the padres received from the interior and the specific services that all the missions provided to other frontier agencies. Even if professed goals indicated otherwise, the special character of the missions encouraged the trend towards self-preservation and exclusivity, setting these institutions on a road which kept them isolated from the currents that drew settlers and presidiales together. Nevertheless, by the end of the eighteenth century, proximity, interdependence, economic and social interaction, and forces beyond their control broke down the walls of separation and moved the missions towards integration with the wider community.

Missionary Goals and Traditions:
The Foundations of Exclusivity

In delineating and executing their strategies for evangelizing the natives, the Franciscans who arrived on the frontier in the late 1600s drew upon the immediate postconquest tradition of settling the Indians in permanent villages. After the fall of the Aztec Empire, missionaries began their task of converting the inhabitants of central Mexico by ministering to them in the towns where the concentration of population facilitated instruction and control. The padres often focused on converting the leaders, which resulted in the acceptance of the new faith by the masses. Although the friars visited small settlements in the countryside, they preferred to work in larger villages and thus encouraged, and sometimes forced, the relocation of Indians in remote areas into reducciones, or compounds. In rationalizing this strategy the friars argued that living scattered in the mountains or the hinterlands went counter to natural law since such an isolated existence deprived the natives of the services of the missionaries and made impossible the mutual assistance that neighbors usually provide one another. The missionaries also recognized that stable settlements encouraged long-lasting, monogamous unions in which Christian family and sexual ideals would be realized.[10]

Actually, the tactic of moving the Indians into towns did not need justification from the friars; it had been adopted early on as the most effective technique by which all the agents of conquest – missionaries, individual Spaniards, and the authorities – controlled the native population. When the Indians were numerous but not settled, gathering them was essential for implementing the encomienda and (later) the repartimiento, the systems through which conquistadores obtained free labor as a reward for participation in the conquest. The tight-knit social structure of the Indian communities lent itself to the manipulation of the natives by the encomenderos, by the regidores who managed the repartimiento, and by missionaries who were spreading the new faith. Those with vested interests in the native population were further served by the segregation of Indians in the República de Indios (the Indian corporate body) in the countryside from which would-be competitors for Indian services and loyalties could be easily barred. Additionally, the organization of the natives in distinguishable and quantifiable units facilitated the exercise of the Crown's sovereignty over Indians, civilians, and religious. Thus, while striving for very different goals—authority over New World residents, the exploitation of the natives' labor, or the salvation of their souls—all Spaniards had been committed since the first years of the colonial period to congregating the natives in villages in a completely separate area.[11]

Out of this initial experience of shared objectives of congregating the Indians emerged a formal mission system in the mid-1500s that was later extended to the far northern frontier. Expansion of the colony in this direction was blocked by warring Chichimecos who plundered caravans on the main roads that linked the Valley of Mexico with the new mining towns in the north. After aggressive campaigns against these Indians failed, the viceroy sent missionaries to persuade the nomads to gather in villages and take up the peaceful occupations of grazing, farming, and trade. Less costly to royal coffers than the endless cycle of attack and retaliation by both sides, the mission system also reduced the shameless spectacle of slave raiding by settlers. Although the success of the religious did not preclude war "by fire and blood" altogether, wherever resistance was broken Jesuits and Franciscans introduced mission programs that were very similar: isolated Indian communities which strove towards Christianization and self-sufficiency through the introduction of European economic enterprises.[12]

The missionaries tended to view their objectives and those of the Crown as the same, but they sought to place themselves beyond the control of the criollo (New World) church and settlers. To this end they established special jurisdictional lines that assured them independence even from their Franciscan provincials in New Spain. Accordingly, the priests and lay brothers who spearheaded the advance to the northeast belonged to colleges administered by the order's superior general in the peninsula and the viceroy in Mexico City. With this strong backing, friars from the Colegio Apostólico de Santa Cruz de Querétaro (founded in 1683) and later those from its counterpart, Nuestra Señora de Guadalupe de Zacatecas (founded in 1707), dedicated themselves to reviving the order's original task of preaching in parishes and to the evangelization of the indios gentiles (unconverted natives). They were thus able to attend to their spiritual goals and resist local and regional demands for mission lands and the exploitation of the Indians.[13]

The Franciscans' independence on the frontier was furthered by the crucial material assistance they received from their order and from the Crown. Monasteries in New Spain and in the peninsula recruited and prepared zealous men willing to live on the edge of Western civilization. Fellow Franciscans in the colony solicited contributions wherever they preached and organized vital procurement and supply trains that took food, clothing, tools, utensils, church wine, vestments, and other articles to the northernmost missions. The viceroy's treasury paid the friars an annual salary, which they generally used to make their operations run smoothly. Periodically the Crown also funded new missionary enterprises that expanded the Kingdom of God as well as Spain's territories, but when government officials wavered in their commitment or a particular mission found itself in economic difficulties, other missions came to the rescue, and the colegios took up the slack, striving always to maintain the frontier institutions at the original levels of support.[14]

The padres also obtained important assistance from the military. By the early seventeenth century, when the Franciscans with military escorts pushed into Nuevo León and Coahuila, joint religious and military expeditions had become the norm. Padres and presidiales gathered Coahuiltecans into a mission at Monclova in 1685 and five years later speared into East Texas in search of French intruders and Indian converts. Armed soldiers provided safety for the priests on recruiting visits to Indian campsites, and, when necessary, they intimidated the natives into joining the reducciones. Throughout the new province, as elsewhere on the northern frontier, garrisons guarded the various mission centers and provided presidiales to aid the padres in training the natives.[15]

In implementing their goals on the frontier, the friars relied on long-established techniques. The first encounters with the natives required communicating with them through Indian or mestizo intermediaries or by means of sign language. Professing friendship, the padres usually offered gifts, which, as expected, drew the Indians' awe and curiosity. The friars then outlined the advantages of a settled life and the Christian faith and proposed to the Indians that they gather in mission pueblos.[16] To their amazement, the padres at times discovered that some natives had "as good acquaintance with the 'Spanish' skills of building houses and planting as the most efficient missionary could teach them." Indians like these were usually prepared to settle down and sometimes asked that missions be organized for them. So did groups who were threatened by other stronger and more aggressive tribes and who therefore stood to gain from the protection the friars and soldiers could extend.[17]

But most of the natives were not eager to join the missionaries, sometimes prompting the padres to use coercion in recruiting the nomads. On occasion the padres lured some groups by promising to secure for them their relatives held captive by the settlers. The friars drew still others by offering food or by threatening them outright. As Fray Benito Fernández de Santa Ana explained to the viceroy, "There are Indians who are hungry, and they accept the faith through the enticement of food . . . and there are those who . . . require the weapons of Your Majesty to bring them into civil society."[18]

Once the natives agreed to settle down, the padres procured the formal recognition of the Indians' rights to the land and established the social and administrative structure necessary to run the new communities. Acting in the place of the governor and accompanied by the friars, presidial Captain Juan Valdez executed the appropriate ritual in the founding of Mission San José. "I grasped the hands of the . . . Indian chiefs, and taking them through the site, gave them . . . possession of the land and water. . . . [Then] going through the area, they pulled up grass, threw rocks, [and] cut off branches from the bushes" as a sign of their control and ownership. Following these rites, Captain Valdez added, "I appointed Juan, Chief of the Pampopas, as Governor [of the mission community]; Nicolás, Chief of the Suliajame tribe, as Judge and Alcalde [mayor of mission town council]; Alonzo of the Pastía nation as Constable; and Francisco of the Pampopa tribe and Antonio of the Suliajames as Aldermen. To each I gave the insignia befitting his office so that he might be obeyed." [19]

On other occasions the padres themselves performed the ceremonies and other formalities, which included bestowing titles and symbols of authority on native officials. In order to provide the new Indian magistrates with the necessary respect and obedience from the mission residents, the friars gave the leaders items of clothing and utensils that were finer than those distributed to the others. More importantly, the missionaries backed their actions by threatening to punish those who defied the new officials. Thus guided by the padres and their lieutenants, each pueblo would become, according to one friar, a new Jerusalem, where the faithful lived the communal life of the evangelical church. [20] More immediately, mission society resembled the organized villages of central Mexico, with native chiefs directing life in the Indian community while a Spaniard (in this case, the padre) made the basic work decisions.

Forces of Exclusivity in Mission Life

Although certain facets of mission life seemed to encourage the eventual integration of the Indians into Hispanic colonial society, overall the padres strove to build and maintain communities that were completely separate from the neighboring settlement of San Fernando. In the missions natives were to become acquainted with farming and grazing and certain crafts, gain some fluency in the Spanish language, and adopt selected cultural traditions. The overriding goal of the friars was, after all, to settle the Indians and inculcate in them the Christian faith and the moral virtues it required, all very important elements of Spanish society and culture.[21] However, acculturation of the natives was not absolutely essential to the functioning of mission pueblos and the fulfillment of the friars' goals. As for assimilation of the Indians into the Hispanic society of San Fernando, it does not appear to have been seriously considered. Quite the contrary, the work and life in the missions and the building programs directed by the padres were designed to create permanent communities completely separate from the other institutions on the frontier.[22] The survival and development of the missions for almost a century attests to the strength of those ideals of segregation and independence.

A dispute in 1736 between the missionaries and the governor in San Antonio concerning a bridge over the river that separated Mission San Antonio de Valero and the town-presidio settlement exemplifies this commitment of the friars to build and maintain separate communities. The bridge had been built by the Indians under the direction of the padres to facilitate mission business with the presidio, but no sooner had the crude span been set up than settlers and soldiers began using it to visit the Indian pueblo for personal reasons. This unrestricted access to the mission interfered with the scheduled work, the teaching of crafts, and catechism and prayer. Some of the intruders allegedly cheated the neophytes out of food and household goods or stole these outright. Supposedly the soldiers also slaughtered mission cattle, indulged in public drunkenness, and molested native women. To prevent these disruptions and abuses the missionaries removed the beams that served as a bridge. Thereupon the settlers and soldiers affected by this action took their objections to the top provincial authority, Carlos Franquis de Lugo, who eagerly jumped into the fray on their side. Without hesitation the governor brazenly ordered the missionaries to send some Indians to help reconstruct the bridge. The friars refused, but the soldiers forced a handful of natives to carry out the governor's wishes nonetheless. The padres retaliated by posting a guard in front of the mission, an action that enraged Franquis de Lugo. Set on resolving the conflict personally, he dashed across the river, forced his way into the mission, and confronted the religious superior in his cell, threatening him with his cane. The missionary stood his ground, however, and, although the bridge remained, the friars discontinued the tradition of allowing settlers and soldiers to worship in the mission chapel.[23]

The bridge story is illustrative of the friars' attempts to control all interaction between the natives and all others and to protect mission property. Fray Benito Fernández de Santa Ana observed that, while presidiales and townspeople could trade with the mission residents, these outsiders should not be allowed to enter the Indian pueblo or even talk to the natives unless supervised by a missionary. By the same token, intruders and squatters on mission lands were to be assessed the stiff penalty of 200 pesos and evicted.[24] The maintenance of two distinct societies was critical to the functioning of the friars' institutions. Indeed, as padre Mariano Francisco de los Dolores y Viana reminded the governor, strict separation of Indians and Spaniards was decreed by the laws of the realm.[25]

As prescribed by the friars, life and work within the mission walls was directed to the exclusivity and permanence of those institutions. The friars set out to teach the Indians to farm and graze livestock and to build suitable dwellings, but they did so at the most elementary levels. The evidence suggests that the missionaries utilized the neophytes mostly in work gangs that provided unskilled manual labor. Bolstered by supply trains which brought a variety of finished or nearly finished goods to the missions, the padres could direct the energies of the residents to clearing the fields, constructing the irrigation canals, and erecting the buildings needed in the pueblo. Occasionally some Indians took up butchering, tanning, tailoring and sewing, smithing, carving, and sculpturing. Most frequently, however, Spaniards or mestizos from the villa or from central Mexico were in charge of these skilled tasks, while the natives were engaged in the labor-intensive functions that ensured the subsistence, profit, and long-range endurance of the missions.[26]

These overriding objectives interfered with goals directed to the acculturation of the natives, such as teaching the Spanish language. The padres did prefer their own mother tongue over Indian dialects, which lacked the terms for the new tools and crops and, most importantly, for the abstract concepts of Christianity.[27] But teaching Spanish to the natives proved to be more difficult than learning the Indian languages. The use of a Coahuiltecan dictionary-catechism in the missions bears this out and in fact suggests that the padres even attempted to establish a Coahuiltecan lingua franca among the natives. To have carried out an efficient acculturation program as their ideals called for, the friars would have needed to have started each mission with only a few Indians, as one friar advised, and increased their numbers only gradually.[28] But that process would have impeded the construction projects, which involved many workers, and learning Spanish did not appear to be as important for missionization and Christianization as did the work habits and moral behavior fostered by a settled village life.

The friars had, in fact, directed substantial efforts in the early years to Hispanicizing the Indians, but these endeavors were thwarted by their own manpower limitations. Ideally one of the two friars stationed at a mission was to devote himself entirely to teaching the new language, Spanish customs, and Christian doctrine and morals, but, given the relatively large number of Indians, this was hardly sufficient for effective cultural change.[29] Consequently the friars demanded that some mission families send their young boys to reside in the monastery wing in order to imbue them with the European world view, values, and traditions. By midcentury, when widespread commitments drained available personnel and only one priest was assigned to each mission, the friars deemphasized cultural endeavors and at times even spiritual ideals and placed more attention on the "temporalities" in order to guarantee the primary goal of institutional survival.[30]

The building program reflected the self-sustaining impulse pervasive in the missions. Generally the first structures erected after a mission's founding were makeshift, temporary jacales (mud and stick, thatched-roof huts) because the padres wanted to ascertain the location's suitability and because priority was given to clearing the fields and digging the acequias, undertakings that required a couple of decades to complete. However, small stone churches were built shortly after a permanent site was selected. Typically these structures were converted into other uses once the major projects were well on the way in the 1740s and construction began on bigger churches and on conventos (monasteries for the friars). In the following decade storage buildings and workshops were erected. Later, stone houses were built for the residents, and the pueblos were enclosed. Within these fortresslike villages the friars then expanded the churches and conventos, impressing residents and visitors alike with the success of the mission enterprises. From their pulpits and offices the padres directed mission life and operations, fully confident that their institutions would always form important, separate communities in the area.[31]

Even serious demographic changes did not alter for a long time the direction of these institutions towards exclusivity. When a decline in the mission population became evident in the 1780s, the friars shifted construction priorities from the addition of decorative features in the churches to the expansion of utilitarian structures such as mills, granaries, and workshops. Most of the buildings had, in fact, been erected previously, in the early period which coincided with population peaks (from the 1740s to the 1770s). [32]

During those years, and indeed since their foundation in the 1720s, the San Antonio missions had averaged more than 150 residents, having at times as many as 260 (in one exceptional year Mission San José reported 350 Indians). But in the mid-1770s the population of each institution declined by 50 to 100 natives. Then, in the late 1780s, it dropped precipitously, reaching the lowest marks after 1792, approximately when partial secularization began. In those twilight years the still physically imposing structures housed very few Indians (from twenty-seven to forty-five residents each).[33] However, given the more than sixty years of sustained relatively high populations and strong support from the interior of the colony, the mission communities stood apart and independent from the other institutions in San Fernando.

This trend towards creating insular communities, so evident in the drive for mission self-sufficiency and in the physical barriers, minimized the need for interaction between Indians and the soldier-settlers and town dwellers. Consequently the movement of acculturated natives to San Fernando – if, in fact, it was ever intended – appears minimal until the end of the century. The number of mission Indians marrying outside their racial group was inconsequential.[34] The mission system was simply not designed towards making integration a reality. Indeed, contrary to prevailing historical interpretation, the padres did not, until the very end, contemplate the demise of their institutions and full assimilation of the natives into the Hispanic society. Throughout most of the century the letters and reports of the missionaries never expressed a desire for a fully integrated society. Quite the opposite, the padres' words and actions attest to the hope of permanent, separate towns. Up until the 1790s the friars launched new building programs, continued to consolidate their institutions, and even made efforts to expand their landholdings. These mission complexes, with prominent churches and conventos, reflected a large-scale, somewhat utopian, plan to create distinct Indian communities directed by the friars – a re-creation of the centuries-old República de Indios common to central Mexico.

Forces of Integration:
Limitations to Missionary Goals

The independence of the missions could not be sustained indefinitely, however. Along with the pull towards exclusion, the system contained internal pressures directing it towards integration. Furthermore, external forces, such as governmental policies and economic and social developments beyond the control of the padres, interfered with mission objectives. The friars themselves also had a change of heart, or at least of interest, in their work in Texas, and this also weakened the intrinsic institutional drive for autonomy. Consequently by the end of the century the missions were shorn of their corporate status and secularized. Lands were deeded to residents and opened to settlers, while the religious duties of missionaries were turned over to the diocesan clergy. The dissolution of these once-separate religious entities broke down the barriers to their becoming a part of the larger Béxar community.

To a certain extent, the seeds of the dissolution of the missions were evident in the very foundation of the province. The padres had never been able to implement their goals in East Texas, where large groups, such as the Hasinai, who lived on isolated farms, proved "insolent" and "obstinate," resisting the padres' pressures to congregate them. For a time the missionaries were heartened by the number of deathbed baptisms (it appears that the Indians who were seriously ill hedged their bets on the hereafter by availing themselves of both Indian and Spanish rituals). Eventually, however, since the padres were unable to procure the military support to create the necessary social structure for conversion, they became disillusioned with their work among these Indians and retreated to the San Antonio River valley.[35]

The Béxar "way stations" quickly became the core religious settlements from which missions for the large northern Indian groups were planned and launched. However, these ambitious new efforts failed. The Comanches, the Wichitas, and other northern tribes were prospering in their commerce with the French and remained beyond direct Spanish control throughout the colonial period. When Spain did try to bring the Norteños (Nations of the North) into its sphere in the mid-1700s, the Crown adopted a policy of trading with these natives rather than attempting to settle them. For geopolitical reasons, the government also refused to assist the missionaries in reducing and Christianizing the Apaches. Still, in the face of these failures and constraints, the padres never questioned their strategy for evangelization; rather, they continued to be committed to their vision of creating permanent Indian villages.[36]

Unable to evangelize the larger native groups, the missionaries contented themselves with recruiting from small Central-Texas and coastal bands, a limitation which was an asset in many respects but which ultimately proved to be the undoing of the missions as separate communities. Small bands of Coahuiltecans and Karankawas, which were easily recruited and controlled, were the most likely candidates for missionization.[37] Having a dozen or so of these groups in a mission provided an element of stability to the work force because, if one band left with all its members (as happened on one occasion at San José), the entire pueblo's population would not suffer significantly, and the construction projects could continue without interruption. This strategy of depending on small bands worked well until the last quarter of the eighteenth century. At that time, these groups no longer subjected themselves to the padres' demands for social and cultural conformity to Spanish ways and turned instead to the Norteños to improve their lot.[38] The lack of neophytes to replenish mission populations would in time spell the end of those institutions.

Recruitment was critical for the survival of the missions since the Indian towns were unable to increase, or even maintain themselves, numerically. At Valero, for example, during the sixty years for which data is available (which includes mostly years with high populations), births outnumbered deaths only in five years. On the average, for every seven babies born annually, ten persons died. The disproportionate death rate was directly linked to a high infant and childhood mortality. Over two-thirds of 319 Indians baptized and buried at Valero died during the first three years of life. Only fifty reached what may have been considered adulthood, twelve years of age. Of these, only fourteen lived into their twenties, and a mere eight into maturity (thirty to forty-five years).[39]

Various factors contributed to the overall low rate of natural increase among mission Indians. For example, there were considerably fewer women than men, a phenomenon that resulted from the numerous deaths of mothers while giving birth and possibly from female infanticide. This latter practice appears to have been a common form of population control among Indians facing limited resources, and the natives may have continued this custom even after missionization. Fatal accidents, murders, and deaths at the hands of attacking Indians contributed minimally. Plagues also took their toll on the mission residents because of the Indians' lack of immunity to European diseases, but the data suggests that deaths occurring during epidemic years were not considerably higher than usual.[40] It appears, however, that the most important contributor to the high death rate was the generally poor health of the mission Indians.

According to the missionaries, the Indians themselves were to blame for this condition. Fray Mariano observed that common illnesses were fatal to the natives because they ate unwholesome foods gathered in el monte (the wilderness) nearby. Supposedly these had debilitating effects on all, especially on nursing infants. Moreover, the padre noted, the Indians were usually dirty and did not use purges, sweating, or other accepted remedies, relying instead on wild herbs for their cures. They also engaged in "sexual excesses," which resulted in the spread of venereal diseases. Fray Mariano also complained that the natives did not adequately protect themselves from the elements. They appeared more concerned with eating and roaming than with building comfortable houses and weaving in order to clothe themselves.[41] While Fray Mariano's observations may reflect a strong European prejudice, they may also suggest that the missions were not attracting physically strong bands and that life in the mission did not substantially alter the lifestyles of those Indians or make up for the poor health in which they arrived.

Indeed, mission life itself may have had limited effects on the Indians and may have, in fact, exacerbated the Indians' health problems. Undoubtedly the nutrition of mission residents improved – sufficient corn and beef appears to have been distributed year-round, and vegetables and fruits were available seasonally – but the very change of diet may have affected the Indians' health. Whereas, during their roaming days the natives had eaten a large variety of roots, fruits, nuts, wild game, and fish, their mission fare was largely starches (corn) and red meats (beef). Then, too, while their caloric intake may have been suitable for moderate activity, Indians were made to work in different and more demanding work patterns than their previous tasks required. The highly supervised life of labor, prayer, and learning was probably very stressful for these once-free natives, and constant psychological pressures, we now know, are as injurious to health as any virus or malnutrition.[42]

Besides being more constrained and crowded in the Indian pueblos than they had been in el monte, the natives actually did not enjoy adequate housing in the missions. The construction program had concentrated on clearing the fields, digging the acequias, and building the churches and storage rooms. Indeed, as late as 1776, Fray Benito Fernández de Santa Ana admitted that some "Indian houses . . . [were still] impermanent and rickety, their household goods . . . [were] few, not much more than a metate [corn-grinding stone], a skillet, and a thin mat on which to sleep."[43] Despite benefits natives received by accepting the padres' invitation, life in their new surroundings apparently did not improve their health significantly and may have worsened it. Whatever the cause, the troubling reality was that mission populations had serious difficulties maintaining themselves.

Indian resistance to demands of mission life also contributed to the demise of those institutions. The task of changing the natives' cultural outlook and lifestyles was a major challenge for the missionaries, who continually had to exhort and pressure backsliding neophytes to comply with their new religious responsibilities. The padres' charges did not easily give up their sexual mores or their mitotes (nature-dance rituals). Under the observant eyes of friars and soldiers, the mission Indians were marched to church like schoolchildren to attend mass, sing the alabanzas (hymns), and fulfill the Easter duty of receiving the Sacrament of Penance.[44] In the confessional the neophytes rarely volunteered any information on their offenses, acknowledging them only when prodded and excusing their reticence by claiming "You did not ask me" or "I thought it would upset you." When pressed to admit sexual sins, they usually denied these were willful acts. But the missionaries were not discouraged by their limited success in changing the natives. They merely doubled their efforts of persuasion and force, including greater supervision and the use of whips and stocks to discipline those remiss in their obligations.[45]

Chafing under the monastic work-and-prayer routine, the Indians resorted to passive protests such as carelessness and work slowdowns or desertion. "It takes four of them to accomplish what I can do alone," grumbled one missionary, adding that the simple task of cleaning the sanctuary lamp would not get done unless the priest supervised the assignment.[46] The neophytes often claimed ignorance or lack of dexterity as reasons for not performing their duties, or they feigned illnesses, a strong sign, according to one friar, that they were preparing to desert. Indeed, when pressed too severely to comply with the work rules or to change their ways, many residents simply ran away. "These Indians are not difficult to convert," observed one padre, meaning that they could be easily persuaded to enter the mission, "but they are bothersome [to keep]," thus explaining the large population turnover in the missions.[47]

Desertions aggravated the demographic crisis. Unbeknownst to the natives, in joining the missions they had entered into a binding legal commitment, equivalent to receiving baptism, matrimony, or Holy Orders, or to taking religious vows. Thus, when the Indians abandoned their new homes to go back to their old habitats, they became "apostates," individuals rejecting the faith or abandoning the monastery. Usually soldiers accompanied the padres to ensure the return of escapees, but the padres did not receive this assistance after midcentury. By then the government had adopted a policy of befriending and trading with the larger Indian nations and refused to alienate them by demanding they surrender mission runaways who had joined them. This inability to retrieve escapees, coupled with a decline in new recruits, dealt a heavy blow to the missions.[48]

The demographic crisis led to greater contact between the religious institutions and the town. Despite restrictions, mission residents had, in fact, always traded with the soldier-settlers and interacted with them in various other settings. On occasion Indians accompanied the presidial companies on military campaigns against warring Indians, and some soldiers were almost always stationed in the missions because their assistance, as Fray Mariano observed, was indispensable "in order to direct and instruct them [the natives] in their work, and to subdue, teach, control, and punish" them.[49] Without the soldiers' help, another missionary advised, the Indians would revert to their inherent laziness, neglect to plant and harvest the corn crop, and commit all kinds of excesses and crimes right under the very roof of the mission. Furthermore, unless closely watched, the natives might just run away.[50] Two or three soldiers sufficed to maintain order and work because their presence reminded the Indians that the entire presidial company was nearby.[51] Towards the end of the century the influence of these few presidiales increased as fewer natives remained in the missions.

The same happened with other outsiders. The padres had always hired some five to ten vecinos (townspeople) in each mission for skilled crafts. As the Indian population declined, additional outsiders worked at the missions in order to keep them economically viable. The vecinos residing in the Indian pueblos increased not only in absolute numbers but also in proportion to the declining native population. For every one Spaniard, mestizo, or mulatto living in the missions, there was an average of twenty-eight Indian residents in 1772, thirteen in 1792, and only six in 1806.[52] As the proportion of vecinos from San Fernando working and living in the missions grew, their cultural impact on the remaining natives increased, a situation that hastened secularization. Thus, while the friars had at first insisted on segregation, in time they increasingly brought into the missions more soldiers and townspeople who unavoidably acted as agents of acculturation for the mission residents, and by the end of the century the once-Indian pueblos came to resemble Hispanic villas in practically everything save legal status.

A downturn in the economic fortunes of the missions further weakened those once self-sufficient institutions and threatened their very survival as separate communities. In the 1750s San José had been a thriving enterprise with approximately 2,000 sheep and 3,000 head of cattle, bustling carpentry and smithing workshops, active looms where the Indians made most of their clothing, a full granary, and a sugarcane storage building.[53] But "now [three decades later] everything, everything is turned around," lamented one of the friars. "There are few Indians and many hired hands. There are few cattle, and even so, no one to sell them to because there are too many grazers. Even if the missions had an abundance of corn, there are too many farmers, so many that some have abandoned agriculture. The resources that [once] sustained the missions have [now] been reduced."[54] As this observer suggested, part of the padres' problem stemmed from developments outside the mission walls. By the second half of the century some of the town dwellers from San Fernando had not only secured their agricultural resources but also had expanded their cattle-grazing enterprises. These ranchers had found a market for their herds in Louisiana and prospered from this trade, openly disregarding the royal decrees prohibiting it. The padres, who relied on subsidies from the Crown, could not act so boldly. Furthermore, as the roundup of wandering, unbranded cattle spread throughout the river valley down to the coast, the rancheros competed vigorously with the missions, with the result that the institutional herds dwindled considerably and the padres found themselves in a serious economic impasse.[55]

An expensive and futile cattle roundup for San José in 1785 reflects the missionaries' problem. That year the priest in charge spent 250 pesos, a sizable amount, hiring nonresident vaqueros (cowhands) to gather a small herd of animals that turned out to be so lean they had to be set free.[56] As this was repeated at the end of the century, the friars faced mounting difficulties in keeping their operations viable, and even the application of their personal salaries to mission coffers and the arrival of supply trains from the interior did not remedy the needs of their institutions.

Yet these economically depressed and demographically small communities continued to control immense properties, resources that the town dwellers and the soldiers quite naturally wished to exploit. To achieve that goal, the latter urged the government to end the corporate privileges of the missions and allow them (the settlers) to exploit the lands and herds used by so few residents, who were only technically "Indian."[57]

The Crown agreed in part with the petitioners and applied to the mission herds the same tax it collected on all mesteños (unclaimed livestock on the range). The vecinos avoided the assessment on their herds by various appeals and by ignoring the decree altogether, but the padres apparently lacked the stamina for the long, drawn-out legal battle and, more importantly, did not have the manpower to compete with the settlers in the race to round up the remaining livestock. By the end of the century the herds were largely depleted, and the issue of the tax became moot, even though the padres repeatedly blamed the decline of the missions on the levy on mesteños.[58] Faced with all these difficulties, the friars found the governing of the missions an all-consuming task. Overseeing the farming and grazing operations took so much time, one padre complained, that he had little time for the doctrina (religious education for the natives) and even for his own prayer and meditation. Maintaining the missions was draining the resources available locally and straining the order's assets and its ability to raise funds for the San Antonio institutions.[59] Furthermore, the expulsion of the Jesuits from the Spanish Empire in 1767 had left an enormous vacuum in the northwestern frontier, a vacuum the Franciscans were called upon to fill. Facing this new challenge and disappointed by their ventures in Texas, the friars willingly agreed to partial secularization in the 1790s and all but abandoned the province in the early 1800s.[60]

Conclusion

When the missions were secularized, title to many of their lands was turned over to individual residents. Some Franciscans remained to minister spiritually to their former charges, but the mission era was over. The institutions that had dominated the San Antonio valley from the early 1700s to the 1780s experienced a rapid decline in the last decade of the century.[61] Originally established with the idealistic goal of "civilizing" and Christianizing the natives, the missions developed into separate Indian pueblos but ended as Hispanic communities barely distinguishable from the neighboring town of San Fernando. At the close of the century that villa, its military establishment, and the missions merged into the settlement later known as San Antonio.

In a sense, the closing of the missions and the distribution of lands was in keeping with the friars' long-range goal of integrating the Indians into the Hispanic society, and to that extent the missions accomplished the purpose for which they were founded originally. In reality, however, the friars had not operated their institutions with this end in mind. They had set out to establish segregated Indian towns with certain corporate legal rights and a very distinct character. Many aspects of mission life were geared towards self-sufficiency, permanence, and the exclusion of external influences. Nevertheless, critical demographic patterns beyond the control of the padres worked against the survival of those autonomous Indian pueblos. In this regard, the problem of desertions was aggravated by minimal or nonexistent population growth, leaving the missions dependent on continued in-migration, which ceased once the economically dependent bands found a better alternative in joining the Norteños. When the prospects of recruiting neo-phytes at the earlier levels faded, it then became impossible to justify the cost and personnel involved in maintaining those large enterprises for so few residents. Challenges by the towns-people and the government resulted in the termination of the autonomous corporate status the missions had enjoyed. By the time this happened, those institutions were already changing. Vecinos and soldiers had moved into the missions, and Indians had been drifting into the civilian town. Thus the once-separate Franciscan-Indian pueblos merged with the larger community of the villa of San Fernando de Béxar.

V

Immigrants and Integration in Late Eighteenth-Century Béxar

Gerald E. Poyo

Introduction

During 1718-1731 several hundred settlers inhabited the farming and ranching community of San Antonio de Béxar, but by the end of the century their number had increased to almost 1500. Most of this growth came from immigration. The hardships and isolation of New Spain's northeastern frontier produced high rates of infant mortality, and only immigration provided the source for demographic expansion.[1] Statistical information on migration to Texas during this period is scarce, but census documents provide data regarding Béxar's non-native-born population and its position within the community.

Migrants to Béxar came mostly from the northern provinces, reflecting Texas' strong regional ties with Saltillo, Camargo, Monterrey, Monclova, and Rio Grande. But newcomers also traveled from farther south. During the 1790s Béxar received immigrants from Querétaro, Mexico City, Guadalajara, San Luis Potosí, and Aguascalientes, among other places.[2] Many of these immigrants arrived in Texas with the military and, after serving in presidios such as Los Adaes, San Xavier, San Sabá, or La Bahía, often retired and established themselves in Bé- xar.[3] Others simply joined migratory streams and ended up in Texas. Deteriorating economic conditions in New Spain toward the latter part of the century created considerable migratory pressures which drove people north, where they believed that they could find opportunities for economic stability and secu- rity.[4] Béxar also received immigrants from the east; some came from Louisiana, but most came from the East Texas set- tlement of Los Adaes. These immigrants were actually refugees who were forced to leave their homes in 1773 by order of the Spanish Crown. As such, they came with special status and received extra attention when they arrived in Béxar.

Bexareño Society in the Late Eighteenth Century

By the final third of the eighteenth century Béxar emerged as a community with a clearly stratified social structure. Eco- nomic status and racial background divided Béxar's population, and, while the interactions between class and race were very complex, the structure itself is evident in the census data of the 1790s.

The idea of race played a significant role in Bexareño soci- ety, although race itself did not often create insurmountable barriers for individuals aspiring to status and influence within the community. Despite the fact that Béxar's original mixed- race presidio population was often classified as Spanish in official documents, racial background did not at first seem to be of great social consequence in this isolated frontier settle- ment.[5] But the role of race in Béxar's society began to change with the arrival of the "Spanish" Canary Islanders, who brought with them traditional European attitudes. Seeking to become the region's elite, the Islanders made much of their Spanish heritage and linked it to status within the community, injecting a new concern about race later reflected in the 1793 census.

In that year 74 percent of Béxar's native-born population was classified as Spanish, while 26 percent was Indian and casta (mixed blood).[6] Since this high percentage of Spanish residents was not consistent with the mixed racial character of the Mexican population of New Spain, obviously a social mechanism based on a local definition of what constituted Spanish allowed a majority of Bexareños to claim that category. By the final decades of the century the idea of race still contributed to the definition of social boundaries, but the fluidity of definition meant that designations of race were less a statement about one's actual racial background than of an individual's overall status within the community.

A more important factor in defining an individual's status in the community was accumulation of wealth and political influence. Béxar's prominent families of the 1790s descended from the mixed-blood Mexican soldier-settlers and Canary Islanders who resided in Béxar during the initial distribution of farm and ranch lands (1730s-1760s). While race exerted some influence on their position as economic and political elite in the community, the determining factor in defining their status was control of local land and water resources, which gave them accessibility to Béxar's cabildo.

The socioeconomic group with the greatest influence in the community was the labrador, a census occupational category for individuals with direct access to land through ownership or as tenants. Labradores were an economically diverse group which included the wealthiest ranchers and farmers as well as owners or renters of modest lots with small gardens and orchards. Labradores composed 23.5 percent of Béxar's heads of household in 1793. Among the sixty-three native-born household heads (16.1 percent of Béxar's total) classified as labradores, fifty enjoyed the racial designation of "Spanish." The only non-Spanish native-born labradores in the community included twelve Indians and one mulatto. Indian labradores were primarily mission Indians who had found their way into the town and obtained land by virtue of their long-standing relationship with the community.

The fact that all except one non-Indian landowner were Spanish suggests that, technically at least, castas were ineligible to control land. This land-tenure pattern helps explain the high proportion of Spanish residents in a town where one would expect to see an inverted demographic composition. In fact, individuals of mixed racial heritage did receive land and, along with their property title, grantees gained a new Spanish racial status in official documents.

Béxar also had a group of native-born merchant-artisans and professionals, who, except in one case, were Spanish. Three merchants, two blacksmiths, two carpenters, two tailors, a shoemaker, an ecclesiastical notary, and a schoolteacher formed this group, which represented 3 percent of Béxar's total household heads. While not classified as labradores, many of these twelve owned land and so probably shared equal status with those thus classified. The 1793 census also included forty-five native-born heads of household who were Spanish widows (12.8 percent of total), with no occupation listed. Some were from prominent Bexareño families and also owned land.

The remainder of Béxar's native-born heads of household (25.1 percent) were presumably landless and were classified as jornaleros (day laborers) and criados (servants). Castas and Indians were overrepresented in these occupational categories, demonstrating the relationship between work and race among native-born Bexareños. While Indians and castas made up only 18 percent of landholders, they composed 40 percent of day laborers and servants.[7]

The community's political leadership was recruited from the Spanish labrador and merchant, artisan, and professional classes. Officers in the cabildo during the 1790s were almost all from the traditional Bexareño elite families formed during the first half of the century. And, among these elite, certain members carried the honorific title of "don," which identified them as respected individuals in the community. Twenty-nine of fifty native-born heads of households classified as Spanish labradores carried the title of "don." In addition, three Spanish merchants, a Spanish carpenter, a Spanish tailor, and the Spanish notary of the ecclesiastic tribunal were also dons. Only four Spanish day laborers used the honorific title, and they were probably members of established families.[8]

Limits to Integration in Béxar

For its first half-century of existence Béxar offered newcomers and new generations of Bexareños ample opportunity for settlement through the distribution of lands within the presidio's defense perimeter. During these formative years Mexican soldier-settlers and Canary Islanders, and their descendants, established their claim on community resources. They held the only irrigable farmlands and most of the ranch lands in the vicinity of Béxar. Furthermore, they dominated the community's most important political institution, the cabildo.[9] By the final third of the century untapped resources were at a premium, and immigrants found a less-open society within which to settle.

After the 1770s immigrants to Béxar could not necessarily count on receiving land outright. Vacant lands within the town were no longer plentiful, and the possibilities for the extension of the presidio's defense perimeter were not good. Most of the villa's population lived between the San Antonio River and San Pedro Creek. South of the villa's plaza were the irrigated farmlands (labores de abajo) which had been granted originally to the Canary Islanders. The pasture east of the plaza had been subdivided into solares for residential use beginning in the 1750s. North of the plaza, the town's original propios had also been granted to residents for homes, gardens, and orchards. Farther north of this residential area a new acequia had been constructed, linking San Pedro Springs and the San Antonio River, which made possible a second distribution of irrigated farmlands (the labores de arriba) during 1778-1779. These lands, however, did not go to immigrants but to members of the long-standing presidio community which had never received grants. Most arrivals after the 1760s received grants for homes west of San Pedro Creek, but this new residential area was less desirable than others because of its vulnerability to

Indian harrassment. All lands east of the San Antonio River belonged to Mission San Antonio de Valero and were thus not available for settlement by new immigrants. The land along the river south of San Antonio had been granted as sitios for cattle ranching.[10]

All of this area was under the effective protection of the presidio company, whose primary responsibility was to maintain security from Indian depredations. But, already by the 1770s, the presidio's resources were insufficient. Residents could not live on their ranches for fear of the Indians, and often they would not even risk gathering cattle. The vast expanses of land beyond the protective perimeter could not be effectively utilized, which created clear limitations to spatial growth. Only additional Crown investments in the form of an expanded presidio company or another military installation in the region could provide the infrastructural support necessary for Béxar's physical growth. This the Crown would not then consider, and only with the secularization of the missions beginning in the early 1790s and the arrival of a mobile presidio company from Parras after the turn of the century were additional lands available for distribution and the defense perimeter expanded.

The Immigrant Elite in Béxar

The frontier conditions that limited Béxar's expansion affected the fluidity of socioeconomic mobility within the community. By the 1770s native-born Bexareños controlled most of the community's limited resources, and land-granting became increasingly selective as the century wore on. Immigrants had to find other ways to establish themselves.

Immigrants successful in acquiring stability and status did so through a combination of factors, including marriage, utilizing previous connections, or personal skills and other resources. The number of immigrants in Béxar by the 1790s was significant. In 1793 about 43 percent of households were headed by non-native-born individuals. Among the 167 immigrant household heads in Béxar, twenty-nine (17 percent) were labradores, five (3 percent) were merchants, twenty-seven (16 percent) were artisans, thirty (18 percent) were widows, and seventy-six (46 percent) were day laborers and servants. With castas and Indians making up 51 percent of the immigrant household heads, newcomers brought greater racial heterogeneity to Béxar.[11]

Immigrant labradores, less than half of native labradores, accounted for 7 percent of Béxar's household heads. But at least ten of the immigrant labradores managed to obtain the necessary economic resources, social contacts, and political influence to become important members of Béxar's elite by the 1790s. Those identified in this category met three criteria: they enjoyed access to land, they were referred to in the census records as "don," and they served in the cabildo.

Two immigrant merchants managed to become members of the town's ruling elite. A Corsican by birth, don Angel Navarro arrived in Béxar in the mid-1770s and married María Josefa Ruiz y Peña, a descendant of two of Béxar's ranching families. Navarro entered into commerce and served on the city council at various times during the 1770s-1790s.[12] Don Francisco Xavier Galán migrated to Béxar from La Bahía during 1788 and married María Erlinda Bustillos, daughter of another well-established Bexareño family. He too served on the city council during the 1790s and later became postmaster of Béxar. During his first six years in Béxar Galán purchased three pieces of land from Isleños—José Curbelo, José M. Granados, and Antonia de Armas.[13]

Six of the immigrant labradores who joined Béxar's elite became important in ranching around Béxar. Among them was don Felis Menchaca, of Béxar's Menchaca family, who was born in the Presidio de Rio Grande where his father was stationed. He had little trouble using his family connections to establish himself as one of Béxar's leading citizens. By the 1770s Menchaca was an active rancher and served often as alcalde and senior councilman in the cabildo.[14] The other five emigrated from various areas: one from Castille, one from Aguascalientes, one from Santa Rosa, and two from Saltillo. In each of these cases, the individuals apparently established their prominence through marriage.

The Castillian, don Miguel Gortari, probably arrived in the early 1760s, perhaps with the military. He married the daughter of Vicente Alvarez Travieso, one of the original Canary Islander immigrants. They had a child in 1764, and Gortari served as the cabildo's alcalde in 1767. He held three more cabildo positions in subsequent years, including the jobs of town constable for one year after his father-in-law's death. During 1769 he acquired two adjacent solares between the San Antonio River and the acequia madre, which no doubt became his residence. He then turned his attentions to ranching activities and by the 1790s owned two ranches east of Salado Creek.[15]

Don Ygnacio de la Peña, don Ignacio Calvillo, don José de la Santa, and don Marcos Zepeda followed similar patterns in their rise to ranching prominence. They too came as young men in the 1760s and 1770s and quickly married into influential local families, including the Urrutias, Arochas, Floreses, and Alvarez Traviesos respectively. By the 1780s and 1790s they were active in ranching, and several owned ranch lands in the vicinity of Béxar.[16]

Two additional immigrant labradores who became part of the local elite occupied their time in farming. Don Joaquín Orandáin and don Vicente Amador both obtained irrigated lands for farming. Originally from Saltillo, Orandáin probably arrived in Béxar with the military in the late 1750s. He married Josefa Leal, of the prominent Islander family, and they had a child in December 1760. In 1771 he had another child with a second wife, Michaela Romero, the daughter of an early presidio family of San Antonio. By 1774 he was a lieutenant stationed at the Cíbolo Fort, south of Béxar on the San Antonio River. Two years later he retired from military service and participated in digging an acequia from San Pedro Springs to the San Antonio River, for which he obtained two suertes of irrigable farmlands. He was elected to the cabildo in 1789 and again in 1793.[17]

Vicente Amador arrived in Béxar as a tailor in 1756 from Celaya and married Manuela Banul, the widow of a Canary Islander, Manuel Leal, and daughter of Manuel Banul, a long-time resident who worked as a blacksmith at Mission San Antonio de Valero. Amador received two grants of land in 1762 and 1771. He served as city attorney (1791) and alcalde (1792) and became alcalde and landowner of irrigable farmlands at Valero when it was secularized in 1793.[18]

All of these immigrants who became part of Béxar's elite married into influential local families. They may have had other advantages as well, such as being Spaniards or possessing a skill or funds with which to make a start, but it is obvious that marriage selections were important for immigrants attempting to establish themselves in the community. Of the twenty-nine immigrant labradores, eleven carried the designation of "don." Nine of the eleven were married to local españolas of well-established families. One was single but had other family contacts (Menchaca), and the other married a woman from Saltillo with family connections in Béxar. Among the remaining eighteen labradores not called "don," only five married españolas of Béxar, of whom only one seems to have been from an elite family.[19] Thus, a "good" marriage clearly enhanced an immigrant's standing in Béxar.

Immigrant Artisans

While marriage opened the possibility of entering Béxar's ruling elite, personal skills provided possibilities for at least securing one's niche in the community. Immigrants who entered Béxar with specific artisanal skills enjoyed an advantage since few native-born Bexareños pursued the urban trades in their predominantly rural-based economy.

Immigrants dominated the trades in Béxar. Twenty-seven immigrant artisans in 1793 included six shoemakers, nine tailors, four blacksmiths, three carpenters, and five other trades. They represented 7 percent of Béxar's household heads, double the figure for native-born artisans. While all of the native-born artisans were Spanish, those that immigrated were of a variety of racial categories. In fact, 52 percent were castas and Indians. The immigrant artisans came from diverse places, including the Canary Islands, New Orleans, Natchitoches, Los Adaes, Saltillo, and many communities throughout New Spain.[20] But, unlike the native-born artisans, these immigrants were not influential socially in the community, and none served in the cabildo. Still, some did generate enough wealth through their trades to purchase land, and at least one managed to "change" his race.

Among the tailors, four were Spanish, one was French, and three were Indian. Perhaps the best established was Sebastian Monjarás, who married Gertrudes Flores, of one of Béxar's Flores families. It was probably through this marriage and perhaps with funds earned as tailor that Monjarás extended his interests into ranching. He conducted many cattle drives and for a time even served as tithe collector. While he no doubt practiced his trade when he first arrived in Béxar, he seems to have spent most of his energies in ranching.[21]

Another tailor, Juan Manuel Ruiz, also did quite well in Béxar. He immigrated from Querétaro and in the early 1760s married Manuela de la Peña, daughter of Ygnacio. Their daughter married the merchant Angel Navarro. Along with his father-in-law, Ruiz also turned to ranching and by the 1790s had purchased a ranch on the Medina River west of Béxar. Despite his economic successes and social ties, however, Ruiz apparently never served in the cabildo.[22]

Three carpenters also immigrated to Béxar. The most successful was Pedro Huízar, a mulatto from Aguascalientes who also worked as a sculptor, according to the 1779 census. He probably arrived in Béxar early in the 1770s. Huízar worked at Mission San José, where he married a coyota (Indian-mestizo mixture), Trinidad Enriques, and had several children, the first in 1779. He then purchased lots from prominent Bexareños in San Fernando during the early 1780s, which suggests that his employment at San José was financially rewarding. Interestingly, Huízar was listed as Spanish in the 1793 census, again demonstrating how economic prosperity overcame racial exclusivity. Huízar also surveyed. In 1791 he conducted a survey in La Bahía to determine the feasibility of digging an irrigation system off the San Antonio River, and in 1794 he surveyed the mission lands that were distributed during secularization. After the missions became dependent pueblos, Huízar became an alcalde at the former San José mission.[23] At least one other artisan managed to acquire property. An Indian from Guadalajara, Juan Blanco, one of six shoemakers (the others included four Indians, a mulatto, and a coyote) also experienced relative prosperity and purchased property during 1806.[24]

Immigrant artisans did not become leading citizens in Béxar by the 1790s, but they did possess skills that gave them the opportunity to purchase land in a community where grants were increasingly difficult to obtain. This was an advantage that placed them in a better position than the landless inhabitants who worked as day laborers and servants.

Landless Immigrants: Day Laborers and Servants

Forty-six percent of immigrants in Béxar were jornaleros and criados, approximately equal to the 44 percent of native-born in the same occupational categories. Whether immigrant or native-born, a significant proportion of the population failed to establish an independent livelihood through acquisition of land or the practice of a specific skill. Among the seventy-six immigrant day laborers and servants in Béxar, 58 percent was casta and Indian, again reflecting the overrepresentation of this group in the lowest and least-mobile occupational categories of Bexareño society.

Since land ownership or renting were the basis of economic stability, immigrant and native-born day laborers and servants alike lived a very marginal existence indeed. Béxar did not lack for unemployed to fill jobs as servants or workers. Some found a measure of stability and security in the service of Béxar's elite families, but the community's economic production could not have employed the approximately 45 percent of the population without access to land. It is thus likely that this sector of Béxar's society was highly transient in nature and resided in the community only intermittently. On many occasions throughout the century the cabildo ordered the town's unemployed to secure some means of livelihood or else leave the community.[25]

Immigrants from Los Adaes

In addition to the economically induced migratory flows from the south, Béxar also received refugees. The single most important migration to Béxar during the eighteenth century came from Los Adaes in the early 1770s. The settlement of Los Adaes grew from the presidio and missions established in East Texas by the expedition of Captain Domingo Ramón during 1715-1716. Besides Ramón, twenty-five mounted soldiers, and twelve priests, the expedition included close to thirty-five or forty civilian settlers, stock drivers, and Indian guides. This initial Spanish presence in East Texas provided a buffer to French advances into New Spain from Louisiana, but their situation was highly precarious. Difficult conditions resulted in the virtual abandonment of the region in 1719, which prompted the Crown to dispatch another expedition. In 1720 the Marqúes de San Miguel de Aguayo, newly appointed governor of Texas, departed Monclova with some 500 soldiers. The missions were reestablished, as was the presidio, which again was garrisoned with twenty-five men.[26]

During the next fifty years the community of Los Adaes emerged. At first the presidio provided the primary means of economic livelihood, but in time residents farmed, raised cattle, and traded with the nearby French garrison of Natchitoches. The twenty-five Mexican soldier-settlers from Coahuila, which group later grew to sixty-one, provided the initial male population base. Most were of mixed racial heritage. According to a presidio roster in 1731, only twenty-nine members of the presidio were designated español by Governor José Antonio de Bustillo y Zevallos, but even most of these were probably descendants of mixed-blood frontiersmen. The other thirty-two members of the presidio were openly (contrary to tradition) classified as mestizos, mulattoes, lobos, coyotes, and indios. While some no doubt brought their families, it is quite likely that many soldiers married other frontier inhabitants, including Indians of the region, residents of Natchitoches or Béxar, or other immigrants from New Spain, producing a population of castas typical of much of Mexico.[27]

By the late 1760s Los Adaes included about 500 inhabitants and provided a barrier to French movement into Texas. But with the signing of the Treaty of Paris ending the Seven Years' War in 1764, Louisiana passed into Spanish hands, and shortly thereafter, as part of a larger reorganization plan of the entire northern frontier of New Spain, the Crown ordered the abandonment of Presidio de los Adaes and the removal of its inhabitants to Béxar in 1772. Though deeply resentful, most of the community obeyed Crown orders.[28]

Almost as soon as the Adaesanos arrived in Béxar, however, some began to seek a way to return to East Texas. With the help of Governor Ripperdá, Adaesano leader Antonio Gil Y'Barbo received permission to establish the town of Bucareli on the Trinity River in 1774. This location did not suit the Adaesanos, and several years later they founded Nacogdoches.

But not all followed Gil Y'Barbo back to East Texas. Many remained and eventually found their place within Bexareño society, though this was not accomplished without struggle. Initially the Adaesanos scraped out a livelihood in a variety of ways. The eighteen Adaesanos who served in the presidio were perhaps the most secure of all those transplanted. As members of the extinguished presidio of Los Adaes, they merely transferred to an enlarged military garrison at Béxar. Curiously, however, seven of the Adaesanos petitioned for and received discharges from the military between 1778 and 1784.[29]

Twenty Adaesanos found employment at the missions. By the 1770s the number of Indians at the missions had dwindled considerably, leaving the missionaries without a suitable work force. Eager to have the Adaesanos work on the mission lands, during 1778 Fray Pedro Ramírez de Arellano formally offered to allow the Adaesanos to cultivate irrigable lands at the missions or simply to hire them as salaried day laborers. Those already at the missions probably continued there, but most did not want to improve lands that were not their own and feared that acceptance of the friar's offer would delay acquisition of grants. They refused Fray Ramírez's offer.

Those Adaesanos who chose not to work at the missions found employment elsewhere in the community. Twenty-seven worked as servants or day laborers, probably on farms or perhaps rounding up cattle for prominent members of the community. Several members of Béxar's elite hired Adaesanos to work for them, including don Jacinto Delgado, Macario Sambrano, José Antonio Bustillos, Marcos de Castro, Francisco Flores, Juan José Flores, Bartolo Seguín, and Sebastian Monjarás. All these individuals were active in the cattle industry and, except for Monjarás, prominent in the cabildo.

Seven other Adaesanos were self-employed. An Indian named Cristóbal Ballejo owned two carts, which provided him a livelihood. He was hired, for example, to move Los Adaes's cannons to Béxar. Four others, including two Indians, were tailors. One, Antonio Brito, apparently earned enough to purchase a piece of land in 1784. Miguel Antonio Losoya, a carpenter, worked "at whatever was available." Finally, Marcos Hernández became an active rancher and used his knowledge of East Texas and Louisiana to drive cattle to that region. During 1775 he was arrested for contraband, and several years later he received permission to take cattle to Louisiana. Nevertheless, Hernández apparently never secured a grant for a cattle ranch and thus was unable to establish himself as one of Béxar's prominent ranchers.[30]

At the same time that the Adaesanos sought to make a living, they lobbied for their own land, essential for establishing a secure foothold in the community. And they were quite successful. By 1793 fifteen of thirty-eight (39.4 percent) heads of household from Los Adaes were classified as labradores.[31] This was proportionally higher than the 17.3 percent of immigrants as a whole or the 23.5 percent for all household heads in Béxar. Their special status is demonstrated by the fact that, except for Béxar's mission Indians and the case of one mulatto, the Adaesanos were the only immigrant landholders in Béxar who were not required to be classified as Spanish. They included three Spaniards, seven mestizos, and five Indians. Furthermore, an additional ten households headed by widows from Los Adaes may also have owned land. Given the circumstances of their arrival at Béxar, Adaesanos obviously received greater consideration than other immigrants.

Adaesano lands probably represented solares on which they built their homes and engaged in limited dry farming. The cabildo and governor regularly considered petitions for land from residents, and, generally speaking, petitioners justified their claims for land on the basis of long residence in the community, compensation for military service, or connections with important families in the community. At least two Adaesanos petitioned for and received land on the basis of their service to the king. Francisco Guadalupe Calahorra stated in his petition that he had served the king at Los Adaes for fourteen years, and he asked for a piece of land that had been denied to Antonio Rincón (another Adaesano) because "he had not resided at this presidio the required length of time." Simón de Aragón also received a grant in 1769 and declared that he had come to the province thirty-two years before and had served the king at the presidio of Los Adaes. Both plots were in the potrero east of the villa's plaza. Finally, the former lieutenant of the Los Adaes company, Manuel Antonio Losoya, in 1784 purchased a twelve-vara plot that included a jacal with a kitchen.[32]

The Adaesano Struggle for Farmlands

Having been ordered to abandon their homes and lands in East Texas, the Adaesanos were not satisfied just with solares, and, as a group, they organized politically to obtain more resources in Béxar. In January 1778, some five years after arriving in Béxar, the Adaesanos (perhaps after failing to obtain land through the normal community procedures) formally petitioned the Crown to help them. In response to their petition the comandante of the Interior Provinces, don Teodoro de Croix, ordered the various authorities in the province of Texas to consider their plight. The governor, commander of the presidio at La Bahía, and the cabildo of San Fernando offered various suggestions, including settling them on the San Marcos, Guadalupe, or Cíbolo rivers. These solutions, however, required stationing additional troops for protection from the Indians. Croix and his asesor general, Pedro Galindo Navarro, preferred a cheaper solution: the secularization of Mission San Antonio de Valero and the distribution of its lands to the Adaesanos. On June 8, 1779, Croix ordered Governor Domingo Cabello y Robles of Texas to implement the ruling.

Local authorities took no action, prompting Adaesano leader Bernardo Cervantes, a sixty-year-old Indian, to set out for Chihuahua to see Croix during October 1780 in defiance of Cabello's opposition to the trip. Cervantes told Croix of the Adaesanos' decade-long struggle to find security within the community of Béxar.[33] Croix again ordered Mission San Antonio de Valero's lands secularized and distributed to the Adaesanos. The missionaries no doubt objected and probably succeeded in stalling the implementation, but ultimately the solution was too attractive for Crown authorities to ignore. Settling the Adaesanos on mission lands not only solved the problem of these displaced frontiersmen, but also eliminated Crown expenditures for the maintenance of the missions. Finally in 1794 Governor Manuel Muñoz secularized Mission San Antonio de Valero and distributed irrigable farmlands to fourteen Indian families, forty-two Adaesano heads of household, and fourteen others. Among those receiving lands were eighteen of the original sixty-three petitioners in 1778. After twenty years many of the inhabitants of the former presidio community of Los Adaes finally secured a potentially stable and profitable means of livelihood.[34]

Limits to Adaesano Influence

Despite the Adaesanos' success in acquiring lands, during their first twenty years in Béxar they did not achieve social or political prominence in the community. Only two individuals from Los Adaes managed to marry into prominent families and serve in the cabildo. Manuel Berbán's marriage to Teresa de Armas, daughter of Canary Islander Ignacio Lorenzo de Armas, for example, apparently provided him the possibility of entering the cabildo, where he served as a councilman (1796) and attorney (1801). As councilman in 1796 Berbán oversaw the irrigation system and even became engaged in a legal tussle with Santiago Seguín for attempting to enforce the irrigation allotments. Berbán's marriage and political connections also resulted in a changed racial designation in the census. In 1779 Berbán's real mulatto race was indicated. By 1793 he had made the transition to mestizo, and by 1803 Berbán was a Spaniard.[35]

Even more successful was don Marcos de Zepeda, although his Adaesano connection was less firm. Classified "Spanish" in the census, Zepeda was from Santa Rosa and only served in Los Adaes presidio during 1768-1772. He arrived in Béxar in 1770 with the transfer of Los Adaes company and apparently left military service shortly thereafter. In Béxar he married Justa Travieso, daughter of Vicente Alvarez Travieso, thereby establishing a crucial social link. They had their first child in 1771. By 1780 he was elected to the cabildo as second alcalde. He also served as councilman during 1781, 1785, and 1789. During the 1790s Zepeda held the important posts of alguacil and senior regidor. As part of the Alvarez Travieso family Zepeda engaged in the ranching business and became an influential political leader in support of his family's ranching interests.[36]

With the exception of these two men, immigrant Adaesanos did not break into the ruling circle in Béxar. Their economic successes, as defined by acquisition of lands, resulted primarily from their status as refugees and their ability to win the support of Crown officials, who felt an obligation to help them reestablish their livelihood. Nevertheless, since they were not of the primeros pobladores (first settlers) and had few family connections in Béxar, their possibilities for access to social influence and political power in their adopted town were minimal. It was their children who eventually found full acceptance in Béxar.

Conclusion

Immigrants played a vital role in Béxar's growth and development during the final third of the eighteenth century. Despite the emergence of a clearly structured society by the 1770s, the town's social structure continued to be sufficiently fluid to allow newcomers the possibility of entering society at all levels. Immigrants became influential ranchers and political leaders. They established a firm artisanal tradition, and they worked as laborers and servants. Furthermore, they brought greater ethnic diversity to the town and region. Immigrants included European Spaniards, French, Spanish criollos, mestizos, mulattoes, lobos, and Indians.

Integration in the town was accomplished in a variety of ways. The most effective way to enter elite circles was through marriage, but this was biased in favor of those considered Spanish. Béxar's elite criollo families clearly preferred to marry their daughters to Spaniards if possible. Only a few castas apparently used this strategy successfully, although racial designations were not rigid, which makes categorical statements about race tenuous at best. But if obtaining elite status was problematic for immigrant castas, security was not beyond their reach. Numerous individuals of mixed racial background who arrived in Béxar with artisanal skills used them to accumulate wealth and purchase land. Indeed, most of the artisans in Béxar were immigrants of mixed-blood and Indian heritage.

At the same time, Béxar was not particularly attractive for immigrants who failed to establish social ties and lacked specific skills. Many who worked as servants or laborers stayed in Béxar just a short time. Perhaps they moved to other frontier communities such as Nacogdoches or La Bahía where land and water resources were more easily acquired, or maybe they returned to the more settled areas of New Spain to the south. It may be that outmigration was as significant as immigration among these unestablished groups.

Some historians have argued that frontier communities are by their very nature open and teeming with opportunity for those rugged enough to outlast the difficulties. Béxar's experience seems to indicate that, while immigrants were able to integrate into the town at all levels, their possibilities were subject to restraints imposed by the community's social structure, racial attitudes, land-granting policies, and relationships with the surrounding Indian groups. Indeed, these restraints to immigration and integration may explain stagnation in Béxar's demographic growth after approximately 1790.

VI

Indians and Their Culture in San Fernando de Béxar

Gilberto M. Hinojosa and Anne A. Fox

Introduction

The story of the Indians residing in San Fernando de Béxar is perhaps the most neglected aspect of the town's history. Studies on the Spanish actors – the governors, the missionaries, and the Canary Islanders – and to some extent on the mestizo soldier-settlers have drawn considerable attention and over-shadowed the scant references in the available literature on the role of the natives in the villa. For a long time archaeologists have examined remnants of the material culture of area nomads, and lately historians have paid some attention to mission Indians and to natives belonging to the larger groups in the province, but few scholars have related their findings to the Indians in the town. New historical perspectives, however, have encouraged the use of previously untapped eighteenth- and early nineteenth-century censuses and archaeological findings that reveal a substantial Indian population and culture in the community of Béxar.[1]

An examination of the census and archaeological data reveals that the countercurrents of exclusion and integration that affected other groups in the community also determined the fate of native residents of the town. Changing racial/ethnic classifications, probably altered because these were self-referents, may have allowed Indians to move up socially. The diversity of occupations among native residents and the ability of some of them to own land suggests that such mobility was indeed possible or that the community recognized that they had some rights. Furthermore, the presence of numerous fragments of Coahuiltecan artifacts in the town proper indicates a widespread acceptance of Indian culture. Very importantly, however, natives residing in the villa lacked a formal, corporate legal status as a group, granting them communal privileges such as those held by the Isleños, the presidiales, and the mission town dwellers. Lacking a power base, Indians were at a disadvantage, and some may have been relegated to a certain marginality. This limitation apparently set them apart even as other forces in eighteenth-century Béxar were bringing them into the mainstream of the community.

The Indian Demographic, Occupational, and Social Profile

The Indian population in the northern provinces of New Spain was very substantial, but the actual size is difficult to ascertain since estimates and tabulations sometimes refer to all Indians, sometimes only to those settled. For example, the estimate of 50,000 natives in Coahuila in the late 1600s reflects mostly the size of unsettled groups beyond Spanish control. A later count of 7,900 in 1810 represented an enumeration of only the settled natives, including the Tlaxcaltecans who had migrated to San Estevan, adjacent to Saltillo. Nevertheless, this substantially lower number may have reflected an ongoing decline of the Indian population due to disease and warfare. Censuses and reports from Nuevo Santander for 1755, 1770, and 1795 showed the settled Indian population there also decreasing, cut in half in each subsequent reporting year from the high of 14,298 first listed. In Nuevo León, however, the numbers of settled Indians grew from 1,260 in 1740 to about

4,000 eighty years later.[2] All the records seem to indicate numerous nomadic groups at the time of first European contact and a subsequent disastrous decimation of the native population. Still, Indians were clearly a constant presence in the towns, and their numbers may have been larger than the census figures indicate, since it is very likely that some changed their status to mestizos, mulattoes, or other castas (mixed bloods). Texas also had large numbers of Native Americans. Various official reports indicate that the independent Indians, including those in small groups along the coast and in the Rio Grande region as well as the large Norteño tribes, were quite numerous. In 1778 Teodoro de Croix, commander of the Interior Provinces of New Spain, estimated more than 7,000 indios bárbaros y gentiles (unsettled and un-Christianized Indians).[3] In the missions the native population at one point reached 800, outnumbering the settlers in the town-presidio complex.[4] Thus a sizable Indian population hovered in the immediate proximity of Béxar and in the province of Texas, and this Indian presence was bound to influence the demographic structure and the culture of the town.

The Indian population of the villa of San Fernando amounted to approximately a tenth of the town inhabitants in the late 1700s. The 1779 census did not provide racial designations for all residents, only for heads of households. Listed among these were twenty natives whose households contained a total of eighty-seven members, not all of which may have been Indians. By 1793, however, the number of natives had risen to 126, or 9.5 percent of the 1,321 residents of San Fernando.[5] The available records, therefore, indicate a strong, growing Indian representation in the community in the later decades of the eighteenth century.

Native residents in the town in 1793 did not constitute a homogeneous group, as is evident from the listing of Indians for whom there is birthplace information. About half of these natives were born in San Fernando; the remainder moved there voluntarily from elsewhere in the province and the colony's interior. The immigrants, thirty-eight in number, made up 52 percent of the adult Indian population (seventy-three), while the 183 other newcomers made up 20 percent of the non-Indian adults (895) who lived in San Fernando. The vast majority of the Indian adults who had moved to San Fernando were born outside Texas, mostly in the northern provinces, though two listed Mexico City as their place of origin. Of the six from Texas itself, four were from Los Adaes, one was from La Bahía del Espíritu Santo, and the other from the Tonkawa nation. In sum, about half of the Indian men and women were not from San Fernando, a larger portion of outsiders than the other town dwellers. These Native American citizens of New Spain had apparently joined the migratory stream to the frontier in larger proportions than their fellow countrymen.[6]

The sizable immigration may have involved large numbers of fully established families. This may account for the fact that the percentage of Indian births, as reflected by the number of baptisms, is on the average considerably lower than the 10 percent of the population constituted by natives. In 1745 natives christened in the town church made an impressive 42 percent of all individuals baptized, but that was a one-year phenomenon. In the seventy-seven years of the colonial period for which baptismal records are available (1744 to 1821), Indian christenings composed only 5 percent or less in sixty-one (over two-thirds) of those years, between 5.1 and 10 percent in eighteen years, and between 10.1 and 23 percent in nine years. Many of the years with the larger native baptisms occurred after the secularization of the missions, when Indians who had lived in those institutions enjoyed greater freedom and apparently moved to the town or had their children baptized there.[7]

The reasons for the relatively low number of native christenings are not clear. Since Indians did not have significantly lower fertility rates than other groups in San Fernando, it appears they were not baptizing their offspring regularly, suggesting that many natives may not have been fully hispanicized or Christianized.[8] The relatively fewer Indian christenings may also indicate substantial geographical and social mobility. Quite possibly natives were caught in the economic currents that pushed landless people in and out of the town. Or perhaps some resident Indians, along with natives moving into San Fernando, changed their racial designation in order to improve their social standing. The low rate of Indian baptisms suggests that, in spite of the significant number of native residents, Indians either did not enjoy full permanence or did not compose a fully distinct group within the community and were integrating rapidly.

This ambivalent status of Indians is reflected in the fact that many Indian infants were baptized without surnames, suggesting a certain marginality, at the same time that other natives enjoyed long-time standing in the community. Those individuals lacking surnames often began their lives in the villa as orphans or as children of servants without a complete Hispanic identity or as adoptees of important Bexareños. Between 1745 and 1773, for instance, eighty-four Indians were baptized in the church of San Fernando, but of these, fifty-eight, or 70 percent, bore no surnames. The remaining twenty-six natives christened in the town actually were part of the Roxo and Segura families, indicating that only two Indian families were clearly established in San Fernando's early town life. Individuals baptized without surnames as infants may have subsequently enjoyed that same membership in the community as the Roxos and Seguras, or perhaps even a greater one, because many were "adoptees" in Hispanic households and were probably very acculturated. Upon reaching adulthood these Indians may have taken the surname of their adoptive parents or their godparents and may have become indistinguishable from the mestizos and other castas in the town.[9]

Such integration may have been assisted by the fact that a few of those baptized with no surnames were adoptees of well-established San Fernando families. This particular pattern of Indian adoptees is exemplified in the enumeration of the household of don Francisco Travieso, a scion of one of San Fernando's leading clans. Along with the family members, the report lists a Lipan Apache girl, four years old. Other census entries list "orphaned sons (and daughters)" or simply "orphaned children," as was the case in the enumeration of the households of don Pedro Flores, doña Visenta Treviño, doña Juana de Ocón y Trillo, and José Antonio Saucedo. While not a common occurrence, given the nearly 400 households in San Fernando in 1793, the process of informally adopting Indian children was frequent enough to have been well accepted.[10]

There are indications that some adoptees were acquired in slave-gathering excursions. Occasionally the friars complained that retaliatory campaigns against certain Indian groups were, in fact, slave raids. On a recruiting expedition by Fray Francisco Durá of Mission Concepción to the Arrinconada del Río Grande, the pocket or corner formed by the coast on the river's east bank, the missionary's mayordomo (chief lieutenant) and other members of the party were told of Spaniards coming into the area to mine la sal del rey (the king's salt flats) and forcing Indian women to trade their infants in return for piloncillos (sugar cones). Technically the territory in question was part of Nuevo Santander, and it appears that the men implicated were from that same province as well, but the viceroy's expressions of concern to Juan María Barón de Ripperdá, governor of Texas, suggests that he believed that some of the captives may have ended up in Béxar.[11]

The instability and marginality that Indians experienced as a result of being unacculturated immigrants and adoptees was mitigated by the strength in local roots of an equal number of Hispanicized Indian Bexareños. While the movement of natives from the missions to San Fernando does not seem to have been great, it is possible that many Indians listed as "de esta villa" (born in this town) were actually mission residents who had lived in the civilian settlement since time immemorial. As the missions became secularized and lands were alloted, residents of those Indian pueblos understandably became linked to the outlying towns rather than to San Fernando. Nevertheless, the 1793 census does record at least three former mission residents in civilian towns.[12]

The life stories of some mission Indians reflect their mobility to the larger community. For example, Hermenegildo Cuserio, a member of a Papanac band which entered the Mission San Antonio de Valero in the 1730s (or possibly earlier), was baptized on April 13, 1749, when he was a six-day-old infant. His godparents were don Joseph Bueno de Rojas, a retired soldier, and doña María Curbelo, a Canary Islander. Cuserio grew up in that same mission and by age twenty became its fiscal, or band leader. By 1793, after secularization of Mission San Antonio de Valero, he and his third wife were residing in San Fernando with their twelve-year-old daughter. Cuserio listed his occupation as farmer. In another case, Miguel Carvajal, possibly an adoptee from the town, married Eugenia Huízar, a mulatta from that well-known Aguascalientes family. Sometime after the birth of their second child in 1783 the mother died, and Carvajal moved into Mission Concepción, where he married into the Castañeda family in 1790. Carvajal and his new wife, María Guadalupe, then left the mission to reside in the presidio community. She died shortly after giving birth, as did their baby boy. Carvajal then moved into the villa, where he was employed as a servant and cared for his two sons, ages nine and ten (in 1793), from the previous marriage. As these cases were repeated, particularly after the secularization of the missions, Indians from those institutions became a part of the villa.[13] There these natives found other Coahuiltecans and Indians from the interior, particularly from the northern provinces, and, despite residency in a segregated neighborhood, filled a variety of occupations and often married outside their group, thus becoming an integral part of the larger community.

Either as immigrants to Béxar or as native-born, Indians exhibited great stability in their family structure. They had the lowest ratios of single-parent families: 5 percent of all Indian families in 1779 and close to 8 percent in 1790. This contrasted sharply with ratios of Spaniards, mestizos, and the other castas in San Fernando. Among the latter, single-parent families made up from 17 to 42 percent of all families in each group and from

17 to 36 percent, respectively, in the two censuses. The size of Indian families was the highest of any group in 1779 (3.1 children per family), but this declined drastically in the 1790 census (1.3, the lowest in that tabulation), perhaps suggesting harder times for natives towards the end of the century. Still, the family unit remained strong.[14]

Family stability may have contributed to integration of the community to the extent that it encouraged intermarriage with non-Indians. The census of 1793, for example, listed 257 married couples. Eighty of these were interracial unions, of which thirty-two involved Indians marrying Spaniards (eleven), mestizos (eleven), mulattoes (seven), coyotes [Indian-mestizo mixture] (two), and Negroes (one). Possibly because of the relatively small size of the native group, Indian exogamous marriages outnumbered endogamous ones thirty-two to twelve. In the racial/ethnic intermarriages native males outnumbered females three to one, reflecting how the world of gainful employment facilitated intergroup contacts. [15]

Indeed, natives held a variety of skilled occupations, even though they were strongly represented in the lower-rung positions of "servants" and day laborers. Of the nineteen heads of households in the 1779 census, about half of the native vecinos (townspeople) farmed or tended flocks, as one would expect for the region. But among the other half, four were day laborers, three were cart drivers, one was a shoemaker, and another a stone mason. The racial identity of the "servants" was not indicated in that particular census, but it is highly likely, given information from previous and later counts, that many of them were Indians. That was the case for the 1793 enumeration. In that instance, four-fifths of the native workers were "servants," day laborers, and farmers. Still, Indians are also listed in craft positions that reflected the variety of occupations of the town's overall population.[16]

The type of employment that native residents of San Fernando reported was closely related to their stability or mobility. For example, the craftsmen, including the four shoemakers that serviced the Bexareños' footware, were from the interior of the colony, but farmers were all from either Los Adaes or San Fernando itself. Understandably, craftsmen and laborers were more likely than farmers to join the migratory stream. By the same token, local origin or long-time residency were prerequisites for farming and land ownership. In petitioning for land, for example, Indian labradores (farmers) Josef Marcos Pereida and Juan Josef Segura cited their respective ten- and fifteen-year residencies in the town, with the former also mentioning his five-year stint as a soldier, which included service at San Sabá on the frontier. Segura was listed as owning a huerta, or garden, in the 1779 census, while Pereida boasted of three huertas and a "piece of land." Thus some Indians, particularly Texas residents, managed to establish a foothold in San Fernando.[17]

Coahuiltecan Culture in San Fernando

Despite the relatively small numbers of area Indians in San Fernando, the impact of their culture on Béxar was significant. Native pottery, tools, blankets, and other articles were present abundantly in San Fernando homes. These items were produced in the villa or were acquired through trade and treaties between the Norteños and the town dwellers. Similar goods were exchanged between mission Indians and the San Fernando residents. Letters and reports from the friars to religious and Crown officials allude to this trade, which was not without problems for the padres. The interaction between the settlers and soldiers and the Indians interfered with the separate Indian society the missionaries sought to create. Notwithstanding the friars' objections, the very proximity of these mission pueblos and of the nomadic groups to the Hispanic settlement and the utility of native artifacts facilitated the interchange of goods and brought Indians and the villa residents into close contact.

The native goods used by Bexareños were basically the same as those produced by South Texas Indians in the premission era. At the beginning of the eighteenth century Coahuiltecans in northern Mexico and the Rio Grande plain and Karankawas along the coast searched for food in seasonal hunting-and-gathering migrations across the vast wilderness of

South and Central Texas. Threatened almost to the point of extinction by larger groups to the north and by European diseases spreading in the vanguard of Spanish settlement, Coahuiltecans and Karankawas organized themselves in small bands, utilizing the scant resources of the area to construct their impermanent shelters, to hunt, and to prepare their food. From bones, stone, and tree limbs they constructed small huts covered with animal skins, fashioned spears, bows, and arrows to kill deer, wild pigs, javelinas, and other animals, and to use against their enemies in the occasional, small-scale warfare. These Indians also produced a variety of tools, utensils, and clay pots which they used in the preparation of their meals and the preservation of food. Some, if not all, of these natives were also acquainted with the rudiments of netting and weaving, and they manufactured needed objects from natural fibers harvested in the areas where they lived. Given the widespread evidence of all of these objects, area natives spent a large portion of their lives hunting and gathering and preparing the roots, nuts, berries, and animal products that sustained them.[18]

Still, as among all peoples, South Texas Indians also participated in certain communal celebrations. Theirs were called mitotes and involved dancing, singing, and the ingestion of hallucinogens such as peyote. Remains of bone flutes, rattles, and other instruments recovered from various area archaeological sites confirm the spirited character of these festivities. Betraying their own prejudices, missionaries and other European observers found the Indian rituals frenzied and boisterous, depicting the worst of the native "barbaric" cultures, which they (the Spaniards) hoped to change once the Indians were settled in the missions.[19]

The latter institutions were, in fact, introduced to systematically "reduce" (gather and settle), acculturate, and Christianize the nomadic bands encountered by Spaniards as they pushed north from the core of New Spain. Mission life made new demands on the natives, altering their lifestyles in profound ways. The friars restricted the Indians' freedom, forbidding them to migrate across the South Texas plain and regulating their daily activities. Even their eating and resting periods were scheduled by the padres, who also controlled the distribution of food, clothing, tools, and artifacts. The natives were introduced to new and stringent sanitation rules, to unfamiliar tasks such as farming and ranching, and to very different religious practices and beliefs.[20] One scholar has concluded that "missionization brought changes to native cultures that were so rapid as to be traumatic."[21] While not all researchers are so extreme in their judgment, all point to the problems which the new demands created for the Indians, at least when they first entered the missions.

Despite the many problems with their new lives, natives actually continued as before in many ways. Some new foods required complex preparation techniques, but many dishes were not completely unlike traditional Indian recipes. While some household articles – for example, metal comales (skillets) – distributed by the friars were not available before, other Spanish goods resembled Indian wares. The European items were preferred because they were more durable or simply more readily available than those devised by South Texas natives. Yet many Indian artifacts remained in use in conjunction with Spanish-introduced items. Native stone tools and grinding slabs, for example, continued to be made long after metal knives and volcanic rock metates were brought into the area. Ceramic vessels like those fashioned in the wilds were also produced and employed in the missions, altered only by shapes common in Spanish colonial society.[22]

Likewise, despite the availability of domesticated animals and agricultural products, wild animals and foods remained a significant part of the diet of mission Indians. Archaeological inventories of bones recovered from the mission sites include not only cows, sheep, goats, chickens, and ducks, but also deer, javelina, various kinds of fish and turtles, wild turkeys, rabbits, raccoons, squirrels, and other small animals, all of which had been the staff of life for the Indians in el monte. A certain amount of food-gathering in the wilds also continued. Indian women would leave the mission complex towards evening, reported a friar at Concepción, to gather tunas, berries, nuts, and other fruits and roots. Obviously, the old lifeways were not entirely replaced by the new.[23]

Crafts in the mission can also be seen as extensions and developments of skills the Indians had practiced for generations. For example, pottery making continued in the traditional way, with the vessels fired over open flames. While the preparation of cotton and wool and the spinning of yarn called for the acquisition of new skills, weaving with thread was not radically different from weaving with plant fibers. Similarly, the use of metal tools and the construction of durable structures undoubtedly required some adjustment and training, but Indian men were well versed in working with stone and wood and applied these skills to mission tasks.[24]

Along with their artifacts and abilities, the natives also brought their religious traditions. The same bone flutes and rattles found in South Texas campsites were unearthed in mission trash heaps, indicating that mitotes and possibly other rituals also survived missionization. In fact, the friars found it difficult to suppress these cultural expressions altogether. Some padres wisely preferred to alter or supervise Indian traditions rather than ban them altogether, lest the Indians steal away to observe them anyway.[25] Thus Indian ways crept past the military and spiritual guards and entered through the wooden gates of the missions.

But native traditions, somewhat changed or enhanced, also moved out of those walled structures. Although the natives were familiar with the preparation for warfare and with some fighting techniques, they had to be introduced to the care and handling of guns and the building of stone and earthen fortifications. They also had to be drilled in Spanish military strategies. The constant preparedness was not new, however, since most of the native groups settled by the padres had faced raids by the Apaches before. Military training and preparation of the natives were essential for safeguarding their communities and indeed the entire settlement. For this the padres periodically sent mission Indians to assist the presidial soldiers in scouting and tracking as well as fighting on campaigns against marauding groups.[26]

This interaction between Indians and soldiers, along with the trade between mission residents and all town dwellers, introduced Coahuiltecan and Karankawan goods and traditions into San Fernando. Findings from archaeological research in the town church, in the governor's dwelling and office, and in a small residential site on the south side of the central plaza exemplify the Indian influence in the very heart of the town. These excavations have yielded eighteenth-century tools, chert cores from which the tools were made, and the debris that resulted from their manufacture. The choice of raw material and the method of flaking as well as the appearance of the implements created reflect the same activities carried out in prehistoric campsites and later at the missions. Evidence that such tools were not only used in the town but also were being made there indicates a general acquaintance with the Indian technology and perhaps even a preference for it or at least a reliance on it when the Spanish settlement experienced shortages of metal.[27]

As with tools, Indian-made pots, jars, and bowls appear to have predominated in the kitchens of the community. Since more sophisticated vessels had to be brought by mule train from the interior, the use of native artifacts seems to have been a practical solution. In fact, these utensils remained popular even after other unglazed wares were produced locally in substantial numbers. Towards the end of the eighteenth century, however, Indian containers were phased out, possibly because the Coahuiltecan and Karankawa population both inside and outside the mission declined or because more durable vessels became available as the San Fernando community prospered. In any case, the popularity of Indian pottery for most of the 1700s reflects the important influence of the surrounding native cultures.[28]

Moreover, the use of Coahuiltecan ceramics may be representative of a larger assortment of Indian-made goods commonly used by the villa's citizenry. Various reports describe a considerable amount of weaving done at the missions, suggesting that blankets and cloth produced by the natives were in demand in the town. Other perishable items, such as matting and baskets, the production of which utilized skills common among area Indians, may have been bartered or purchased from mission residents or may well have been made by Indian women residing in San Fernando.[29]

Conclusion

Thus the historical and archaeological record demonstrates the very strong and clear cultural impact of the area natives on the San Antonio community. Indian artifacts found in the town center reveal traditions existent in the missions and, beyond that, in the prehistoric sites of South Texas. The popularity of native tools and pottery among the town dwellers may indeed be indicative of widespread cultural borrowing and, as Elizabeth A.H. John suggests, of considerable interaction between the Indians of Texas and the Hispanic settlers of San Fernando. This acceptance of things Indian contributed to the integration of the settlement by the end of the century.

The native demographic presence was of at least equal importance. While there is evidence of exclusion and separation, such as the possible existence of an Indian neighborhood, the high number of Indians who were servants or who bore no last names in the baptismal records, and the great fluctuations in rates of native births, there are also many signs of inclusion and integration. Indians held as wide a variety of occupations as other San Fernando residents and accounted for the largest ratio of intermarriage. The presence of a considerable number of acculturated natives from the interior may have helped ease the acceptance of area natives and Indian culture in the town. Even the process of adopting native children, which may have involved slave raiding, in time may have contributed to the softening of racial bias and the breaking down of barriers. Certainly the presence of other mixed groups, the coyotes, tresalvos (mixture of mestizo and Indian), mulattoes, and mestizos, while in some way accentuating racial and ethnic differences, probably furthered a tolerance that would have been missing had divisions been few and clearly marked. All these factors increased and strengthened the bonds between the Indian residents and the rest of the community, resulting in lasting native traditions in the town and a progressively integrated Indian-Hispanic society in San Fernando de Béxar.

This process of integration was not unlike that in other communities of the far north, as a study of Saltillo reveals. In that town Hispanic residents procured Indian servants and laborers through encomienda arrangements that allowed the enslavement of area bands. In the early years of the settlement of Saltillo natives in the wilds were captured en masse, but the eventual scarcity of nomads necessitated the development of a wage system which provided closer interaction between Indians and the town dwellers. Native-Hispanic relations in San Fernando were not exactly like those in Saltillo, but they were similar. Perhaps because the Texas settlement was established considerably later in the colonial period, slave raiding was not as formalized and blatant in this far-northern province as in Saltillo, which was founded in the seventeenth century, but the use of captured natives as servants and laborers was clearly in evidence in San Fernando. However, as the century progressed Indians there were occupied mostly as independent laborers, farmers, and craftsmen. Possibly, as in Saltillo, a shortage of labor in Texas and the presence of Indian immigrants from the interior also gave rise to a free wage system on this frontier and facilitated the eventual integration of area natives into the community.[30]

The secularization of the missions undoubtedly contributed to a blending of different groups into San Fernando. Missions had not been established in the Saltillo area, but a separate Indian town (San Estevan) settled by transplanted Tlaxcaltecans was founded adjacent to the Hispanic settlement. Unlike the San Antonio missions, however, San Estevan was able to maintain itself demographically and economically and remained independent well into the nineteenth century. It was thus in a better position to resist the dissolution that occurred in the religious institutions along the San Antonio River. However, to the extent that the Indian pueblos in the Texas settlement continued as autonomous corporations after secularization, their experience was similar to that of San Estevan, with the possible exception that the Béxar postmission towns included numerous settlers from San Fernando. In this regard, the process of integration of separate Indian societies and of area and immigrant natives was more complete in the Texas settlement than in Saltillo.[31] Certainly, the Indian demographic, occupational, and social structure in the town, as well as the presence of native artifacts, demonstrates that by the end of the century, the larger San Antonio community had drawn native groups rather successfully into its social and economic life.

VII
Independent Indians and the San Antonio Community
Elizabeth A.H. John

Introduction

Independent Indians" rings more politely to the modern ear than the "indios bárbaros" of eighteenth-century usage. In either case, in the context of the Hispanic frontier, the reference is to those natives who remained outside the mission program, which taught not only the Catholic faith but also the rudiments of Hispanic civilization. "Los bárbaros" carries a connotation of ferocity or bellicosity, but the accuracy of that description depends upon which tribe and which period of time is considered. Nowhere were those variations over the years more significant than in San Antonio.[1]

Hostile or friendly, indios bárbaros had a formative impact on San Antonio from the outset. It was the menace of far-riding Apache warriors that first drove countless small Indian groups in this region to ask for admission into the missions that became the nucleus of San Antonio. Perhaps they were attracted by what they saw of Christianity at missions in northern Coahuila; but certainly those Indians needed the secure subsistence and

123

the protection from enemies that missions and their supporting soldiers offered.

The Path toward Coexistence

Sporadic hostilities with Apaches dominated life in San
Antonio through its first three decades. In the early 1700s
Apaches were fleeing Comanche enemies on the north even as
they themselves overran the helpless small bands to the south.
A vanguard of the southward-moving Apaches clashed with
Spaniards from San Antonio about 1720. Thenceforward, old
vendettas between Apaches and the local tribes, along with
grievous new provocations on all sides, fueled intermittent warfare. San Antonio's mission Indians, soldiers, and settlers ce-
mented their interdependence as comrades-in-arms against the
common foe.

Overt wars with the Apaches ended in 1749, when wors-
ening pressures from enemy Indians on the north drove the
Lipan and Natagé Apaches to respond to long-standing peace
overtures from San Antonio, frankly seeking refuge in a Spanish
connection. On the military plaza of Béxar they celebrated the
treaty of peace and alliance that made them vassals of the king
of Spain and thus, at least nominally, friends and brothers of
the San Antonians. Thenceforth, Lipan Apaches frequented San
Antonio, trading, visiting, proving their usefulness and reli-
ability as scouts for their new allies. Many Lipans moved close
to San Antonio for safety; some begged for a mission there.

Although some mutual confidence evolved between Lipans and Spaniards, the ingrained hatred and fear of Apaches
among mission Indians ruled out any congregation of Apaches
at San Antonio. Hence, in 1757, the Franciscans founded a separate mission for Apaches at a prudent distance northwestward
on the San Saba River (at present Menard). In so doing the good
fathers accidentally opened a new front in the wars that had
driven the Apaches to peace with the Spaniards. Sundry tribes
from the Red River, Trinity, and Brazos basins joined in hunting their Apache foes to the San Saba and, in the fury of tribal

vengence, destroyed the new mission. Now, in the same way that the Crown's responsibility to protect San Antonio's mission Indians had drawn the Spaniards into the vendettas of those people with the Apaches, the treaty commitment to the Apaches thrust the Spaniards unwittingly and unwisely into much more dangerous and complex intertribal wars.

Norteños, or Nations of the North, was the name under which San Antonians lumped the diverse Indian peoples who lived northward to the Red River: various groups whose descendants we now call Caddos, Wichitas, and Tonkawas. Loosely associated with the Norteños were the newly arriving Comanches. Their ready rapport with Norteños stemmed from mutual hatred of Apaches as well as from earlier Comanche alliance with Wichitan bands in the upper Arkansas basin.

At first the Norteños bore no active animosity towards Spaniards, but persistent Spanish favors to Apaches soon exhausted the Norteños' tolerance. By the mid-1760s Norteño warriors routinely attacked Spanish soldiers whom they found protecting Apaches. Next, Comanches, Taovayas, Wichitas, Tawakonis, and Tonkawas started harrassing San Antonio, where they were provoked by the town's conspicuous Apache visitors as well as tempted by its concentration of horses. Random incidents burgeoned into a desultory war that imposed great suffering on all sides and seemed to threaten the destruction of Spanish Texas. Certainly San Antonio could not thrive when farmers dared work their fields only under armed guard and when livestock herds attracted raiders who could be as dangerous to people as to property.

Imagine, then, how incongruous it may have seemed at San Antonio when, in the 1770s, the Crown proclaimed that its foremost objective on New Spain's northern frontier would be peace and alliance with the Comanches and, in Texas, their Norteño associates. Yet, within less than two decades, patient diplomacy and tenacious defense brought all of those groups to San Antonio to celebrate treaties of peace and alliance. The effort climaxed at San Antonio in the autumn of 1785, when delegates from the eastern Comanches came to negotiate the treaty of peace and alliance without which there was no hope of tranquillity or prosperity in Texas. Now the San Antonio community, which had weathered nearly seven decades of intermittent hostilities, faced the more complex challenges of peaceful interaction with countless Indian visitors of diverse languages and customs, among whom there were potentially dangerous intertribal enmities.

Indian Interactions at San Antonio

Although Indians of any or all of the allied nations might be found in San Antonio at any given time, Comanche visitors predominated from the 1790s onward. Trade was a prime factor. Indians brought hides, tallow, meat, and sometimes horses and even captives to exchange for textiles, clothing and ornaments, metal implements, weaponry, and foodstuffs, especially the dark, sweet piloncillos, the sugar cones of which there could never be enough to sate Indian appetites. Services also figured in the economic interchange, especially blacksmithing, because gun repairs were so important to the Indians, and tailoring, particularly of Spanish-style uniform coats and trousers for Indian leaders.

Social interaction was no less crucial. Visiting was a vital component of Indian friendships and unstinting hospitality a prime value in Indian cultures. Reciprocity was important. As the Comanche connection with Texas evolved towards stability in the 1790s and early 1800s, San Antonians traveled freely into the Comanchería to hunt, trade, and explore, often enjoying generous hospitality in Comanche camps and accompanying their hosts in hunting buffalo or catching mustangs. Comanches flocked to San Antonio, frequently bringing entire families, not only trading but also visiting with the local citizenry and among the assorted Indian guests. There they met Indian allies and mounted, or rested from, campaigns southward and eastward against Lipans. There too they received the Crown's annual presents, presumably at the governor's residence, where tribal leaders always presented themselves for long talks with the governor. When large groups came to trade, the authorities often proclaimed a feria (a trade fair or market day) to facilitate commerce between Indian visitors and local residents, so that the town's plaza bustled with barter.

The necessity of frequent and often extended entertainment of Indian guests led to the construction in 1786 of a huge jacal for that purpose. About 144 feet long by 15 feet wide, it was partitioned into four 36-foot rooms to facilitate lodging visitors from different nations. Chief interpreter Andrés Courbière donated its site beside his own home in the potrero (the area within the U-shaped bend in the San Antonio River, directly east of the main plaza), right next to the river so as to accommodate the Indians' exotic habit of bathing daily in a stream. Local residents contributed the labor of construction, although they were not altogether cheerful about the governor's decision not to pay them, since all members of the community had so much to gain from the peace and commerce fostered by the structure.

And gain they did. Quite apart from the obvious benefits to the community of peace as opposed to war, the lodge became a local profit center. There Indians were supplied with all they could eat and smoke and plenty of firewood for cooking and for dancing and sometimes for warmth. That meant profit for the local farmers, stockmen, and woodcutters from whom the government purchased that food and wood, and thus a welcome flow of cash into a local economy that was always short on currency. Still more cash flowed from the government's expenditures on such services as gun repair and tailoring for Indian guests, and local people were sometimes hired to cook or clean at the lodge. In addition to the special services rendered by such soldier-interpreters as Andrés Courbière and Francisco Xavier Chaves, one or more soldiers from the presidio were routinely assigned to the duty of Indian hospitality. In sum, San Antonio spared no effort to ensure that its Indian guests suffered no want or inconvenience and in the process found its own economy bolstered.

What was the outcome of such extensive interaction among such unlike peoples? Some warm personal friendships developed between San Antonians and Indians, with important long-term effects. For example, the Menchacas became particular friends of the Lipans and thus useful channels when Spanish authorities or Lipans wished to communicate with each other. Friendships between certain San Antonians and Comanches entailed reciprocal hospitality in each other's homes. Those visiting relationships benefited the whole community when such Comanches came to warn their San Antonio allies of dangers brewing within the Comanchería and even volunteered to support the Spaniards in case hostilities should occur.

Of course, there were dangerous as well as favorable outcomes. The community suffered when rebellious or lawless San Antonians took refuge in the camps of friendly Indians, sometimes enlisting Indian associates in their illegal activities. Conversely, San Antonio sometimes served as a refuge for nonconforming Indians: most notably, adulterous Comanche couples trying to elude the harsh penalties that adultery evoked under Comanche law. Moreover, increasingly after the first decade of the nineteenth century, there was the thorny problem of "white Indians," non-Indian criminals—Hispanos and Anglos—operating in Indian guise to evade identification.

It was never expected that peace treaties between nations could eliminate all clashes among persons from those nations. The best hope was that offenses by those of one nation against those of another should invoke law enforcement rather than war. Therefore, the treaties between Spaniards and Indians provided that leaders report such offenses to each other. Each society pledged to curb its own wrongdoers and make restitution for their crimes. Spanish authorities rigorously punished members of their own society for offenses against Indians, but they understood that such procedures were new and difficult in Indian societies. Therefore, the Spaniards displayed great forbearance so long as Indian leaders strove faithfully to fulfill their commitments. Horse theft, the most frequent offense on all sides, was especially difficult for Indians to relinquish because it was not only profitable but also had come to be greatly honored within their societies. Comanche leaders especially struggled to curb horse thefts, making restitution as fully as possible for crimes reported to them. They too showed forbearance, most importantly in 1802, when they rejected the provocation to tribal war after several young Comanches were killed in the San Antonio region, apparently by Spaniards.

After that dramatic demonstration of Comanche commitment to the peace, San Antonian fortunes became intertwined increasingly with those of their Indian allies. Great communal buffalo hunts, with Comanche assistance, loomed so large in the community's subsistence as to diminish the importance of traditional livestock in their economy. Products traded by or to the Indians composed the bulk of San Antonio's growing trade with Saltillo, which was its principal link to the economy of New Spain. Unfortunately no one in San Antonio possessed the capital required to make the most of the opportunity presented by the Indian trade.

Indios Bárbaros, San Antonio, and Mexican Independence

Of course, the eruption of Mexico's struggle for independence in 1810 eventually disrupted Indian relations at San Antonio. All across the northern provinces royalists and insurgents vied for Indian support. Royalists fared better at first because the tribes' loyalties focused on the king as the "great father" and because many Indians had personal friends among his officers. In 1811 Comanche and Lipan warriors helped crush the insurgents in Coahuila. Meanwhile, in Texas some Indians took advantage of growing disarray at San Antonio to steal more horses than usual, but none went to war. Indeed, Comanche leaders strove particularly to uphold their alliance in Texas in spite of the turmoils, volunteering measures to improve treaty compliance by their followers. Still more difficult tests of Indian loyalties and judgments came in 1812 with the invasion of Texas by the oddly assorted band of American filibusters and Spanish insurrectionists, who destroyed the Crown's authority in Texas by April 1813.

Although the invaders presumed Indian support, most tribes in fact held aloof from their enterprise. Some disaffected Comanches, Tawakonis, and Taovayas exploited the opportunity to raid for horses in Texas and Coahuila, but none of these Indians responded to the invaders' urgent appeal for help in ousting the royalists. The insurrectionists' slaughter of the governor and commandant, whom they captured at San Antonio, must have appalled the Comanche leaders with whom those officers had cooperated closely; it is hardly surprising that Comanches stood aloof from San Antonio during the invaders' brief ascendancy. Some 200 Lipans did join the insurrectionists at San Antonio, probably because their long-time friends, the Menchacas, espoused the cause.

When the royalists recaptured San Antonio in August 1813, some Tejano insurgents fled northward and westward for refuge among Indians. Some could rely upon friendships established in years of interaction with Indian visitors at San Antonio. They could also exploit fresh grievances among Comanches, Tawakonis, and Taovayas: a party from those nations suffered casualties when chased by royalist troops marching towards San Antonio. Over the next seven years many warriors of those nations, and Lipans, too, would help the fugitive insurgents wage a deliberate war of attrition designed to make Texas and Coahuila untenable for the Spanish Crown. They nearly destroyed San Antonio's economy in the process, and of course the continuing warfare wrecked the community's viability as a center of Indian trade.

But as the war for independence wore to a close, both the Crown and its erstwhile Indian allies in Texas were groping toward a restoration of peace. Mexico's new national government promptly pursued the pacification effort inherited from the viceroyalty, in a purposeful effort to revive the colonial legacy of an imperfect peace that was mutually useful to Hispanos and Indians, and infinitely preferable to war. San Antonians served as the primary agents in renewed negotiations; some were official representatives of San Antonio's ayuntamiento, which energetically supported the national government's peace objective. By the end of 1822 all of the tribes had renewed their treaties at San Antonio, and delegates from most had ridden on to Mexico City to ratify those treaties with the new national government.

It was never possible to mend completely the torn fabric of Indian relations at San Antonio, partly because Mexico's resources were inadequate to sustain its commitments on the northern frontier. Moreover, the influx of Cis-Mississippi tribes and subversive Anglos sorely disrupted Indian affairs in Texas. But the restored Comanche alliance functioned reasonably well until the Texas Revolution began. As late as August 1835, when representatives of the moderate Anglo colonists came from San Felipe de Austin to San Antonio seeking permission to carry their case to Commandant General Martín Perfecto de Cos at Matamoros, Comanche Chief Casimiro and his principal associates were in San Antonio, also seeking permission to go to Matamoros to talk with General Cos. Accompanying those Comanche leaders were some 300 men, women, and children, camped as usual in the outskirts of the town and peacefully pursuing their usual errands.

Astonishingly, Anglo accounts of that episode made no mention of those 300 Comanche visitors, who surely must have been quite conspicuous in a San Antonio of little more than 2,000 inhabitants. But the Anglos, with their overriding presumption of Indian hostility, appear to have been unable to see peaceful Indians. They soon made San Antonio a place of terror for Indians, and one that was none too comfortable for most Hispanos as well.

Inclusion of Indios Bárbaros in the San Antonio Community

A long-neglected dimension of the history of San Antonio is the actual incorporation of indios bárbaros – almost always women or children – into the community. Consider three examples of that process:

In 1759, when Lipan allies helped a punitive Spanish expeditionary force wipe out a Yojuan camp in North-Central Texas, the Lipans captured an eight-year-old Yojuan boy, whom they later sold to retired soldier don Baltasar Peres of San Antonio. Reared in the Peres home and taking the family's name, Miguel Peres grew up thoroughly Hispanicized, married a young Indian girl from a local mission, and lived as a model resident of the settlement. In the 1770s, when the Tonkawas became allies and regular visitors at San Antonio, Miguel discovered that his father and brother had escaped to join the kindred Tonkawas, among whom they had won considerable influence. Although Miguel had no wish to return to the Indian life, he often visited his natural father and brother and became a very useful communications link between San Antonio and the Tonkawas. In the 1780s he carried to his relatives a crucial message from Governor Domingo Cabello which helped preserve the alliance.[2]

Several other indios bárbaros blended into the San Antonio community through purchase from their Indian captors by the humane soldier-interpreter Francisco Xavier Chaves, who himself had grown up as a captive, first of Comanches and then of Taovayas. Early in the nineteenth century Chaves ransomed from Comanche captors a Lipan woman and her little girl – baptized as Guadalupe and Trinidad, respectively – who were incorporated into the Chaves household. About 1810, not long after puberty, Trinidad produced a son whom she voluntarily gave to Chaves to rear and educate. The child was sired by militiaman Joaquín de Almaguer, with whom Trinidad apparently lived for a time. When their son, christened Miguel de los Santos, was about three, Trinidad married Joaquín del Mages, for whom she bore another son before she died three years later. Meanwhile, for the first six years of his life, Miguel de los Santos had lived principally with his adoptive parents, the Chaveses, who provided all his care after his mother's death.

In 1822, when eleven-year-old Miguel was beginning to have some economic value, the stepfather took legal action to claim him. Chaves protested that Mages had never made any provision for nor accorded any recognition to the child, even during his marriage with the mother, letting the child be reared as a member of the large family of Chaves. When San Antonio's alcalde ruled in the stepfather's favor, Chaves appealed to Governor Antonio María Martínez. The governor ordered that the natural father be located and noted that Chaves had the right to demand the costs of rearing and educating the child if compelled to relinquish him.[3]

The natural father, Joaquín de Almaguer, acknowledged paternity of Miguel de los Santos and attested that Chaves had indeed cared for the boy after the mother's death. Almaguer himself had wanted the child back to help him in his work, but Miguel always wanted to go back to the Chaves home, so it was never satisfactory to have him. Almaguer would not impede Miguel's return to the Chaves household; he denied liability for costs that Chaves had incurred in rearing and educating the boy. Either stepfather Mages lost the case at that point or his enthusiasm vanished upon contemplating the costs he would owe to Chaves. Apparently Miguel de los Santos remained in the Chaves household until the age of independence.

Some integration of indios bárbaros into the San Antonio community resulted from direct capture. A striking instance began in September 1830 when a punitive force from San Antonio surprised and routed an encampment of Tawakonis on the San Gabriel River. Found amidst the camp debris were four little Tawakoni boys – three of them suckling infants and one a few years older – whom members of the expedition undertook to carry to San Antonio. One of the babies proved too young to survive the journey on the thin gruel that was the best diet the soldiers could improvise; they baptized him before he died. But militiamen José Antonio Salinas and Juan Casanova managed to carry the other two babies to San Antonio in time for compassionate nursing mothers to save their lives. The babies were soon firmly established in the hearts as well as the homes of Salinas and Casanova. Salinas counted on rearing his little Tawakoni as his only son, with all the proper legal formalities of adoption. Casanova already had children with whom he wished to rear his little Tawakoni, and he too intended legal adoption.[4]

So those two citizens protested vigorously in January 1831 when San Antonio authorities received the commandant general's order that the four captured Tawakoni children mentioned in the battle report be sent on to Monterrey. Salinas and Casanova contended that these two suckling infants would surely die en route to Monterrey just as the third had died before reaching San Antonio. Moreover, they pleaded their great love for the children as the natural result of having cared for them. Both the jefe político and the military commandant vouched for the reality of these citizens' affection for the infants and argued that humanity dictated leaving the children with them. The commandant general consented, on condition that the jefe político be responsible for monitoring their education and welfare. The jefe político responded that he had already observed the situation carefully from the moment the children arrived, in order to remedy any possible deficiencies in their care, and would continue to do so.[5]

The fourth, older boy appeared to be epileptic. Comanche visitors familiar with those Tawakonis explained that the child's seizures had resulted from an accident sometime after infancy. Soldier Francisco Calvillo cared for that youngster in his home until the commandant general's order resulted in his transfer to Monterrey. Local Commandant Principal José Antonio Elozúa made careful arrangements for the transfer, authorizing full provisions for the journey and entrusting the child to a soldier of Aguaverde Company for delivery to the commandant of Laredo, who would entrust the child to two other soldiers for delivery to Monterrey via Punta de Lampazos. If further help should be needed en route, it was to be kindly furnished; any bills could be sent to the Comisario of Monterrey with expectation of prompt payment.[6]

Those three instances of Indian integration into the San Antonio community stand out in the Béxar Archives because they entailed some official involvement, through service to the governor in the first example and through legal action concerning custody in the second and third. It is impossible to know how many more indios bárbaros were absorbed by the community through informal processes that left no clear paper trail, but there is reason to suppose such occurrences not to have been uncommon. The qualities of compassion and particular love of children attested by these examples constitute compelling contradictions to the pervasive and pernicious myth of Spanish cruelty.

It is also impossible to know how many Spaniards were absorbed into the communities of indios bárbaros. Many captives never had the opportunity to return to Spanish communities, but there are documentary traces of others who chose to remain in Indian societies. Some Tejanos voluntarily lived among the Indians from time to time: some were fugitives from the law, as noted above, and some were merely poor or discontented Tejanos seeking a better life for themselves in Indian societies. Many returned eventually to San Antonio, greatly enriching that community's pool of expertise concerning various indios bárbaros.

One of the tragedies of Texas history was the distrustful Anglo-American Texans' failure to avail themselves of the San Antonio community's well-developed skills in dealing with Indians and its established avenues of communication with Indian communities. Then, as now, ignorance and bluster proved to be dangerous substitutes for patient understanding.

CONCLUSION

The Emergence of a Tejano Community

By focusing on the main population groups that settled San Antonio de Béxar, this collection of papers has provided glimpses of the economic, social, cultural, and political processes that shaped the emergence of Béxar's Tejano community during the eighteenth century. Originally the settlement began as three distinct societies: the missions, a military garrison, and a civilian town. At first the members of the separate colonial institutions that composed the settlement (friars and Indians, Mexican soldier-settlers, and Canary Islanders) promoted their group rights and prerogatives instead of cooperation and unity. But in time the realities of life on the frontier forced the original settlers, who were joined during the century by Indian, mestizo, mulatto, criollo, and European immigrants, to collaborate and build a unified society.

Economic expansion was critical to the emergence of an integrated community in Béxar. In the early days competition and conflict over control of local resources threatened to destroy the fledgling settlement. The missions' acquisition of vast properties, their struggle to control water rights on the San Antonio River, and the threat of Indian attack limited the availability of farmlands for the soldier-settlers and Canary Islanders. Faced with the reality of scarce resources, the early inhabitants engaged in numerous heated controversies that undermined the emergence of a community-wide economic vision. But the search for resources on which all could rely eventually overcame selfish group interests. Bexareños cooperated with one another to enhance an economy built on farming and ranching and linked commercially to Louisiana and Coahuila.

Béxar's settlers initially focused their energies on farming. At first irrigable farmlands were in the hands only of the missions and the Canary Islanders, but in time new grants to soldier-settlers and immigrants, sales of property by Canary Islanders, and the secularization of the missions and distribution of their lands to settlers opened farming activities to many in Béxar. By 1800 those engaged in farming included all segments of the local society: Indians on former mission lands; descendants of the original soldier-settlers and of the Canary Islanders; and immigrants from New Spain and Los Adaes, including some Indians. This broadening of the productive social base brought security to a larger segment of Béxar's inhabitants and provided them with the economic means to participate meaningfully within the community.

If farming established the nutritional necessities in Béxar, ranching developed as the most important commercial pursuit. The missions first exploited the cattle resources in Texas on their extensive lands along the San Antonio River between Béxar and the settlement of La Bahía to the south. Franciscan friars and Indian vaqueros pursued what became a relatively lucrative enterprise of rounding up cattle that roamed freely on mission and surrounding lands. Prominent members of the original presidio families were the first civilians to follow the lead of the missions. These Mexican military settlers received land grants along the San Antonio River and began to take advantage of a sizable demand for Texas cattle and horses in

Louisiana. In return, the presidios received European goods and tobacco. Realizing the advantages of this trade and the limitations on farming imposed by inadequate technologies and limited markets for agricultural products, the Canary Islanders in time also entered ranching. Those who took up ranching soon obtained large land grants and became the most prominent and influential citizens of Béxar.

The distribution patterns of Béxar's resources during the eighteenth century determined the nature of the community's social structure. Through their control of irrigable farmlands during the 1730s, the Canary Islanders became the settlement's socioeconomic elite. Within the next two decades, however, they shared this status with many members of the presidio community who established their own economic base in the ranching sector or purchased farms from Islanders. Frequent intermarriage between Isleños and presidiales resulted in the formation of an integrated ruling elite. Once the ruling families emerged, entry into this elite circle occurred through further intermarriage, the accumulation of wealth, or inheritance. Later in the century wealth was not easily acquired, since most of the land and water resources were already in the hands of the dominant families. But many immigrants to Béxar managed to become members of the elite through strategic marriages.

The relationship between economic condition and social status in Béxar is clear, but that between ethnic and social standing is complex and difficult to characterize. Béxar's elite were almost exclusively "Spanish" in their ethnic designation, revealing the advantage of such a status. However, social attitudes were sufficiently flexible to allow individuals of non-Spanish backgrounds to attain economic or political prominence. In fact, along with the attainment of status came changes in ethnic designations, as is evident in the frequent transition of mulattoes or mestizos to "Spanish" in official documents. Indeed, the racial/ethnic designations in Béxar's census often reveal more about an individual's social position and reputation in the community than about his actual background.

The blending under the rubric of "Spanish" and the merging of ranching and farming interests among Bexareños produced specific political concerns and a particular regional identity. A strong impulse for autonomy, based on the community's relative self-sufficiency, gave rise to an independent Tejano spirit. This emergent identity enhanced the community's desire and willingness to pursue local interests and objectives even when they contradicted Crown policies.

Changes in political attitudes were reflected in Béxar's cabildo. At first the Canary Islander-controlled cabildo served the political interests of that group, but, in time, as others in the community gained economic or social influence, they too participated in the cabildo. By the final third of the century the city's ruling council no longer represented the interests of an ethnically defined Isleño group, but rather the interests of the region's farmers and ranchers, regardless of ethnic background, against the encroachment of Crown authority. The integrative forces that led to economic growth, the formation of a social system, and the need for political autonomy also produced a unique cultural expression that borrowed from the various ethnic traditions of Mexicans of mixed racial heritages, Indians, and Canary Islanders.

Cultures blended as groups adopted each other's traditions. The Canary Islanders, for example, arrived with their Old World protectress, Nuestra Señora de la Candelaria, but soon accepted New Spain's mestiza Virgen de Guadalupe as their own. Mexican settlers who married Canary Islanders accepted their Isleño identity, as did their children. Indians who lived in Béxar, or who came from the Norteño tribes to trade, introduced many aspects of their material culture which were readily adopted by Béxar's Mexican and European citizens. Interactions with Indians in the missions, Indian immigrants and residents, as well as the various independent Indian peoples even further enriched the cross-cultural experience of the Hispanic inhabitants.

As the various groups interacted and exchanged traditions, synthesis produced a specific Tejano culture which may be thought of as a regional identity. Although not easily defined, this identity involved the adaptation of a Mexican ranching culture to the Texas frontier. Mission Indians, Mexican soldier-settlers, Canary Islanders, and later immigrants accepted a ranching lifestyle as their own. Whether it was utilizing certain accouterments, developing a distinct vocabulary, accepting the hardships associated with cattle roundups and drives, side-stepping legal strictures against exporting cattle to Louisiana, or developing political attitudes related to their particular socioeconomic condition, the residents of Béxar accepted these traditions as the basis of a shared Tejano cultural heritage.

This process of community and identity formation, it must be pointed out, was never all-inclusive. Those most integrated into the community were Bexareños with a direct stake in the farming and ranching economy, whether as elite or working-class residents. But many in Béxar existed without access to a stable economic existence, social contacts, or political influence. Census documents of the 1790s reveal that many individuals appear and disappear from the settlement year to year. Their experience is in sharp contrast to Béxar's established families, which, along with their employees or servants, are consistently recorded in the documents.

Nevertheless, by the end of the eighteenth century Béxar was a unified though socially stratified Tejano community. The residents of the town underwent considerable change during the century as they established their socioeconomic order, which produced its related regional political and cultural expressions. After 1800 the processes of economic, social, political, and cultural change so vital for understanding the community's formation continued and even accelerated as Béxar felt the cross-currents of Mexican politics and United States expansionism through the end of the century.

The Anglo-American westward movement had serious and often disastrous effects on Bexareños as they made the transition to ethnic minority in their own land, but, as Arnoldo De León and others have pointed out, their society was not destroyed. The original community survived changes in sovereignty, political tradition, cultural expression, and economic system and emerged with a still vibrant and more focused and crystalized Tejano self-image, a process of adaptation that continued and shaped the nineteenth- and twentieth-century Tejano and Mexican-American identity.

NOTES

Introduction

[1] Andrew Anthony Tijerina, "Tejanos and Texas," p. 333.

[2] The complexity of the interplay between diversity and sense of identity in Chicano history is discussed in a recent historiographic essay by Alex Saragoza, "The Significance of Recent Chicano-related Historical Writings," pp. 25-62. See also Arnoldo De León, "The Tejano Experience in Six Texas Regions," and Richard Griswold del Castillo, "Tejanos and California Chicanos."

[3] Carlos E. Castañeda, ed. and trans., *History of Texas, 1673-1779, By Fray Juan Agustín Morfi*, pp. 190, 92.

[4] José María Sánchez, "A Trip to Texas in 1828," pp. 249-88.

[5] H. Yoakum, *History of Texas from Its First Settlement in 1685 to Its Annexation to the United States in 1846*, I: 141-42.

[6] George Pierce Garrison, *Texas: A Contest of Civilizations*, p. 53.

[7] T.R. Fehrenbach, *Seven Keys to Texas*, pp. 1-2. See also T.R. Fehrenbach, *Lone Star*.

[8] On traditional Spanish Borderlands historiography, see Gerald E. Poyo and Gilberto M. Hinojosa, "Spanish Texas and Borderlands Historiography in Transition," pp. 393-416.

[9] Paul S. Taylor, *An American-Mexican Frontier*.

[10] Carey McWilliams, *North from Mexico*.

[11] J. Frank Dobie, ed. *Puro Mexicano*. For an overview of Dobie and his work, see Don Graham, "J. Frank Dobie," pp. 1-7.

[12] O. Douglas Weeks, "The Texas-Mexican and Politics in South Texas," pp. 257-78. For a more comprehensive interpretation, see Evan Anders, *Boss Rule in South Texas*.

[13] William Madsen, *The Mexican-Americans of South Texas*; Arthur J. Rubel, *Across the Tracks*. For a critique of the trends in midcentury sociological literature, see Octavio Romano-V, "The Anthropology and Sociology of the Mexican-Americans," pp. 26-39, and Nick C. Vaca, "The Mexican-American in the Social Sciences," pp. 17-51.

[14] Frederick C. Chabot, *With the Makers of San Antonio*; Rubén Rendón Lozano, *Viva Tejas*; Jovita González, "Social Life in Cameron, Starr, and Zapata Counties," and "Tales and Songs of the Texas Mexicans," pp. 86-116; Alonso Perales, *El méxico-americano y la política de sur de Tejas* and *En defensa de mi raza*.

143

[15] Thomas D. Hall, *Social Change in the Southwest, 1350-1850.* See also Edward H. Spicer, *Cycles of Conquest,* and D.W. Meinig, *Southwest.*

[16] Arnoldo De León, *The Tejano Community, 1836-1900;* David Montejano, *Anglos and Mexicans in the Making of Texas, 1836-1986.*

[17] Américo Paredes, *"With His Pistol in His Hand";* José Limón, "El Primer Congreso Mexicanista de 1911." For a brief interpretative synthesis of Chicano historiography, see essays by David J. Weber and Roger W. Lotchin in "The New Chicano History: Two Perspectives," pp. 219-47. On Tejanos, see Arnoldo De León, "Tejano History Scholarship."

[18] De León, *Tejano Community,* pp. 23, 206.

[19] Mario T. García, *Desert Immigrants.*

[20] Juan Gómez-Quiñones, "Toward a Perspective on Chicano History."

[21] Gilberto M. Hinojosa, *A Borderlands Town in Transition,* p. 113.

[22] On this recent Tejano research, see Poyo and Hinojosa, "Borderlands Historiography."

[23] Fane Downs, "The History of Mexicans in Texas, 1820-1845," p. 3; Tijerina, "Tejanos and Texas"; Jesús de la Teja and John Wheat, "Béxar," pp. 7-34; David J. Weber, *The Mexican Frontier, 1821-1846.*

I. Béxar: Profile of a Tejano Community 1830-1832

This chapter was originally published in *Southwestern Historical Quarterly* 89, no. 1 (July 1985): 7-34. Reprinted with permission of the Texas State Historical Association.

[1] Two unpublished works dealing with Tejanos during the Mexican Republic and early statehood years are Tijerina, "Tejanos and Texas," and Downs, "History of Mexicans." See also Arnoldo De León, *Tejano Community,* pp. 1-22.

[2] Jean Louis Berlandier, *Journey to Mexico during the Years 1826-1834,* II: 291.

[3] Census report of La Espada and San Juan Capistrano missions, 1819, Béxar Archives (hereafter BA), University of Texas at Austin, Barker Texas History Center (hereafter BTHC). Unless otherwise noted, all documents cited in this article are from BA. Documents are arranged in the Béxar Archives by date, whether or not that date is correct. Dates of documents in this article indicate, therefore, where the documents are filed in the archives. If only a year is given, the document is filed after the last day of that year; if only a month and a year are given, the document is found after the last day of that month in that year.

[4] José Erasmo Seguín to Antonio María Martínez, Dec. 28, 1820; election returns for missions, Dec. 23, 1827. For the secularization of the missions, see Carlos E. Castañeda, *Our Catholic Heritage in Texas, 1519-1936,* V: 35-66; VI: 317-22.

5 Marion A. Habig, *The Alamo Chain of Missions*, pp. 70-71; monthly report
of the Veteran Cavalry Company of San Carlos de Parras, Nov. 30, 1819;
census report of the Presidial Company of Béxar, Dec. 14, 1819; Weber,
Mexican Frontier, pp. 107-15.

6 Ayuntamiento instructions to provincial deputation, in Martínez to Am-
brosio Aldasoro, Nov. 15, 1820; José Félix Trespalacios to Gaspar López,
Oct. 18, 1822; Juan Castañeda to junta gubernativa, May 21, 1823; provincial deputation to Castañeda, May 23, 1824; Rafael González to
Antonio Elozúa, Oct. 22, 1825; Ramón Múzquiz to Elozúa, Nov. 6, 1832.

7 Edict creating wards in San Fernando de Béxar, Oct. 5, 1809, Nacogdoches
Archives Transcripts (BTHC; these transcripts are cited hereafter as
NAT); Berlandier, *Journey to Mexico*, II: 289-91. For genealogies of the
important San Antonio families, see Chabot, *Makers of San Antonio*.

8 Tijerina, "Tejanos and Texas," pp. 29-32; Hinojosa, *Borderlands Town*, p. 42.
The census figures, of course, are not exact. The 1820 estimate is based
on the following: censuses of Indians for San Juan Capistrano, San
Francisco de la Espada, and San José de Aguayo missions, Nov. 12,
1818; list of persons drowned (on July 5, 1819), July 8, 1819; monthly
report of the Veteran Cavalry Company of San Carlos de Parras, Nov.
30, 1819; census report of the Presidial Company of Béxar, (Dec. 14,
1819); census report of La Espada and San Juan Capistrano missions,
1819; census report of Béxar, Jan. 1, 1820; Tomás de León's report of
election returns for election of judge at Mission San José, Dec. 20, 1822.
The 1830 estimate is based on the following: census report of Barrio
del Norte, July 19, 1829; census reports of the Cuartel del Norte,
Cuartel del Sur, Cuartel de Valero, and jurisdiccion de misiones, Aug.
10, 1829; military report of Texas troops, Aug. 28, 1829; census report
of Barrio de Valero, July 7, 1830; census report of Barrio del Sur, July
9, 1830.

9 List of persons paying taxes on shops during January 1824; census for tax
on dulas (irrigation water), at the San Antonio missions (1824);
Hinojosa, *Borderlands Town*, p. 35; Weber, *Mexican Frontier*, pp. 216-17.
Widows enjoyed certain legal privileges and a degree of social accept-
ability not afforded to abandoned women or unwed mothers (see Colin
M. McLachlan and Jaime E. Rodríguez O., *The Forging of the Cosmic
Race*, pp. 237-48).

10 Hinojosa, *Borderlands Town*, pp. 32-33; Weber, *Mexican Frontier*, pp. 214-
15. For the 1820 population figures, see note 8. The outline of the debate on race and social structure can be found in Patricia Seed, "Social
Dimensions of Race," pp. 569-606.

11 Census summary for reporting municipalities of the state of Coahuila y
Texas, Jan. 2, 1832, NAT.

12 Ayuntamiento minutes of Apr. 15, 1823, in Ayuntamiento Minutes Book
(1821-1825), Jan. 17, 1821 (hereafter cited as Minutes Book I); Nettie
L. Benson, *La diputación provincial y el federalismo mexicano*, pp. 82-84.

The story of the insurgency in Texas during this period is told in Julia
Kathryn Garrett, *Green Flag over Texas.*

[13] Tijerina, "Tejanos and Texas," pp. 227-40; Charles A. Bacarisse, "The Union
of Coahuila and Texas," pp. 341-49.

[14] José Ramírez to Martínez, Aug. 30, 1820; James McReynolds, "Mexican
Nacogdoches," p. 30; Eugene C. Barker, "The Government of Austin's
Colony, 1821-1831," pp. 244-45.

[15] Selection of constitutional ayuntamiento, July 25, 1820; Martínez to ayuntamiento, Dec. 16, 1821; election returns for Béxar ayuntamiento
(1822-1826), Dec. 21, 1822; election returns for Béxar ayuntamiento,
Dec. 9, 1827, Dec. 21, 1828.

[16] See, for instance, ayuntamiento to Martínez, Nov. 15, 1821; municipal
revenues and expenditures, Dec. 24, 1821; ayuntamiento to Agustín
de Iturbide, June 24, 1822.

[17] Plans for funds formed by the ayuntamiento, Oct. 20, 1823; account book
of municipal funds (1826-1827), Jan. 1, 1826; ordinance issued by
Múzquiz, Dec. 7, 1830.

[18] Barón de Bastrop to Juan Martínez de Veramendi, Mar. 12, 1825; José
Antonio Saucedo to ayuntamiento, May 22, 1826; Múzquiz to José
María Viesca, May 9, 1830; Elozúa to Rudencindo Barragán and
Francisco Padilla, Sept. 9, 1830; Nicolás Flores, request for loan, Apr.
14, 1831; law no. 634, May 8, 1829, Manuel Dublán and José María
Lozano, *Legislación mexicana,* II: 106. For the establishment of the bank,
see Carlos E. Castañeda, "The First Chartered Bank West of the Missis-
sippi," pp. 242-56.

[19] State law no. 37 (June 15, 1827) redefined the jurisdiction and powers of
Texas municipalities, while state law no. 39 (June 21, 1827) set forth
the bases of a code for the administration of justice in Coahuila y Texas.
Law no. 37, June 15, 1827, Coahuila y Texas, General Printed Series,
BA (hereafter cited as GPS). For law no. 39, see Clarence R. Wharton,
The Jurisdiction of the Alcalde Courts in Texas Prior to the Revolution,
pp. 5-6, 26-57.

[20] *Bando de buen gobierno,* Feb. 1, 1824, articles 12-14; *Ordnanzas* [sic]
*municipales para el gobierno y manejo del ayuntamiento de la ciudad de
San Antonio de Béxar, (Leona Vicario, 1829),* articles 28-32 (hereafter cited
as Ord[e]nanzas [1829]).

[21] Múzquiz to citizens, Feb. 26, 1830; prison reports of Béxar jail (1826-1830),
Jan. 1, 1826.

[22] José Salinas to Martínez, June 28, 1822; Martínez to Salinas, June 30,
1822; theft trials (1820-1831), Feb. 28, 1829.

[23] Records of conciliatory judgments, June 4, 1822, Mar. 21, 1825, Jan. 18,
1829, Jan. 14, 1831; state decree no. 25, in Saucedo to Salinas, Dec.
11, 1827, Juan N. Seguín and Luciano Navarro to ayuntamiento, Nov.
18, 1829. By a state decree of Aug. 27, 1827, the alcalde had to prove

the theft charge against the defendant at a hearing with two conjueces (one chosen by each party) in order to impose a sentence. State decree no. 7, H.P.N. Gammel, comp., *The Laws of Texas, 1822-1897*, I: 176-78.

[24] Criminal proceedings against Agapito A. (1824-1825), Aug. 5, 1824, Oct. 22, 1828.

[25] The state decree of Aug. 27, 1827, formalized penalties for various degrees of theft. Gammel, *Laws of Texas*, I: 176-78. See also Victor Blanco to tobacco administrator for Béxar, Aug. 28, 1827; theft trials (1829-1831), Feb. 28, 1829; report of contributors according to state decree no. 90, 1829. State decree no. 90 provided for a graduated income tax. Gammel, *Laws of Texas*, I: 123-26; *Bando de buen gobierno*, Feb. 1, 1824; record of fines and imprisonments (1832-1833), Jan. 14, 1832; *Ord[e]nanzas* (1829), articles 52-56.

[26] Prison report of Béxar jail (1826-1830), Jan. 1, 1826; lists of tools bought by the ayuntamiento for the use of convicts (1828-1829), Nov. 27, 1828; account of days worked by prisoners on private houses and the church (1829-1831), Apr. 8, 1829; theft trials (1829-1831), Feb. 28, 1829.

[27] *Bando de buen gobierno*, Feb. 1, 1824; *Ord[e]nanzas* (1829), articles 19-21.

[28] Ayuntamiento to Martínez, May 2, 18, 1820; López to Trespalacios, Nov. 11, 1822; Mateo Ahumada to J.E. Seguín, Nov. 30, 1825; Lucas de Palacio to J.E. Seguín, Jan. 21, 1827; José Flores to Saucedo, Feb. 8, 1827. The best summary of medical efforts in this period is Pat Ireland Nixon, *The Medical Story of Early Texas, 1528-1853*.

[29] Nixon, *Medical Story*, p. 126, offers contemporary evidence of a native curandera, giving medical testimony in a Laredo trial in 1824.

[30] Ibid., pp. 130, 138. San Antonio was ravaged, however, by a resurgence of cholera in 1834.

[31] Martínez to ayuntamiento, May 4, 1820; reports of smallpox cases by barrio, Mar. 6, 1831; establishment of the junta de sanidad, Jan. 22, 1831; junta de sanidad minutes, Jan. 23 (to Mar. 13), 1831; list of persons vaccinated, Feb. 20 (to Mar. 18), 1831.

[32] Woodrow Borah, "Social Welfare and Social Obligation in New Spain," IV: 45-57; census report of Béxar, Jan. 1, 1820; jail regulations, article 10 (June 30, 1828); *Ord[e]nanzas* (1829), article 40.

[33] Minutes Book I, Feb. 6, 1823; ayuntamiento to Trespalacios, Feb. 6, 1823; Saucedo to ayuntamiento, Jan. 23, 1825; ayuntamiento to Múzquiz, June 18, 1830, and Múzquiz' statement of smallpox relief expenses, July 15, 1831; Múzquiz to Elozúa, Nov. 6, 1832; ayuntamiento minutes, Apr. 1, 1830, Spanish Minutes Book II, 1830-1835, San Antonio City Records Transcripts (BTHC; hereafter cited as Minutes Book II [SACRT]).

[34] List of persons drowned (on July 5, 1819), July 18, 1819; ayuntamiento report on distribution of relief funds, Mar. 10, 1820; Fr. Miguel Muro to Martínez, Mar. 13, 1820; Martínez's report on distribution of relief

funds, May 14, 1820; ayuntamiento reports on distribution of relief funds, Dec. 24, 1821. The flood is described in detail in Martínez to Joaquín de Arredondo, July 8, 1819, Nacogdoches Archives, Archives Division, Texas State Library, Austin; a copy of the letter appears in Virginia H. Taylor, ed. and trans., *The Letters of Antonio Martínez, Last Spanish Governor of Texas*, pp. 241-43.

[35] Weber, *Mexican Frontier*, pp. 232-33; constitution of Coahuila y Texas, Title 6, article 215, Gammel, *Laws of Texas*, I: 451. The story of educational efforts in Béxar, from colonial times to 1834, is told by Isaac Joslin Cox, "Educational Efforts in San Fernando de Béxar," pp. 27-63.

[36] Minutes Book I, Mar. 15 and Aug. 4, 1822, June 8, 1823; minutes of ayuntamiento, May 25, 1820; ayuntamiento to Saucedo, Apr. 14, 1825; ayuntamiento to José Ignacio de Arispe, Apr. 14, 1826; ayuntamiento to Arispe, Mar. 15, 1827, draft enclosed in Arispe to ayuntamiento, Feb. 10, 1827; school fund ledger (1828-1835), Jan. 1, 1828; Chabot, *Makers of San Antonio*, pp. 34, 199, 203.

[37] Minutes Book II (SACRT), Jan. 7, 28, and July 1, 1830, Apr. 14, July 28, 1831; J.N. Seguín to Múzquiz, June 7, 1829; Múzquiz to ayuntamiento, Nov. 18, 1829; contract for teacher, July 28, 1831; Cox, "Educational Efforts," pp. 46-47.

[38] Writing exercises, Mar. 13, 1832; report on school, Dec. 31, 1832; school regulations, Mar. 13, 1828.

[39] Múzquiz to ayuntamiento, Feb. 12, 1828; José María Letona to Múzquiz, Oct. 12, 1831; Minutes Book II (SACRT), Jan. 26 and Feb. 6, 1832.

[40] Saucedo to Veramendi, Oct. 21, 1825; minutes of meeting at Jefatura, Jan. 22, 1831; "*Receta para la chólera morbo, dada por d. Pascual de Aranda, profesor de medicina,*" reimpreso en Monclova, GPS, governmental undated; Múzquiz to Miguel Arcinega, Dec. 29, 1830.

[41] GPS, governmental and nongovernmental documents. The mail carrier between San Felipe de Austin and Béxar earned 740 pesos per annum in 1826, not an insubstantial amount. Agricultural workers, by comparison, earned only half that sum. Post office account ledger, Apr. 4, 1826; report of contributors according to state decree no. 90, 1829. The shortest possible amount of time for round-trip correspondence with Mexico City was approximately two months (see, e.g., Arredondo to Martínez, June 13, 1820).

[42] Eugene C. Barker, "Notes on Early Texas Newspapers, 1819-1836," p. 127; Lota M. Spell, *Pioneer Printer*, p. 69; Marilyn McAdams Sibley, *Lone Stars and State Gazettes*, p. 40-42; ayuntamiento of Monclova to Trespalacios, May 10, 1823; José Angel Benavides to publisher of the *Correo de Texas*, May 21, 1823; ayuntamiento of Sombrerete to governor of Texas, May 26, 1823; bill for printing services, July 10, 1823; Luciano García to Felipe de la Garza, July 17 and 22, 1823. For examples of the documents printed in Béxar, see "Noticias del govierno de Texas,"

June 11, 1823, and "Junta gubernativa de la provincia de Texas," July 8, 1823, GPS, governmental.

[43] A number of financial and administrative documents shed some light on the quantity, if not the quality, of the social life of Béxar. Travelers' accounts also describe some of the social events. A good bibliography of these works may be found in Marilyn McAdams Sibley, *Travelers in Texas, 1761-1860*, pp. 201-23.

[44] Minutes Book I, Aug. 23, 1821, Nov. 7 and 14, 1822; junta patriótica program for celebration of Independence Day, Sept. 12, 1829, Sept. 10, 1830.

[45] Celebration of Independence, Sept. 12, 1829. See also celebration of Independence, September 10, 1830.

[46] Celebration of Independence, September 12, 1829.

[47] Ibid.

[48] While 326 pesos was collected for the celebration of the Mexican victory, the town raised only 195 pesos for the actual military effort. Junta patriótica program of celebration of Mexican victory, Sept. 11, 1829; contributions for war effort, Aug. 14, 1829; celebration of Independence, Sept. 10, 1830.

[49] José María Sánchez, *Viaje a Texas en 1828-1829*, p. 30; David Woodman Jr., *Guide to Texas Emigrants*, p. 35. See also Downs, "History of Mexicans," pp. 74-79.

[50] Municipal funds account book (1826-1827), Jan. 1, 1826; plan for funds formed by the ayuntamiento, Oct. 20, 1823.

[51] Minutes Book I, Nov. 21, 1822, July 1, 1824; ordinance issued by Múzquiz, Dec. 7, 1830.

[52] Census for tax on dulas at the San Antonio missions, 1824; census of Barrio del Norte, July 19, 1829; Castañeda, *Our Catholic Heritage*, VI: 307 (quotation), 314-16, 319-21.

[53] Census for tax on dulas at the San Antonio missions (1824). A detailed narrative of the first seventy years of the cattle industry in Texas is provided in the representation of the San Fernando cabildo to Martínez Pacheco, 1787. A translation of the document by John Wheat is available in Béxar Archives Translations (hereafter BAT), Series I, vol. 150, in BA. For roundup rules and problems, see Navarro to Martínez, Aug. 20, 21, and 24, 1821; Navarro to López, Aug. 22, 1821; ayuntamiento statement on roundup, Aug. 23, 1821. For stock exports, see Martínez to Veramendi, Jan. 17, 1822, and ayuntamiento to Saucedo, May 28, 1825.

[54] Census of Béxar, Jan. 1, 1820; census reports for barrios Norte, Sur, and Valero, and for jurisdiccion de misiones, Aug. 10, 1829; report of contributors according to state decree no. 90, 1829. Since both the census reports and the contributors' list give an individual's barrio of residence,

the relative amount of economic activity by neighborhood can be determined. During the entire period under study, the Barrio del Norte was
the most economically diversified part of the city.

[55] Ayuntamiento report, May 1, 1821, typescript, Robert Blake Research
Collection, vol. 10: 232 (BTHC); ayuntamiento to state congress, Dec.
19, 1832.

[56] Béxar censuses for 1820 and 1829; register of foreigners residing in Béxar
(1826-1830), Nov. 2, 1826; list of foreigners residing in Béxar, Apr. 20,
1828.

[57] List of persons paying taxes on shops during January 1824, Jan. (31,) 1824;
merchant invoices for J. Ollie, July 5, 1828; George H. Robb, Sept. 13,
1828; Francisco Ruiz, Apr. 6, 1829; D. Mills and C. Stinnell, May 22,
1830; Ignacio Herrera, Oct. 21, 1830; and various merchants, Oct. 4
(to Nov. 29), 1831.

[58] Dr. John Beales's journal, 1833, in William Kennedy, Texas, p. 396. Further
details on carts and freighting can be pieced together from the following
documents: record of municipal taxes from Béxar merchants (1827-
1831), Jan. 31, 1827; invoices of goods to be brought from La Bahía
by Ignacio Herrera, Oct. 21, 1830; lists of subscriptions to the fund
for rebuilding the parish church, Dec. 31, 1828; invoice and petition
for customs permit from Juan Vilars, Jan. 21, 1831; Luciano Navarro's
list of goods for sale in Santa Rosa by Juan Martín de Veramendi, Feb.
10, 1831; invoice for the sale of goods in Goliad by Eugenio Navarro,
July 9, 1831; and permits issued to Béxar merchants to bring goods
from Leona Vicario, Oct. 4 (to Nov. 29), 1831.

[59] Anastacio Bustamante to Elozúa, Nov. 4, 1827; Saucedo to department of
Texas, Aug. 13, 1826; Bustamante to Saucedo, Oct. 16, 1827.

[60] Ayuntamiento to Bustamante, Oct. 25, 1827; Bustamante to ayuntamiento, Oct. 1827; Veramendi to alcalde, Sept. 11, 1828.

[61] López to Martínez, Oct. 8, 1821.

[62] Instructions to Aldasoro, in Mattie Austin Hatcher, trans., "Texas in 1820,"
pp. 67 (quotation), 68.

[63] Ayuntamiento instructions to provincial deputation, in Martínez to Aldasoro, Nov. 15, 1820; ayuntamiento to state congress, Dec. 19, 1832.

[64] Blanco to Saucedo, Sept. 9, 1826. The standard treatment of this collabora-
tion between Tejano leaders and Anglo colonizers is Eugene C. Barker,
"Native Latin American Contribution to the Colonization and Independence of Texas," pp. 317-35. See also Eugene C. Barker, "The Influence
of Slavery in the Colonization of Texas," pp. 1-33.

[65] Bustamante to ayuntamiento, Oct. 1827; ayuntamiento to Bustamante,
Oct. 25, 1827; Múzquiz to ayuntamiento, May 9, 1828; Veramendi to
ayuntamiento, Oct. 16, 1828 (published as a decree on Oct. 19, 1828).

[66] State decree no. 176, Apr. 29, 1831, Gammel, Laws of Texas, I: 291. The
congressional decree of Sept. 29, 1823, was discussed locally in pro-

vincial deputation to E. Navarro, May 31, 1824. For other exemptions, see Blanco to Saucedo, Sept. 14, 1827, published by Saucedo on Oct. 21, 1827, and Múzquiz to Béxar administrator of revenue, Aug. 2, 1831.

[67] J.N. Seguín and L. Navarro to ayuntamiento, Nov. 18, 1829; Gaspar Flores to Múzquiz, Dec. 3, 1829. Béxar Archives documentation on the final results of the petition is lacking, but a similar petition was made in the memorial of 1832.

[68] Martínez to Aldasoro, Nov. 15, 1820; ayuntamiento to state congress, Dec. 19, 1832.

[69] Weber, *Mexican Frontier*, pp. 125-30, 179-83, 228; Tijerina, "Tejanos and Texas," pp. 239-42, 261-71, 276, 279-81, 295-96.

[70] Ayuntamiento to state congress, Dec. 19, 1832. Reaction to the stopping of immigration is discussed in Alleine Howren, "Causes and Origin of the Decree of April 6, 1830," pp. 378-422, and Barker, "Native Latin American Contribution."

[71] Ayuntamiento to state congress, Dec. 19, 1832. For an excellent translation, see David J. Weber, ed., and Conchita Hassell Winn, trans., *Troubles in Texas, 1832*.

II. Forgotten Founders: The Military Settlers of Eighteenth-Century San Antonio de Béxar

[1] Mexico, Archivo General de la Nación, *Boletín* 28, no. 1 (1957): 64; 28, no. 2 (1957): 357-58 (hereafter AGN, *Boletín*).

[2] Castañeda, *Our Catholic Heritage*, II: 71.

[3] AGN, *Boletín* 29, no. 2 (1958): 305.

[4] The viceroy's fiscal wrote that, in his opinion, "if possible, all the sixty soldiers should be Spaniards, not mulattoes, coyotes, or mestizos, so that the occurrences of 1693 will not be repeated" (AGN, *Boletín* 29, no. 2 (1958): 339). The missionaries had previously complained of the ill effects the behavior of low-caste soldiers toward the Indians had on the first occupation.

[5] "Título de gobernador e instrucciones a Don Martín de Alarcón para su expedición a Texas," AGN, *Boletín* 6, no. 4 (1935): 537.

[6] Olivares to viceroy, June 22, 1718, AGN, Ramo Provincias Internas (hereafter PI), vol. 181.

[7] *Universidad de México* 5, nos. 25-26 (1933): 62-63; Castañeda, *Our Catholic Heritage*, II: 94.

[8] Oakah L. Jones, *Los Paisanos*, p. 247.

[9] David A. Brading, *Mineros y comerciantes en el México borbónico (1763-1810)*, Mexico, 1975, pp. 37-38.

[10] Max L. Moorhead, *The Presidio*, p. 4; Herbert E. Bolton, "Defensive Spanish Expansion and the Significance of the Borderlands," pp. 50-51.

[11] Moorhead, *The Presidio*, pp. 25-26, 182-84, 200.

[12] Governor Pérez de Almazán to viceroy, March 24, 1724, AGN, PI, vol. 183.

[13] Richard G. Santos, ed. and trans., *The Aguayo Expedition into Texas, 1721*, pp. 25, 30-31, 79; Fr. Isidro Félix Espinosa, *Chrónica apostólica y seráphica de todos los colegios de propaganda fide de esta Nueva España*, pp. 452-57; Castañeda, *Our Catholic Heritage*, II: 115-19.

[14] Comparison of the list made of those present in 1718 with the list of officers and soldiers of the Presidio of San Antonio de Béxar, Apr. 25, 1722, in "Autos a consulta hecha del Pe. Fr. Joseph González, Misionero del Presidio de San Antonio Balero Contra el Capitan Don Nicolás Flores por los motivos que expresa," AGN, PI, vol. 32.

[15] Fernando Pérez de Almazán to viceroy, July 11, 1726, in "Carpeta de correspondencia de ls. Proas. Internas por los años de 1726 a 1731 con los Exmos. Sres. Marqués de Casa y Fuerte, y Conde de Fuenclara, . . ." AGN, PI, vol. 236.

[16] "Título de gobernador," AGN, *Boletín* 6, no. 4 (1935): 537.

[17] "Diario de la conquista y entrada a los Thejas," *Universidad de México* 5, nos. 27-28 (Jan.-Feb. 1933).

[18] Ibid., p. 58. See also "Autos sobre diferentes noticias que se han participado a su Exa. de las entradas que en estos dominios hacen los Frances por la parte de Coahuila . . . 1715," AGN, PI, vol. 181; Espinosa, *Chrónica apostólica*, p. 449.

[19] Marriage of Joseph Martínez to Juana de Carbajal, May 8, 1721, no. 31, San Fernando Parish Records, transcribed and translated by John O. Leal, "Mission San Antonio de Valero Marriages" (hereafter SF:VM); marriage of Cristóbal Basques to Ana de Carbajal, Feb. 20, 1722, no. 32, SF:VM; marriage of Diego Camacho to Juana Antonia de Carbajal, June 24, 1723, no. 50, SF:VM

[20] Estimate based on the appearance of married couples as witnesses or participants in San Antonio de Valero Mission marriages and baptisms between 1719 and 1730.

[21] Castañeda, *Our Catholic Heritage*, II: 86-87.

[22] "Autos sobre diferentes noticias . . . 1715," AGN, PI, vol. 181.

[23] Marriage of Juan Pais to Margarita, Sept. 24, 1724, no. 56, SF:VM.

[24] Marriage of Joseph de la Fuente to Clara González, Jan. 3, 1724, no. 52, SF:VM.

[25] Castañeda, *Our Catholic Heritage*, II: 73, 190-91; Elizabeth A.H. John, *Storms Brewed in Other Men's Worlds*, pp. 258-61; William Edward Dunn, "Apache Relations in Texas, 1718-1750," p. 205.

[26] Quoted in Castañeda, *History of Texas*, II: 257.

[27] Governor Pérez de Almazán to viceroy, Oct. 24 and 25, 1724, AGN, PI, vol. 183; Moorhead, *The Presidio*, p. 42.

[28] Castañeda, *History of Texas*, I: 225.

[29] Autos concerning distribution of lands in Béxar, July 31, 1731, AGN, PI, vol. 163; Mardith K. Schuetz, "The People of San Antonio, Part I," in *San Antonio in the Eighteenth Century*, ed. San Antonio Bicentennial Heritage Committee, p. 81; Chabot, *Makers of San Antonio*, pp. 56, 67, 137.

[30] Case against Felipe de Avila for the murder of Nicolás Pasqual, Apr. 12, 1730, AGN, PI, vol. 32.

[31] De León, *Tejano Community*, pp. 2-3; Jones, *Los Paisanos*, p. 248; Santos, *Aguayo Expedition into Texas*, pp. 74-75.

[32] "Diario de la conquista"; "Auto de poseción," July 10, 1731, in autos concerning the distribution of lands in Béxar, July 31, 1731, AGN, PI, vol. 163; Governor Fernando Pérez de Almazán to viceroy, Oct. 24, 1724, AGN, PI, vol. 183; "Relación de los meritos y servicios de Don Fernando Pérez de Almazán" (Madrid, 1729).

[33] "Testimonio de los Autos en virtud de Rl. Cédula sobre que pasen 400 familias para que pueblen la Bahía de Sn. Antonio, misiones de los Adais y los Texas," Feb. 14, 1729, Sevilla, Archivo General de Indias (hereafter AGI), Audiencia de Guadalajara (hereafter AG), legajo 67-4-38, transcription in *Spanish Material from Various Sources*, vol. 23, BTHC.

[34] Castañeda, *Our Catholic Heritage*, II: 301-302.

[35] Ibid., pp. 302-308.

[36] "Ordenanzas q. han de observar y guardar todos los Governadores y Comandtes, de los Presidios y Provinzs. internas pa. el mejor Govo. de ellas, (1729), art. 50," AGI, Audiencia de Mexico, legajo 62-1-41, transcription in *Spanish Material from Various Sources*, vol. 81, BTHC; Toribio de Urrutia to [viceroy], Dec. 17, 1740, in "Autos a consulta de dn. Thoribio de Urrutia Capn. del Presidio de Sn. Antonio de Véjar, . . ." AGN, PI, vol. 32; cabildo meeting, Aug. 25, 1745, BA, BTHC; Order of Colonel D. Angel de Martos y Navarrete, June 25, 1759, in Order of Viceroy D. Agustín Ahumada Villalon, Marqués de las Amarillas, Apr. 7, 1758, BA; Lt. Governor Ramírez de la Piszina to cabildo, Nov. 21, 1760, BA.

[37] Almazán to viceroy, Dec. 1, 1731, AGN, PI, vol. 32.

[38] Petition for land by Juan Banul, Jan. 12, 1734, in "Testimonio del decreto de su Exca. en que contiene varios puntos pertenecientes a los vecinos pobladores de esta Villa de S. Fernando sacado a pedimiento de dhos. vecinos para los efectos que les combenga" (1734). This expediente has

inadvertently been filed within the following: "Testimonio de las disposiciones del Virey respecto a los vecinos y pobladores de la Villa de San Fernando y del Real Presidio de San Antonio de Béjar en las Provincias de las Nuevas Filipinas," 1735, AGN, PI, vol. 163; Auto of Governor, Jan. 29, 1734, AGN, PI, vol. 163; "venta de solar y casa por Matias de la Zerda a favor de José Salinas," July 26, 1761, San Antonio, Bexar County Archives (hereafter BCA), Land Grant Series, no. 67 (hereafter LGS-67).

[39] Antonio Rodríguez Mederos to Francisco Hernández, Apr. 10, 1739; José Cabrera to Antonio Rodríguez Mederos, Jan. 2, 1740; José Padrón to Gerónimo Flores, Oct. 7, 1740; Manuel de Niz to Pedro Ocón y Trillo, May 26, 1741; Juan Leal Alvarez to Toribio de Urrutia, Nov. 25, 1741, in Notary protocol, March 22, 1738, BA.

[40] Petition by the residents of the presidio, Feb. 3, 1733, "Dictamen de Juan de Rebolledo," March 24, 1733, and viceroy's decree, Apr. 8, 1733, in "Autos sobre las providencias dadas por su ex. al gobernador de la provincia de Texas para la pacificación de los Indios Apaches y sus aliados," 1731, AGN, PI, vol. 32.

[41] See "Appendix D: Composition of Béxar's Town Council," in Jesús Francisco de la Teja, "Land and Society in 18th Century San Antonio de Béxar," pp. 407-28.

[42] Castañeda, *Our Catholic Heritage*, II: 275-76, 283-84; "Auto en que se da razon de haver ospedado a los Ysleños y otras providencias," March 10, 1731, AGN, PI, vol. 32.

III. The Canary Islands Immigrants of San Antonio: From Ethnic Exclusivity to Community in Eighteenth-Century Béxar

[1] For discussions of the travels to and arrival at Béxar of the Canary Islands immigrants, see the following: Issac Joslin Cox, "The Founding of the First Texas Municipality," pp. 217-26; Lota Spell, ed. and trans., "The Grant and First Survey of San Fernando de Béxar," pp. 73-89; and Samuel Buck, *Yanaguana's Successors*.

[2] For a discussion of the functions of these offices, see Mattie Alice Austin, "The Municipal Government of San Fernando de Béxar, 1730-1800," pp. 295-328.

[3] For a discussion of the racial and social attitudes of European-born Spaniards in America, see Charles Gibson, *Spain in America*, pp. 112-35.

[4] Apparently the justicia mayor acted as an appellate judge in San Fernando. According to Austin in "Municipal Government," p. 317, "It would seem that the alcalde would try cases and pronounce sentence in disputes between citizens of the villa, and that his decisions were not final, but could be appealed to either the governor or the justicia mayor."

[5] Captain Toribio de Urrutia to the viceroy of New Spain, in Benedict Leutenegger and Marion A. Habig, eds. and trans., *The San José Papers*, I: 89; in 1741 missionaries in Béxar seconded Toribio de Urrutia's request that he be named justicia mayor because they said that within the cabildo "the guilty and the judge come from the same house, relatives, and godfathers in religion." In a lengthy letter to the governor, Fr. Benito Fernández de Santa Ana wrote that "the Islanders know very well that without a major magistrate or with one who is one of their favorites, they can freely inform His Excellency of the untruths they want." The priest concluded the letter by saying that "from all that has been said it is clearly evident that in no way is it good for these Islanders to remain without a higher magistrate, and above all, he should not be one of their number, entrenched in power." Benedict Leutenegger, ed. and trans., *Letters and Memorials of the Father Presidente Fray Benito Fernández de Santa Ana, 1736-1754*, pp. 44-47.

[6] For information on the early activities of the soldier-settlers, see Frederick C. Chabot, *San Antonio and Its Beginnings*, and de la Teja, "Land and Society," pp. 53-71. See also de la Teja's article in this volume, "Forgotten Founders."

[7] Early disputes over land and water between Canary Islanders, missionaries, and soldier-settlers are included in AGN, PI, vols. 32, 163.

[8] Transcription of grant document issued by Governor Bustillos in *Spanish Materials from Various Sources*, 2Q232, BTHC.

[9] Documents granting land to the Canary Islands, Jan. 1734, in AGN, PI, vol. 163.

[10] Documents granting lands to soldier-settlers, Jan. and Feb. 1734, in AGN, PI, vol. 163.

[11] Antonio Rodríguez Mederos to Governor Manuel de Sandoval, Feb. 24, 1734, in AGN, PI, vol. 163.

[12] The Isleño's goals are discussed in Herbert Eugene Bolton, *Texas in the Middle Eighteenth Century*, pp. 24-25, and Castañeda, *Our Catholic Heritage*, III: 103-108. Also see Urrutia to viceroy, Dec. 17, 1740, Leutenegger and Habig, *San José Papers*.

[13] Grant to Domingo Flores de Abrego, May 17, 1738, BCA, LGS-1. See also grant request of Juan Banul, Oct. 24, 1737, in which he asks for a lot "without irrigation water because of the controversies that have arisen in this city concerning grants with water," BCA, LGS-704.

[14] Grant to Ignacio González de Ynclán, June 10, 1739, BCA, LGS-704.

[15] Castañeda, *History of Texas*, pp. 285-86. Morfi accused Governor Franquis of working on behalf of his Canary Islands compatriots.

[16] See San Fernando Parish Records, transcribed and translated by John O. Leal, "San Fernando Church Baptismals," 1742-1760.

[17] See San Fernando Parish Records, transcribed and translated by John O. Leal, "San Fernando Church Marriages," 1742-1760.

[18] The information was found in a variety of sources including Chabot, *Makers of San Antonio*, and Leal, "San Fernando Church Marriages" and "San Fernando Church Baptismals." John O. Leal has also compiled various family genealogies, which are available to researchers in the Bexar County Archives.

[19] For example, the garrison and town of San Antonio in 1780 was 61 percent Spanish, 24 percent mixed-blood groups (i.e. lobo, coyote, entresalvo, color quebrado), 3.5 percent mestizo, and 6 percent Indian. It is certain that many of those designated Spanish were actually mestizo; Alicia V. Tjarks, "Comparative Demographic Analysis of Texas, 1777-1793," p. 324. Tjarks notes that "because of the irregularities in the racial classification as it was carried out in Texas, the term 'Spaniard' can be used only as a classifying category, and not as a pure racial identification."

20. For information on Fermín de Ybiricú, see "Miguel Nuñez Morillo Obligates Himself as Surety for Amount Owed by Fermín de Ybiricú to Francisco Fernández de Ruymayor," Apr. 4, 1736, in BAT, vol. 8, 1736, pp. 44-49 at BTHC.

[21] Grant to Diego Hernández, May 20, 1741, BCA, LGS-316. Information on the Hernández family is available in Chabot, *Makers of San Antonio*, pp. 35-40.

[22] These generalizations are based on a survey of eighteenth-century land grants and private land transactions in Béxar, BCA, LGS, 1730s-1790s.

[23] Buck, *Yanaguana's Successors*, pp. 120-24.

[24] See the following land transactions involving Antonio Rodríguez Mederos and his father-in-law, Manuel de Niz: sale, Rodríguez Mederos to Francisco Hernández, Apr. 10, 1739, BCA, LGS-703; sale, Rodríguez Mederos to Antonio Bueno de Roxas, July 8, 1739, BCA, LGS-704; sale, Joseph Cabrera to Rodríguez Mederos, Jan. 2, 1740, BCA, LGS-674; sale, Manuel de Niz to Joseph Bueno de Roxas, Jan. 7, 1740, BAT, vol. 10; sale, Manuel de Niz to Pedro Ocón y Trillo, May 26, 1741, BCA, LGS-545; sale, Rodríguez Mederos to Pedro Ocón y Trillo, July 26, 1742, BCA, LGS-675; sale, Rodríguez Mederos and Niz to Toribio Urrutia, May 28, 1748, BAT, vol. 18; sale, Toribio de Urrutia to Rodríguez Mederos, May 12, 1749, BAT, vol. 18; sale, Rodríguez Mederos to Miguel de Castro, Apr. 28, 1749, BAT, vol. 18; sale, Rodríguez Mederos to Miguel de Castro, May 21, 1749, BAT, vol. 18; sale, Rodríguez Mederos to Joseph Curbelo, May 22, 1749, BAT, vol. 18. Regarding Rodríguez Mederos's building activities, see BAT, vol. 8, 1736, pp. 61-108; BAT, vol. 20, 1750, pp. 206-207.

[25] See "Records of the Suit for Recovery of Debt Prosecuted by Don Francisco Fernández de Ruymayor," BAT, vol. 4, 1733, pp. 53-60; "Miguel

Nuñez Morillo Obligates Himself for Surety, . . . " BAT, vol. 8, 1736, pp. 44-60; and "Plea for Defense of Rodríguez Mederos," BAT, vol. 20, 1749-1750, p. 187.

[26] "Protocolos of Notary Francisco Joseph de Arocha," BAT, vol. 10. See sales of land, Juan Leal Alvarez to Toribio de Urrutia, Nov. 25, 1741, and Joseph Padrón to Antonio Ximenes, Oct. 22, 1745, BAT, vol. 10.

[27] "Documents concerning Distribution of Water and New Irrigation Canal at San Fernando," Aug. 16-Sept. 2, 1762, BAT, vol. 37, pp. 27-28.

[28] Grant to Juan de la Cruz del Valle, Dec. 20, 1760, BCA, LGS-676; associated document, June 28, 1762, BCA, LGS-678; grant to Ramón Andrés, Aug. 31, 1762, BCA, LGS-550.

[29] See "Certified Copy of the Proceedings Relative to the Visita Made by Martos y Navarrete to the Administration of San Fernando," BAT, vol. 36, 1756-1762, pp. 186-87; "Documents concerning Distribution of Water and New Irrigation Canal at San Fernando," BAT, vol. 37, 1762, pp. 27-39; Andrés Ramón to governor, Aug. 31, 1762, BCA, LGS-550; "Documents concerning Civil Disturbances Caused by Vicente Alvarez Travieso and Francisco de Arocha," Sept. 6-15, 1762, BAT, vol. 37, pp. 40-47.

[30] "Barón de Ripperdá. Decree to Inhabitants of Bexar," Robert Blake Research Collection (transcripts), vol. 69, pp. 310-12, BTHC; "Partition of Lands of the Upper Labores in San Antonio, Texas, and the Acequia, 1776-1784," Spanish Volume Deed Records, Book 3, pp. 317-48, BCA.

[31] The development of ranching in eighteenth-century Béxar is traced in Jack Jackson, Los Mesteños.

[32] Ibid., pp. 51-85; Robert S. Weddle and Robert H. Thonhoff, Drama and Conflict, pp. 143-71.

[33] For an idea of the early conflicts between Leal Goraz and Curbelo, see "Petition from Juan Leal Goraz to Governor Manuel de Sandoval," Feb. 4, 1734, AGN, PI, vol. 163.

[34] See "Petition, Juan Leal Goraz to Governor Manuel de Sandoval," Feb. 4, 1734; "Petition, Antonio Rodríguez Mederos to Governor Manuel de Sandoval," Feb. 27, 1734, AGN, PI, vol. 163. See also "Joachín Miguel de Anzurez to the Viceroy, Don Juan de Vizarrón y Equiarreta, Presenting Complaints of Officials and Settlers of San Fernando against Governor Manuel de Sandoval," Jan. 24-March 15, 1736, BAT, vol. 8, pp. 1-8.

[35] See "Canary Islanders vs. Captain Thoribio de Urrutia and other settlers," BAT, vol. 17, 1745, p. 10; "Petition of Thoribio de Urrutia for Release of Antonio Rodríguez Mederos" and "Antonio Rodríguez Mederos vs. Bizente Alvarez Travieso and Francisco José de Arocha," BAT, vol. 19, 1748-1750; "Brief for Defendant in Suit, Cabildo of San Fernando vs. Antonio Rodríguez Mederos," BAT, vols. 20-21, 1749-1751; "Cabildo of San Fernando vs. Antonio Rodríguez Mederos," BAT, vol. 21, 1749, pp. 1-5.

[36] For information on cabildo officeholders, see BAT, vols. 2-22, 1730s-1740s. See also Castañeda, *Our Catholic Heritage*, II: 308-309; III: 95.

[37] "Documents concerning the Election of the Officials of the Villa of San Fernando from 1763 to 1774," BAT, vol. 38, pp. 18-58.

[38] "Antonio Bucarely y Ursua's Letter to the Barón de Ripperdá Commending His Actions regarding Reinstatement of Don Simón de Arocha," March 9, 1774, BAT, vol. 56, pp. 19-26.

[39] See Jackson's discussion of this in *Los Mesteños*, pp. 143-45, based in part on cattle litigation proceedings included in BAT, vol. 64, 1777, and BAT, vols. 72-75, 1778.

[40] Ibid., pp. 373-75.

[41] "Cabildo of San Fernando to the Viceroy of New Spain," Aug. 25, 1756, BAT, vol. 30, pp. 54-63.

[42] "Protest of Don Vicente Alvarez Travieso and Don Juan Andrés Alvarez Travieso against Claims of the Missions of San Antonio, 1771-1783," *History of Grazing in Texas Collection*, Box 2R340, BTHC; "Memorial from the Government of the Villa of San Fernando and the Royal Presidio of San Antonio de Béxar to Governor Martínez Pacheco, regarding the People's Right to the Mesteña Horses and Cattle of Texas," 1787, BAT, vol. 150; "Petition and Testimony concerning Lands of San Antonio Missions," 1772, Archivo del Convento de Guadalupe, Zacatecas, Microfilm Collection, reel 3, frame 3600-3628, Our Lady of the Lake University.

[43] The details of these conflicts as they related to taxation of the cattle industry are traced in Jackson, *Los Mesteños*. For other kinds of disagreements, see, for example, the cabildo's resistance to Governor Ripperdá's order that local residents help construct a jail and new barracks. BAT, vols. 49-51, 53-54, 1771-1773.

IV. The Religious-Indian Communities: The Goals of the Friars

[1] The friars themselves were the first to record their work, but not until this century did the mission system receive satisfactory nonreligious interpretation. See Herbert E. Bolton, "The Mission as a Frontier Institution in the Spanish-American Colonies," in *Bolton and the Spanish Borderlands*, ed. John Francis Bannon, pp. 187-211.

[2] John, *Storms Brewed*, pp. 191-95, 206.

[3] Fray Antonio de Jesús to Don Joseph de Azlor Virto de Vera, Marqués de Aguayo, Dec. 16, 1719, in Leutenegger and Habig, *San José Papers*, I: 4-5. Occasionally quotations from this and various other published documents were translated by the author of this essay and not by Leutenegger.

[4] Report of the Founding of San José, Captain Juan Baldés, Feb. 23, 1720, in Leutenegger and Habig, *San José Papers*, I: 28- 41. See also Marion A. Habig, *The Alamo Chain of Missions*, pp. 38-39, 84-85, 124-25, 160-63, 202.

[5] Fray Benito Fernández de Santa Ana to Fray Pedro del Barco, Feb. 20, 1740, in Leutenegger and Habig, *San José Papers*, I: 53-56.

[6] Michael B. McCloskey, *The Formative Years of the Missionary College of Santa Cruz de Querétaro, 1683-1733*, pp. 30-32; Benedict Leutenegger, trans., *The Zacatecan Missionaries in Texas, 1716-1834*, p. 40; Robert S. Weddle, *The San Sabá Mission*, pp. 21-22, and *San Juan Bautista*, pp. 238-41.

[7] Fritz Leo Hoffman, ed. and trans., *Diary of the Alarcón Expedition into Texas, 1718-1719 by Francisco de Céliz*, p. 86; Ruth Cowie Buerkle, "The Continuing Military Presence," pp. 47-72; John, *Storms Brewed*, pp. 212, 222-25, 262-65; Herbert Eugene Bolton, *Texas in the Middle Eighteenth Century*, pp. 20-21.

[8] Esther MacMillan, "The Cabildo and the People, 1731-1784," pp. 84-98; John Francis Bannon, *The Spanish Borderlands Frontier, 1531-1821*, pp. 134-36; Bolton, *Texas*, pp. 25-26.

[9] John, *Storms Brewed*, p. 264; Bolton, *Texas*, pp. 21-27; Marion A. Habig, *San Antonio's Mission San José*, pp. 40-43.

[10] Castañeda, *Our Catholic Heritage*, III: 53-56.

[11] Report of Fray Mariano Francisco de los Dolores to Governor Barrio Junco y Espriella, Aug.-Sept. 1749, in Benedict Leutenegger, and Marion A. Habig, eds. and trans., *Letters and Memorials of Fray Mariano Francisco de los Dolores y Viana*, pp. 74-75.

[12] Fray Benito Fernández de Santa Ana expressed these goals in his proposal to establish the new mission of San Xavier. See Fray Benito Fernández de Santa Ana to Viceroy Conde de Revillagigedo, March 10, 1749, in Leutenegger, *Fray Benito Fernández*, pp. 87-89. For the overall policy on the conversion of the Indians and the process it involved, see Robert Ricard, *The Spiritual Conquest of Mexico*, pp. 135-36, 154-55, 267; Cecilia Barba, "The Role of the Church in the Colonization of Michoacan," pp. 10-13, 39; Lesley Byrd Simpson, *The Encomienda in New Spain*, pp. 123-58; Charles Gibson, *The Aztecs under Spanish Rule*, pp. 75-78; Lewis Hanke, *The Spanish Struggle for Justice in the Conquest of America*, pp. 39-41, 83-103.

[13] Philip Wayne Powell, *Soldiers, Indians, and Silver*, pp. 7-8, 93-94, 106, 133, 181-84, 208-209; J. Lloyd Mecham, *Francisco de Ibarra and Nueva Viscaya*, pp. 41, 76, 91, 235-37; Bannon, *Spanish Borderlands Frontier*, pp. 5, 63-64, 72-77; Spicer, *Cycles of Conquest*, pp. 288-98.

[14] Ricard, *Spiritual Conquest*, pp. 52, 136, 142, 150-51, 163-64, 170-71; Gibson, *Aztecs*, pp. 120-35; Hanke, *Struggle for Justice*, pp. 103-105; McCloskey, *Missionary College*, pp. 25-29, 44-46, 98-99.

[15] Bolton, "Frontier Institution," pp. 194-97; "Memorial to the King of Spain, Ferdinand VI, by Fray Francisco Ballejo and the Decreto of the Apostolic College of Our Lady of Guadalupe de Zacatecas," in *The Texas Missions of the College of Zacatecas*, ed. and trans. Benedict Leutenegger and Marion A. Habig, pp. 58-59, 75; Habig, *San Antonio's Mission San José*, pp. 64-65; John, *Storms Brewed*, pp. 79-80, 281.

[16] Fray Mariano Francisco de los Dolores to Fray Francisco Xavier Ortiz, June 12, 1745, in Leutenegger and Habig, *Fray Mariano Francisco de Los Dolores y Viana*, pp. 37-38; Bannon, *Spanish Borderlands Frontier*, pp. 108-23; Bolton, *Texas*, pp. 4-5; Habig, *Alamo Chain of Missions*, pp. 33-40; Weddle, *San Juan Bautista*, pp. 13-18.

[17] Fray Mariano Francisco de los Dolores to Fray Francisco Xavier Ortiz, June 12, 1745, in Leutenegger and Habig, *Fray Mariano Francisco de los Dolores y Viana*, pp. 36-37; Spicer, *Cycles of Conquest*, pp. 25-26, 87-89; Bolton, *Texas*, pp. 14-21; Weddle, *San Juan Bautista*, pp. 63-64, 127-29, 180-85; Habig, *San Antonio's Mission San José*, pp. 36-37; John, *Storms Brewed*, pp. 172-73.

[18] Fray Benito Fernández de Santa Ana to Fray Alonzo Giraldo de Terreros, Feb. 2, 1746; to Viceroy Conde de Revillagigedo, Feb. 23, 1750, both in Leutenegger, *Fray Benito Fernández*, pp. 65, 63; Fray Mariano Francisco de los Dolores to Fray Alonzo Giraldo de Terreros, July 26, 1745; to Governor Pedro del Barrio Junco y Espriella, July 16, 1749; to Viceroy Conde de Revillagigedo, Oct. 8, 1750, in Leutenegger and Habig, *Fray Mariano Francisco de los Dolores y Viana*, pp. 43, 53-54, 130-31. Also see Weddle, *San Juan Bautista*, pp. 22-23, 79, 107, 174; John, *Storms Brewed*, pp. 223-25, 260-61; Mardith Keithly Schuetz, "Indians in the San Antonio Area," pp. 26-28.

[19] "Memorial to the King by Fray Francisco Ballejo et al.," Jan. 15, 1750, in Leutenegger and Habig, *College of Zacatecas*, pp. 55-56; Fray Benito Fernández de Santa Ana to Viceroy Conde de Revillagigedo, Feb. 23, 1750, in Leutenegger, *Fray Benito Fernández*, pp. 164-67.

[20] Report of Captain Juan Baldez, March 13, 1720, in Leutenegger and Habig, *San José Papers*, I: 34, 36.

[21] Fray Benito Fernández de Santa Ana to Fray Alonzo Giraldo de Terreros, Feb. 2, 1746, in Leutenegger, *Fray Benito Fernández*, pp. 62, 64-65; "Instruction for the Minister of the Mission Purísima Concepción of the Province of Texas," c. 1760, in Benedict Leutenegger, ed. and trans., *Guidelines for a Texas Missionary*, pp. 16-17, 25, 30-31; Captain Rafael Martínez Pacheco to the viceroy, Nov. 8, 1772, in Leutenegger and Habig, *San José Papers*, I: 185; Fray José Rafael Oliva, "The Problem of the Temporalities," in *Management of the Missions of Texas*, ed. and trans. Benedict Leutenegger and Marion A. Habig, pp. 18-19.

[22] "Instructions for the Minister," in Leutenegger, *Guidelines*, pp. 37-39, 47-51; Fray José R. Oliva to the missionaries in Texas, Jan. 23, 1787, in *Manage-*

ment, ed. and trans. Leutenegger and Habig, pp. 37-41; Castañeda, *History of Texas,* I: 97; Bolton, "Frontier Institution," pp. 193-94; Mardith Keithly Schuetz, "The Indians of the San Antonio Missions, 1718-1821," pp. 13-20; Weddle, *San Juan Bautista,* pp. 180-85.

[23] In making their case for the missions as vehicles of evangelization, neither the friars nor their historians focused on the independent, self-perpetuating character of the mission system. Even Bolton generally ignored this aspect, although he did allude to it. See Bolton, "Frontier Institution," p. 195.

[24] Captain Juan Baldés to Don Joseph de Azlor Virto de Vera, March 13, 1720, in Leutenegger and Habig, *San José Papers,* I: 40.

[25] Fray Benito Fernández de Santa María to Governor Thomas Felipe Winthuisen, June 1741, in Leutenegger, *Fray Benito Fernández,* pp. 41-42; Fray Mariano Francisco de los Dolores to Fray Miguel Padilla, Dec. 9, 1752, in Leutenegger and Habig, *Fray Mariano Francisco de los Dolores y Viana,* pp. 181, 185-89; "Instructions to the Minister," in Leutenegger, *Guidelines,* pp. 40-41, 48.

[26] Fray Mariano Francisco de los Dolores to Viceroy Juan Antonio de Vizarrón, 1739, in Leutenegger and Habig, *Fray Mariano Francisco de los Dolores y Viana,* pp. 26-27.

[27] "Memorial to the King by Fray Francisco Ballejo et al.," Jan. 15, 1750, in Leutenegger and Habig, *College of Zacatecas,* pp. 49-50; Fray Mariano Francisco de los Dolores to Fray Francisco Xavier Ortiz, June 12, 1745; to Juan Joseph de Montes de Oca, Oct. 8, 1745; to Viceroy Conde de Revillagigedo, Jan. 12, 1752, in Leutenegger and Habig, *Fray Mariano Francisco de los Dolores y Viana,* pp. 37, 46-48, 141.

[28] Fray Benito Fernández de Santa Ana to Viceroy Juan Antonio de Vizarrón, June 8, 1737; to Viceroy Conde de Revillagigedo, Feb. 23, 1750, and July 5, 1752, in Leutenegger, *Fray Benito Fernández,* pp. 23, 169-71, 181-83.

[29] Fray Mariano Francisco de los Dolores to Viceroy Conde de Revillagigedo, Jan. 12, 1752, in Leutenegger and Habig, *Fray Mariano Francisco de los Dolores y Viana,* p. 139.

[30] Schuetz, "Indians of the San Antonio Missions," pp. 271-75; Leutenegger, *Guidelines,* pp. 31-34; Oliva, "Problem of the Temporalities," in *Management,* ed. and trans. Leutenegger and Habig, pp. 31-33, 35-36.

[31] Fray Mariano Francisco de los Dolores to Fray Francisco Xavier Ortiz, March 6, 1762, in Leutenegger and Habig, *Fray Mariano Francisco de los Dolores y Viana,* pp. 343-44.

[32] Habig, *San Antonio's Mission San José,* p. 86.

[33] Fray Benito Fernández de Santa Ana to Viceroy Conde de Revillagigedo, Feb. 23, 1750, in Leutenegger, *Fray Benito Fernández,* pp. 168-69.

[34] Oliva, "Problem of the Temporalities," in *Management,* ed. and trans. Leutenegger and Habig, pp. 30-31; Leutenegger, *Guidelines,* pp. 46-47.

[35] Marlys Bush-Thurber and James E. Ivey, *The Missions of San Antonio*, pp. 16-19.

[36] Schuetz, "Indians of the San Antonio Missions," pp. 182-84.

[37] Bush-Thurber and Ivey, *Missions of San Antonio*, pp. 222-24.

[38] Ibid., pp. 82-85, 95-101, 119-27, 139-45.

[39] Schuetz, "Indians of the San Antonio Missions," p. 128, table 1.4.

[40] John, *Storms Brewed*, pp. 122-23.

[41] Habig, *San Antonio's Mission San José*, pp. 90-92.

[42] Fray Mariano Francisco de los Dolores to Fray Francisco Xavier Ortiz, June 12, 1745, in Leutenegger and Habig, *Fray Mariano Francisco de los Dolores y Viana*, pp. 36-37; Fray Benito Fernández to Fray Pedro del Barco, Feb. 20, 1745, in Leutenegger and Habig, *San José Papers*, I: 59.

[43] Habig, *San Antonio's Mission San José*, pp. 90-92.

[44] Fray Benito Fernández de Santa Ana to Fray Pedro del Barco, Feb. 20, 1740; Fray Ignacio Antonio Crispan to Juan Antonio Abasolo, Oct. 27, 1749; Fray Ildefonso Marmolejo, "Inventory of San José Mission and the Increase Gained in the Year and Ten Months since It Is in My Care," Oct. 14, 1755, in Leutenegger and Habig, *San José Papers*, I: 64, 98, 117, 123, 125-26.

[45] Oliva, "Problem of the Temporalities," in *Management*, ed. and trans. Leutenegger and Habig, p. 31.

[46] Jackson, *Los Mesteños*, pp. 410-15.

[47] "Inventory of San José Mission," Report of Fray José Maria Salas to Fray José Agustín Mariano Falcón, 1785, in Leutenegger and Habig, *San José Papers*, I: 244.

[48] Schuetz, "Indians of the San Antonio Missions," pp. 150, 171.

[49] Fray Mariano Francisco de los Dolores to Fray Francisco Xavier Ortiz, March 6, 1762, in Leutenegger and Habig, *Fray Mariano Francisco de los Dolores y Viana*, pp. 347-48.

[50] Schuetz, "Indians of the San Antonio Missions," pp. 205-15.

[51] Fray Benito Fernández de Santa Ana to Governor Francisco García Larios, Sept. 9, 1776, in Leutenegger, *Fray Benito Fernández*, p. 85.

[52] Schuetz, "Indians of the San Antonio Missions," pp. 154-55, 174-78, 159-70.

[53] Oliva, "Problem of Temporalities," in *Management*, ed. and trans. Leutenegger and Habig, pp. 12, 14; Fray José R. Oliva to the missionaries in Texas, January 23, 1787, ibid., p. 40, and Leutenegger, *Guidelines*, p. 41.

[54] Fray Bartolomé García, *Manual para administrar los santos sacramentos de penitencia, eucaristía, extrema unción, y matrimonio*, p. 104.

[55] Leutenegger, *Guidelines*, p. 10.

[56] Fray Mariano Francisco de los Dolores to Fray Francisco Xavier Ortiz, March 6, 1762, in Leutenegger and Habig, *Fray Mariano Francisco de los Dolores y Viana*, pp. 345-46.

[57] Leutenegger, *Guidelines*, p. 47; Fray Benito Fernández de Santa Ana to Viceroy Juan Antonio de Vizarrón, June 8 and 30, 1737, in Leutenegger, *Fray Benito Fernández*, pp. 22-23, 25; Fray Mariano Francisco de los Dolores to Fray Francisco Xavier Ortiz, June 12, 1745, and March 6, 1762, in Leutenegger and Habig, *Fray Mariano Francisco de los Dolores y Viana*, pp. 36-37, 347; report of Captain Rafael Martínez Pacheco to the viceroy, Nov. 2, 1772; Fray Benito Fernández de Santa Ana to Fray Pedro de Barco, Feb. 20, 1740; report of Captain Toribio Urrutia to the viceroy, Dec. 17, 1740, in Leutenegger and Habig, *San José Papers*, I: 184, 65, 82.

[58] Schuetz, "Indians of the San Antonio Missions," pp. 182-205; Fray Mariano Francisco de los Dolores to Fray Francisco Xavier Ortiz, March 6, 1762, in Leutenegger and Habig, *Fray Mariano Francisco de los Dolores y Viana*, p. 346; Leutenegger, *Guidelines*, p. 30.

[59] Oliva, "Problem of Temporalities," in *Management*, ed. and trans. Leutenegger and Habig, p. 28; Castañeda, *History of Texas*, II: 25-29, 276.

[60] Habig, *San Antonio's Mission San José*, pp. 88-89.

[61] Entries for July 2 and Sept. 4, 1779, Leutenegger and Habig, *College of Zacatecas*, pp. 30-31.

V. Immigrants and Integration in Late Eighteenth-Century Béxar

[1] De la Teja, "Land and Society," pp. 72-88. See also Tjarks, "Comparative Demographic Analysis," pp. 302-19.

[2] Ibid., pp. 332-33.

[3] This is particularly evident in the land-grant documents. Retired soldiers settling in Béxar made numerous requests for grants. See the following: grant to Ramón Diego, Jan. 30, 1745, San Antonio, BCA, LGS-546; grant to Marcos Menchaca, June 19, 1762, BCA, LGS-315; grant to Joseph Sánchez, Sept. 1, 1762, BCA, LGS-600; grant to Pedro Miñon, June 10, 1769, BCA, LGS-377; grant to Ygnacio Estrada, Sept. 11, 1773, BCA, LGS-191.

[4] For information on socioeconomic conditions and migratory patterns in New Spain during the late eighteenth century, see Enrique Florescano, *Precios del maíz y crisis agrícola en México, 1708-1810*, pp. 140-79.

[5] De la Teja, "Land and Society," pp. 54-56, 89-90.

[6] "Padrón de las almas que ay en esta villa de San Fernando de Austria. Año de 1793," Béxar Archives Microfilm (hereafter BAM), reel 24. See a

transcribed and translated version in Carmela Leal, ed., *Residents of Texas, 1782-1836,* pp. 114-41.

[7] Ibid.

[8] For listings of cabildo officials in the 1790s, see election proceedings: BAM, reel 21, 12/20/1790, 12/20/1791; reel 22, 12/20/1792; reel 24, 12/20/1793; reel 25, 12/20/1794, 12/20/1795; reel 26, 12/21/1796; reel 28, 12/21/1797, 12/20/1798; reel 29, 12/20/1799, 12/20/1800.

[9] See chapter 3 of this volume, Gerald E. Poyo, "The Canary Islands Immigrants of San Antonio."

[10] For a good survey of Béxar's physical expansion during the eighteenth century, see de la Teja, "Land and Society," pp. 115-41.

[11] Tjarks, "Comparative Demographic Analysis," pp. 333-35; "Padrón de las almas . . . Año de 1793."

[12] Ibid., household entry no. 134, don Angel Navarro; Chabot, *Makers of San Antonio.*

[13] "Padrón de las almas . . . Año de 1793," household entry no. 19, don Xavier Galán; San Fernando Parish Records, transcribed and translated by John O. Leal, "San Fernando Church Parish Marriage Petitions," Nov. 20, 1789; land sales to Xavier Galán, 1790, BCA, LGS-279; 1792, LGS-280; 1794, LGS-282.

[14] "Padrón de las almas . . . Año de 1793," household entry no. 18, don Felis Menchaca; Jackson, *Los Mesteños,* pp. 143, 164, 179, 189, 194-96, 204-205, 207, 215, 250, 287-88, 305-309, 317, 353-55, 359, 367; Chabot, *Makers of San Antonio,* pp. 103-105.

[15] "Padrón de las almas . . . Año de 1793," household entry no. 113, don Miguel Goltario [Gortari]; grant to Miguel Gortari, 1769, BCA, LGS-259; grant to Gortari, 1769, BCA, LGS-258; sale to Gortari, 1774, BCA, LGS-267; Chabot, *Makers of San Antonio,* pp. 195-96; Jackson, *Los Mesteños.*

[16] "Padrón de las almas . . . Año de 1793," household entry nos. 87, 116, 41, and 323, respectively. All are mentioned in Jackson's *Los Mesteños* as involved in ranching.

[17] "Padrón de las almas . . . Año de 1793," household entry no. 44, don Joaquín Orandayn [Orandáin]; Chabot, *Makers of San Antonio;* BAT, vol. 57, 1774, p. 54; BAT, vol. 63, 1776, p. 12; San Fernando Parish Records, "Baptismal Records," Dec. 1760 and Dec. 1771; "Partition of Lands of the Upper Labores in San Antonio, Texas, and the Acequia, 1776-1784," Spanish Volume Deed Records, Book 3, pp. 317-48, BCA.

[18] "Padrón de las almas . . . Año de 1793," household entry no. 195, don Vicente Amador; Chabot, *Makers of San Antonio,* pp. 194-95; grant to Vicente Amador, 1762, BCA, LGS-3; grant to Amador, 1771, BCA, LGS-8; Castañeda, *Our Catholic Heritage,* V: 42, 44.

[19] "Padrón de las almas . . . Año de 1793," household entry nos. 26, 206, 215, 269, 279, 327, 329-32, 335-38, 346, 350-51, 355.

20 Ibid., household entry nos. 27, 40, 42, 55, 73, 77, 90, 125, 137, 168, 171, 177, 179, 181, 200, 202, 204, 228, 251, 255, 257-59, 265, 267, 275, 325, 381.

21 Ibid., household entry no. 73, Sebastian Monjarás; Jackson, *Los Mesteños*, pp. 138, 143, 163-64, 177-80, 198, 206, 215-18, 241, 252, 272, 300.

22 "Padrón de las almas . . . Año de 1793," household entry no. 27, Juan Manuel Ruiz; Chabot, *Makers of San Antonio*, p. 198.

23 "Padrón de las almas . . . Año de 1793," household entry no. 325, Pedro Guízar [Huízar]; sale to Pedro Huízar, 1783, BCA, LGS-322; sale to Huízar, 1784, BCA, LGS-323; sale to Huízar, 1784, BCA, LGS-278; Castañeda, *Our Catholic Heritage*, V: 40, 42, 51-58, 177, 197.

24 "Padrón de las almas . . . Año de 1793," household entry no. 267, Juan Blanco; sale to Juan Blanco, 1806, BCA, LGS-60; sale to Blanco, 1806, BCA, LGS-62.

25 "Padrón de las almas . . . Año de 1793." See de la Teja, "Land and Society," pp. 284-89.

26 See Elenor Clair Buckley, "The Aguayo Expedition into Texas and Louisiana, 1719-1722"; Castañeda, *Our Catholic Heritage*, II: 33-170.

27 "Lista y relación . . . de los oficiales, y soldados de este Presidio de Nuestra Señora del Pilar de los Adaes, . . ." May 23, 1730, AGN, PI, vol. 163.

28 Herbert Eugene Bolton, "The Spanish Abandonment and Re-Occupation of East Texas, 1773-1779."

29 For a list of Adaesanos in the Béxar presidio, see "Estracto General de la Tropa de dicho [San Antonio de Béxar] Presidio y Vezindario de la Villa de San Fernando en que se Comprende el Padrón de sus Familias, Armamentos, y Bienes Raizes que cada uno tiene. 1, 2, y 3 del Mes de Julio de 1779," AGI, AG, legajo 283. Discharges from the military of Adaesanos are included in the following: BAM, reel 11, 5/12/1777; reel 13, 6/30/1779; reel 16, 4/19/1785.

30 "Expediente promovido por los vecinos del extinguido presidio de los Adaes para que se les conceda algun establecimiento donde pueden subsistir con sus familias," AGI, AG, legajo 103. Copy of transcript in BTHC, Dunn Transcripts, Box 2Q141, vol. 48. For information on Marcos Hernández, see Jackson, *Los Mesteños*, pp. 208-209, 214, 311, 354.

31 "Padrón de las almas . . . Año de 1793."

32 Grant to Francisco Guadalupe Calahorra, 1778, BCA, LGS-118; grant to Simón de Aragón, 1769, BCA, LGS-5; grant to Manuel Losoya, 1784, BCA, LGS-347.

33 "Expediente promovido por los vecinos . . . con sus familias." See Castañeda, *Our Catholic Heritage*, pp. 344-56.

34 "Distribution of Land of Mission San Antonio de Valero, January 11, 1793," BCA, Mission Records.

[35] For data on Berbán, see "Estracto General . . . [San Antonio de Béxar]
. . . Julio de 1779," and "Padrón de las almas . . . Año de 1793," household
entry no. 26, Manuel Bervan [Berbán]; "Padrón de las familias que hay
en esta Villa de San Fernando, y Presidio de Béxar . . . Año de 1803,"
BAM, reel 31; Chabot, *Makers of San Antonio*, p. 177.

[36] For data on Zepeda, see "Padrón de las almas . . . Año de 1793," household
entry no. 323, don Marcos Sepeda [Zepeda]; Chabot, *Makers of San
Antonio*, p. 219; Jackson, *Los Mesteños*, p. 623.

VI. Indians and Their Culture in San Fernando de Béxar

[1] Perhaps the best example of the integration of quantitative, archaeological, and traditional sources on Texas Indians is Schuetz, "Indians of
the San Antonio Missions."

[2] Peter Gerhard, *The North Frontier of New Spain*, pp. 23-27, 331-33, 353-56,
365-67. For a more detailed study of the entire northern frontier, see
Jones, *Los Paisanos*.

[3] For an evaluation of the demographic sources available for Texas, see
Tjarks, "Comparative Demographic Analysis," pp. 291-302.

[4] Schuetz, "Indians of the San Antonio Missions," p. 128.

[5] "Estracto General . . . [San Antonio de Béxar] . . . Julio de 1779," AGI,
AG, legajo 283; "Padrón de las almas . . . Año de 1793," BAM, reel 24.
See a transcribed and translated version of the 1793 census in Leal,
Residents of Texas, pp. 114-41. See also Tjarks, "Comparative Demo-
graphic Analysis," pp. 324-25.

[6] Ibid., pp. 332-37.

[7] San Fernando Parish Records, "Baptismal Records."

[8] Tjarks, "Comparative Demographic Analysis," pp. 313-19.

[9] San Fernando Parish Records, "Baptismal Records."

[10] "Padrón de las almas . . . Año de 1793."

[11] Depositions of mayordomo Juan Nicolás, Lt. don Chrixtóval de Cordova,
and (soldier) Jph. Manuel Martínez taken by don Juan María Ripperdá,
Jan. 16, 1773, BA.

[12] "Padrón de las almas . . . Año de 1793."

[13] Schuetz, "Indians of the San Antonio Missions," pp. 347-48, 303, 356-57.

[14] Tjarks, "Comparative Demographic Analysis," pp. 319-21.

[15] Ibid., pp. 329-31.

[16] "Estracto general . . . [San Antonio de Béxar] . . . Julio de 1779"; "Padrón
de las almas . . . Año de 1793."

[17] Ibid.

Notes   167

[18] Schuetz, "Indians of the San Antonio Missions," pp. 15, 71; T.N. Campbell and T.J. Campbell, *Indian Groups Associated with the Spanish Missions of the San Antonio Missions National Historical Park*, p. 1; W.W. Newcomb, Jr., *The Indians of Texas from Prehistoric to Modern Times*, pp. 43-46; F.H. Rueckings, Jr., "The Economic System of the Coahuiltecan Indians of Southern Texas and Northeastern Mexico," p. 482; Thomas R. Hester and T.C. Hill, "An Initial Study of a Prehistoric Ceramic Tradition in Southern Texas," pp. 195-203; Thomas R. Hester, *Digging into South Texas Prehistory*, p. 50.

[19] F.H. Rueckings, Jr., "Ceremonies of the Coahuiltecan Indians of Southern Texas and Northeastern Mexico," pp. 330-39.

[20] Habig, *Alamo Chain of Missions*, p. 93; Leutenegger, *Guidelines*, pp. 19-21; Newcomb, *Indians of Texas*, p. 43; Mardith Keithly Schuetz, *The History and Archaeology of Mission San Juan Capistrano, San Antonio, Texas, Vol. I: Historical Documentation and Description of Structures*, fig. 19, and *Excavation of a Section of the Acequia Madre in Bexar County, Texas, and Archaeological Investigations at Mission San José in April, 1968*, p. 8. See also Anne A. Fox, Feris A. Bass, Jr., and Thomas R. Hester, *The Archaeology and History of Alamo Plaza*, p. 52.

[21] Schuetz, "Indians of the San Antonio Missions," p. 16.

[22] Anne A. Fox, "What Did They Eat at the Missions?" p. 6; Habig, *Alamo Chain of Missions*, p. 92; Mardith Keithly Schuetz, *The History and Archaeology of Mission San Juan Capistrano, San Antonio, Texas, Vol. II: Description of the Artifacts and Ethno-History of the Coahuiltecan Indians*, pp. 66-67, 69-72; Daniel E. Fox, *The Lithic Artifacts of Indians at Spanish Colonial Missions, San Antonio, Texas*, p. 39.

[23] Fox, "What Did They Eat," p. 5; Leutenegger, *Guidelines*, p. 49.

[24] Schuetz, "Indians of the San Antonio Missions," pp. 275-80.

[25] Leutenegger and Habig, *San José Papers*, I: 149.

[26] Habig, *Alamo Chain of Missions*, p. 97; Bolton, *Texas*, pp. 27-28; Schuetz, "Indians of the San Antonio Missions," p. 281.

[27] See Daniel E. Fox, John Clark, and Dan Scurlock, *Archaeological Investigations at San Fernando Cathedral*; Anne A. Fox, *The Archaeology and History of the Spanish Governor's Palace Park*; Anne A. Fox, I. Wayne Cox, Lynn Highley, and David Hafernick, *Archaeological and Historical Investigations at the Site of the New Bexar County Justice Center in Downtown San Antonio, Texas*.

[28] Virginia H. Taylor, ed. and trans., *The Letters of Antonio Martínez, Last Spanish Governor of Texas, 1817-1822*, pp. 69, 141, 142, 146, 237.

[29] Leutenegger, *Guidelines*, pp. 26, 43-46; Schuetz, "Indians of the San Antonio Mission," p. 240.

[30] José Cuello, "Saltillo in the Seventeenth Century: Local Society on the North Mexican Frontier," (Ph.D. diss., University of California, Berkeley), pp. 364-66.

[31] Ibid., pp. 366-67.

VII. Independent Indians and the San Antonio Community

1 Supporting detail and documentation of the analysis of interactions with "independent" Indians from the founding of San Antonio to the 1790s may be found in Elizabeth A.H. John, *Storms Brewed in Other Men's Worlds*. Analysis of the succeeding decades derives from the author's research for a sequel volume now in progress. Most of the evidence pertaining to this essay is found in the Béxar Archives, University of Texas at Austin, Barker Texas History Center. References in this essay are to Béxar Archives Microfilm (BAM). Some preliminary results appear in Elizabeth A.H. John, "Nurturing the Peace," pp. 345-69. The data on the extensive Indian traffic at San Antonio from the 1790s onward is found principally in the monthly reports routinely submitted by the commandant at the presidio of San Antonio de Béxar found in BA.

Citing the voluminous documentary evidence entailed in this analysis would require such numerous and lengthy footnotes as to overwhelm a brief interpretive essay. Hence, citations are limited to the specific case histories presented as examples of particular kinds of Indian connection with the San Antonio community.

2 John, *Storms Brewed*, pp. 698-99.

3 Census Report of Béxar Company, Dec. 31, 1803, BAM, microfilm reel 31, frame 858 (hereafter BAM 31:858); Francisco Xavier Chaves, petition for custody of Indian child, San Fernando de Béxar, Feb. 18, 1822, BAM 70:771.

4 Ramón Músquiz to José Antonio Elozúa, Béxar, Jan. 12, 1831, BAM 127:819 and 137:807.

5 Elozúa to Terán, Béxar, Jan. 21, 1831, BAM 138:98; Elozúa to Músquiz, Béxar, Jan. 21, 1831, BAM 138:347; Terán to Elozúa, Matamoros, Feb. 19, 1831, BAM 138:865; Músquiz to Elozúa, Béxar, Apr. 2, 1831, BAM 139:283.

6 Elozúa to Monterrey Comisario, Béxar, Jan. 13, 1831, BAM 137:843; Elozúa to Comandante of Laredo, Béxar, Jan. 12, 1831, BAM 137:798; Elozúa to Erasmo Seguín, Béxar, Jan. 12, 1831, BAM 137:798; Elozúa to Erasmo Seguín, Béxar, Jan. 12, 1831, BAM 137:805.

SELECTIVE BIBLIOGRAPHY
on Spanish Texas, 1685-1821

This bibliography contains a selective list of references on Spanish Texas (1685-1821) but also includes references on colonial Latin American history and post-1821 Tejano communities cited in the essays.

*

Abernethy, Francis Edward. "The Y'Barbo Legend and Early Spanish Settlement." *East Texas Historical Journal* 25, no. 1 (1987).

Alessio Robles, Vito. *Coahuila y Texas en la época colonial.* Mexico, D.F.: Editorial Cultural, 1938.

_____, ed. *Diario y derrotero de lo caminado, visto, y observado en la visita que hizo a los presidios de Nueva España Septentrional el Brigadier Pedro de Rivera.* Mexico, D.F., 1946.

Allen, Henry Easton. "The Parrilla Expedition to the Red River in 1759." *Southwestern Historical Quarterly* 43, no. 1 (July 1939).

Allen, Winnie. "A History of Nacogdoches, 1691-1820." M.A. thesis, University of Texas at Austin, 1925.

Almada, Francisco R. *Informe de Hugo de O'Conór sobre el estado de las Provincias Internas del Norte, 1771-1776.* Mexico, D.F.: Editorial Cultural, 1952.

Almaráz, Félix D., Jr. *Crossroad of Empire: The Church and State on the Rio Grande Frontier of Coahuila and Texas, 1700-1821.* San Antonio: Center for Archaeological Research, University of Texas at San Antonio, 1979.

_____. *Governor Antonio Martínez and Mexican Independence in Texas: An Orderly Transition.* San Antonio: Bexar County Historical Commission, 1979.

_____. "Governor Manuel Salcedo of Hispanic Texas, 1808-1813: A Reappraisal." *Texana* 6, no. 1 (Spring 1968).

_____. *The San Antonio Missions and Their System of Land Tenure.* Austin: University of Texas Press, 1989.

_____. "San Antonio's Old Franciscan Missions: Material Decline and Secular Avarice in the Transition from Hispanic to Mexican Control." *The Americas* 44, no. 1 (July 1987).

_____. *Tragic Cavalier: Governor Manuel Salcedo of Texas, 1808-1813.* Austin: University of Texas Press, 1971.

Anders, Evan. *Boss Rule in South Texas: The Progressive Era.* Austin: University of Texas Press, 1982.

Arneson, Edwin P. "The Early Art of Terrestrial Measurement and Its Practice in Texas." *Southwestern Historical Quarterly* 29, no. 2 (October 1925).

_____. "Early Irrigation in Texas." *Southwestern Historical Quarterly* 25, no. 2 (October 1921).

Ashford, Gerald. *Spanish Texas: Yesterday and Today.* Austin: Jenkins Publishing Co., 1971.

Austin, Mattie Alice. "The Municipal Government of San Fernando de Béxar, 1730-1800." *Quarterly of the Texas State Historical Association* 8, no. 4 (April 1905).

Bacarisse, Charles A. "Barón de Bastrop." *Southwestern Historical Quarterly* 58, no. 3 (January 1955).

_____. "The Union of Coahuila and Texas." *Southwestern Historical Quarterly* 61, no. 3 (January 1958).

Bancroft, Hubert Howe. *The History of North Mexican States and Texas.* 2 vols. San Francisco: A.L. Bancroft, 1884-1886.

Bannon, John Francis. *The Spanish Borderlands Frontier, 1531-1821.* Albuquerque: University of New Mexico Press, 1974.

_____, ed. *Bolton and the Spanish Borderlands.* Norman: University of Oklahoma Press, 1964.

Barba, Cecilia. "The Role of the Church in the Colonization of Michoacan." M.A. thesis, University of Texas at San Antonio, 1983.

Barker, Eugene C. "The Government of Austin's Colony, 1821-1831." *Southwestern Historical Quarterly* 21, no. 3 (January 1918).

_____. "The Influence of Slavery in the Colonization of Texas." *Southwestern Historical Quarterly* 28, no. 1 (July 1924).

_____. "Native Latin American Contribution to the Colonization and Independence of Texas." *Southwestern Historical Quarterly* 46, no. 4 (April 1943).

_____. "Notes on Early Texas Newspapers, 1819-1836." *Southwestern Historical Quarterly* 21, no. 2 (October 1917).

Benavides, Adán, Jr., ed. and comp. *The Béxar Archives (1717-1836): A Name Guide.* Austin: University of Texas Press for The University of Texas Institute of Texan Cultures at San Antonio, 1989.

Benson, Nettie Lee. "Bishop Marín de Porras and Texas." *Southwestern Historical Quarterly* 51, no. 1 (July 1947).

_____. *La diputación provincial y el federalismo mexicano.* Mexico, D.F.: El Colegio de México, 1955.

_____. "Texas' Failure to Send a Deputy to the Spanish Cortes, 1810-1812." *Southwestern Historical Quarterly* 64, no. 1 (July 1960).

_____, ed. and trans. "A Governor's Report on Texas in 1809." *Southwestern Historical Quarterly* 71, no. 4 (April 1968).

Berger, Max. "Education in Texas during the Spanish and Mexican Periods." *Southwestern Historical Quarterly* 51, no. 1 (July 1947).

Berlandier, Jean Louis. *Journey to Mexico during the Years 1826-1834.* Translated by Sheila M. Ohlendorf, Josette M. Bigelow, and Mary M. Standifer. 2 vols. Austin: Texas State Historical Association, 1980.

Birge, M. "The Casas Revolution." M.A. thesis, University of Texas at Austin, 1911.

Blake, Robert B. "Locations of Early Spanish Missions and Presidios in Nacogdoches County." *Southwestern Historical Quarterly* 41, no. 3 (January 1938).

Bolton, Herbert E[ugene]. "Beginnings of Mission Nuestra Señora del Refugio." *Southwestern Historical Quarterly* 19, no. 4 (April 1916).

_____. "Defensive Spanish Expansion and the Significance of the Borderlands." In *Bolton and the Spanish Borderlands*, edited by John Francis Bannon. Norman: University of Oklahoma Press, 1964.

_____. "The Founding of Mission Rosario: A Chapter in the History of the Gulf Coast." *Quarterly of the Texas State Historical Association* 10, no. 2 (October 1906).

_____. "The Founding of Missions on the San Gabriel River, 1748-1749." *Southwestern Historical Quarterly* 17, no. 4 (April 1914).

_____. "The Location of La Salle's Colony on the Gulf of Mexico." *Southwestern Historical Quarterly* 27, no. 3 (January 1924).

_____. "The Mission as a Frontier Institution in the Spanish-American Colonies." *American Historical Review* 23 (October 1917): 42-61. (Also in John Francis Bannon's *Bolton and the Spanish Borderlands*, pp. 187-211.)

_____. "The Native Tribes about the East Texas Missions." *Quarterly of the Texas State Historical Association* 11, no. 4 (April 1908).

_____. "Notes on Clark's 'Beginnings of Texas.'" *Quarterly of the Texas State Historical Association* 12, no. 2 (October 1908).

_____. "The Spanish Abandonment and Re-Occupation of East Texas, 1773-1779." *Quarterly of the Texas State Historical Association* 9, no. 2 (October 1905).

_____. "Spanish Activities on the Lower Trinity River, 1746-1771." *Southwestern Historical Quarterly* 16, no. 4 (April 1913).

_____. "The Spanish Occupation of Texas, 1519-1690." *Southwestern Historical Quarterly* 16, no. 1 (July 1912).

_____. *Texas in the Middle Eighteenth Century: Studies in Spanish Colonial History and Administration.* Berkeley: University of California Press, 1915; reprint, Austin: University of Texas Press, 1970.

_____, ed. and trans. *Athanase de Mezieres and the Louisiana Texas Frontier, 1768-1780.* 2 vols. Cleveland: Austin Clark Co., 1914.

_____. "The De León-Massanet Expeditions." In *Spanish Exploration in the Southwest, 1542-1706,* edited by Herbert Eugene Bolton. New York: Charles Scribner's Sons, 1908; reprint, New York: Barnes & Noble, 1967.

Borah, Woodrow. "Social Welfare and Social Obligation in New Spain." *Actas y memorias.* Thirty-Sixth International Congress of Americanists, Spain, 1964. Seville, 1966.

Brooks, Charles M. *Texas Missions: Their Romance and Architecture.* Dallas: Dealy and Lowe, 1936.

Brown, Elise Denison. "The History of the Spanish Establishments at Orcoquisac, 1745-1772." M.A. thesis, University of Texas at Austin, 1909.

Brown, Maury Bright. "The Military Defense of Texas and the Rio Grande Region, about 1766." M.A. thesis, University of Texas at Austin, 1924.

Buck, Samuel. *Yanaguana's Successors: The Story of the Canary Islands Immigration into Texas in the Eighteenth Century.* San Antonio: Naylor Co., 1949.

Buckley, Elenor Clair. "The Aguayo Expedition into Texas and Louisiana, 1719-1722." *Quarterly of the Texas State Historical Association* 15, no. 1 (July 1911).

Buerkle, Ruth Cowie. "The Continuing Military Presence." In *San Antonio in the Eighteenth Century,* edited by the San Antonio Bicentennial Heritage Committee. San Antonio: Clarke Printing Co., 1976.

Bugbee, Lister G. "The Real Saint-Denis." *Quarterly of the Texas State Historical Association* 1, no. 4 (April 1898).

Bush-Thurber, Marlys, and James E. Ivey. *The Missions of San Antonio: A Historical Structures and Administrative History.* Santa Fe: National Park Service, 1988.

Campbell, T.N., and T.J. Campbell. *Indian Groups Associated with the Spanish Missions of the San Antonio Missions National Historical Park.* San Antonio: Center for Archaeological Research, University of Texas at San Antonio, 1985.

Carlson, Paul H. *Texas Woolybacks: The Range Sheep and Goat Industry.* College Station: Texas A&M University Press, 1982.

Casis, Lilia M., trans. "Letter of Don Damian Manzanet to Don Carlos de Siguenza Relative to the Discovery of the Bay of Espíritu Santo." *Quarterly of the Texas State Historical Association* 2, no. 4 (April 1899).

Castañeda, Carlos E. "The First Chartered Bank West of the Mississippi." *Bulletin of the Business Historical Society* 25 (December 1951).

_____. *Our Catholic Heritage in Texas, 1519-1936.* 7 vols. Austin: Von Boeckmann-Jones, 1936-1958.

_____. "Pioneers in Sackcloth." *Preliminary Studies of the Texas Catholic Historical Association* 3, no. 5 (October 1939).

_____. "The Sons of St. Francis in Texas." *The Americas* 1, no. 3 (January 1945).

_____, ed. and trans. *History of Texas, 1673-1779, By Fray Juan Agustín Morfi.* Albuquerque: Quivira Society, 1935.

Chabot, Frederick C. *Military Presidios of Texas at the Place Called San Antonio: With a Description of the Comandancia or the Governor's Palace.* San Antonio: Naylor Co., 1929.

_____. *Mission La Purísima Concepción: Being an Account of Its Founding in East Texas.* San Antonio: Naylor Co., 1935.

_____. *San Antonio and Its Beginnings.* San Antonio: Naylor Co., 1931.

_____. *San Fernando: The Villa, Capital of the Province of Texas.* San Antonio: Naylor Co., 1930.

_____. *With the Makers of San Antonio.* San Antonio: Artes Gráficas, 1937.

_____, ed. and trans. *Texas in 1811: The Las Casas and Sambrano Revolutions.* San Antonio: Yanaguana Society, 1941.

Christiansen, Paige W. "Hugo O'Conór: Spanish-Indian Relations on the Frontiers of New Spain, 1771-1776." Ph.D. diss., University of California, Berkeley, 1959.

Clark, Doris. "Spanish Reaction to French Intrusion into Texas from Louisiana, 1754-1771." M.A. thesis, University of Texas at Austin, 1942.

Clark, Robert C. *The Beginnings of Texas, 1684-1718.* Austin: University of Texas Humanistic Series, 1907.

_____. "The Beginnings of Texas: Fort Saint Louis and Mission San Francisco de los Tejas." *Quarterly of the Texas State Historical Association* 5, no. 3 (January 1902).

_____. "Louis Juchereau de Saint-Denis and the Re-Establishment of the Tejas Missions." *Quarterly of the Texas State Historical Association* 6, no. 1 (July 1902).

Clay, John V. *Spain, Mexico, and the Lower Trinity: An Early History of the Texas Gulf Coast.* Baltimore: Gateway Press, 1987.

Cole, E.W. "La Salle in Texas." *Southwestern Historical Quarterly* 49, no. 4 (April 1946).

Connor, Seymour V. *Texas in 1776: A Historical Description.* Austin: Jenkins Publishing Co., 1975.

Contreras, Roberto. "José Bernardo Gutiérrez de Lara: The Forgotten Man." M.A. thesis, Pan American University, Edinburg, Texas, 1975.

Coopwood, Bethel. "Notes on the History of La Bahía del Espíritu Santo." *Quarterly of the Texas State Historical Association* 2, no. 1 (July 1898).

Cox, Issac Joslin. "The Early Settlers of San Fernando." *Quarterly of the Texas State Historical Association* 5, no. 2 (October 1901).

_____. "Educational Efforts in San Fernando de Béxar." *Quarterly of the Texas State Historical Association* 6, no. 1 (July 1902).

174   Tejano Origins in Eighteenth-Century San Antonio

_____. "The Founding of the First Texas Municipality." *Quarterly of the Texas State Historical Association* 2, no. 3 (January 1899).

_____. "The Louisiana-Texas Frontier." *Quarterly of the Texas State Historical Association* 10, no. 1 (July 1906).

_____. "The Louisiana-Texas Frontier, II." *Southwestern Historical Quarterly* 17, no. 1 (July 1913); 17, no. 2 (October 1913).

Cruz, Gilbert R. "The Cabildo in Texas under the Spanish Bourbons: The Origin and Development of Municipal Life at the Villa de San Fernando, San Antonio, Texas, 1731-1800." M.A. thesis, St. Mary's University, San Antonio, 1970.

_____. *Let There Be Towns: Spanish Municipal Origins in the American Southwest, 1610-1810.* College Station: Texas A&M University Press, 1989.

Dabbs, J. Autrey, ed. and trans. "The Texas Missions of 1785." *Mid-America* 22, no. 1 (January 1940).

Dabney, Lancaster E. "Louis Aury: The First Governor of Texas under the Mexican Republic." *Southwestern Historical Quarterly* 42, no. 2 (October 1938).

Davenport, Herbert. "Geographic Notes on Spanish Texas: El Orcoquisac and Los Horconsitos." *Southwestern Historical Quarterly* 50, no. 4 (April 1947).

Day, James M. *Six Missions of Texas.* Waco: Texian Press, 1965.

De Burgos, Francis. "The Administration of Teodoro de Croix, Commander General of the Provincias Internas de Mexico, 1776-1783." Ph.D. diss., University of Texas at Austin, 1927.

De la Teja, Jesús Francisco. "Land and Society in 18th Century San Antonio de Béxar: A Community on New Spain's Northern Frontier." Ph.D. diss., University of Texas at Austin, 1988.

_____, and John Wheat. "Béxar: Profile of a Tejano Community, 1820-1832." *Southwestern Historical Quarterly* 89, no. 1 (July 1985).

De León, Arnoldo. *The Tejano Community, 1836-1900.* Albuquerque: University of New Mexico Press, 1982.

_____. "The Tejano Experience in Six Texas Regions." *West Texas Historical Association Year Book* 65 (1989).

_____. "Tejano History Scholarship: A Review of the Literature." *West Texas Historical Association Year Book* 61 (1985).

Devereaux, Linda Erickson. "The Magee-Gutiérrez Expedition." *Texana* 11, no. 1 (1972).

"Diario de la conquista y entrada a los Thejas." *Universidad de México* 5, nos. 27-28 (January-February 1933).

Dixon, Helen M. "The Middle Years of the Administration of Juan María de Ripperdá, Governor of Texas, 1773-1775." M.A. thesis, University of Texas at Austin, 1934.

Dobie, J. Frank. "The First Cattle in Texas and the Southwest." *Southwestern Historical Quarterly* 42, no. 3 (January 1939).

———, ed. *Puro Mexicano*. Austin: Texas Folklore Society, 1935.

Dobkins, Betty E. *The Spanish Element in Texas Water Law.* Austin: University of Texas Press, 1959.

Documentos para la historia eclesiástica y civil de la Provincia de Texas o Nueva Philipinas, 1720-1779. Madrid: Ediciones José Porrúa Turanzas, 1961.

Donahue, William H. "The Missionary Activities of Fray Antonio de Jesús in Texas, 1716-1727." *The Americas* 14, no. 1 (July 1959).

Downs, Fane. "The History of Mexicans in Texas, 1820-1845." Ph.D. diss., Texas Tech University, 1970.

Dublán, Manuel, and José María Lozano. *Legislación mexicana.* 19 vols. Mexico D.F.: Imprenta del Comercio, 1876-1890.

Dunn, William Edward. "The Apache Mission on the San Sabá River: Its Founding and Failure." *Southwestern Historical Quarterly* 17, no. 4 (April 1914).

———. "Apache Relations in Texas, 1718-1750." *Quarterly of the Texas State Historical Association* 14, no. 3 (January 1911).

———. "The Founding of Nuestra Señora del Refugio: The Last Spanish Mission in Texas." *Southwestern Historical Quarterly* 25, no. 3 (January 1922).

———. "Missionary Activities among the Eastern Apaches Previous to the Founding of the San Sabá Mission." *Southwestern Historical Quarterly* 15, no. 3 (January 1912).

———. *Spanish and French Rivalry in the Gulf Regions of the United States, 1678-1702: The Beginnings of Texas and Pensacola.* Austin: University of Texas, 1917.

———. "The Spanish Search for La Salle's Colony on the Bay of Espíritu Santo." *Southwestern Historical Quarterly* 19, no. 4 (April 1916).

Eckhart, George B. "Spanish Missions of Texas, 1680-1800: An Outline of Spanish Mission History in Texas." *Kiva* 32 (February 1937).

Erdman, Grace Augusta, comp. "A Compilation of Royal Decrees Relating to Texas and Other Provinces of New Spain." M.A. thesis, University of Texas at Austin, 1930.

Espinosa, Fr. Isidro Félix. *Chrónica apostólica y seráphica de todos los colegios de propaganda fide de esta Nueva España.* Madrid, 1746.

Evans, Kenneth. "The Administration of Manuel de Sandoval, Governor of Texas, 1734-1736." M.A. thesis, University of Texas at Austin, 1928.

Faulk, Odie B. *The Last Years of Spanish Texas, 1778-1821.* The Hague: Mouton & Co., 1964.

———. "The Penetration of Foreigners and Foreign Ideas into Spanish East Texas, 1793-1810." *East Texas Historical Journal* 2, no. 2 (October 1964).

_____. "Ranching in Spanish Texas." *Hispanic American Historical Review* 45, no. 2 (May 1965).

_____. "Spanish-Comanche Relations and the Treaty of 1785." *Texana* 2, no. 1 (Spring 1964).

_____. *A Successful Failure: The Saga of Texas, 1519-1810.* Austin: Steck-Vaughn, 1965.

_____. "Texas during the Administration of Governor Domingo Cabello y Robles, 1778-1786." M.A. thesis, Texas Tech University, 1960.

_____, ed. and trans. "A Description of Texas in 1803." *Southwestern Historical Quarterly* 66, no. 4 (April 1963).

Faye, Stanley. "Commodore Aury." *Louisiana Historical Quarterly* 24, no. 3 (July 1941).

Fehrenbach, T.R. *Lone Star: A History of Texas and Texans.* New York: Macmillan Co., 1968.

_____. *Seven Keys to Texas.* El Paso: Texas Western Press, 1983.

Florescano, Enrique. *Precios del maíz y crisis agrícola en México, 1708-1810.* Mexico, D.F.: El Colegio de México, 1969.

Foik, Paul J. "Captain Don Domingo Ramón's Diary of His Expedition into Texas in 1716." *Preliminary Studies of the Texas Catholic Historical Society* 2, no. 5 (April 1934).

_____. "Fray Juan de Padilla." *Mid-America* 13, no. 2 (October 1930).

Forrestal, Peter P. "The Venerable Padre Fray Antonio Margil de Jesús." *Mid-America* 14, no. 4 (April 1932).

_____, ed. and trans. "Peña's Diary of the Aguayo Expedition." *Preliminary Studies of the Texas Catholic Historical Association* 2, no. 7 (January 1935).

_____. "The Solís Diary of 1767." *Preliminary Studies of the Texas Catholic Historical Society* 1, no. 6 (March 1931).

Fox, Anne A. *The Archaeology and History of the Spanish Governor's Palace Park.* San Antonio: Center for Archaeological Research, University of Texas at San Antonio, 1977.

_____. "What Did They Eat at the Missions?" Paper presented at the Texas State Historical Association annual meeting, Austin, March 1986.

_____, Feris A. Bass, Jr., and Thomas R. Hester. *The Archaeology and History of Alamo Plaza.* San Antonio: Center for Archaeological Research, University of Texas at San Antonio, 1976.

Fox, Anne A., Wayne I. Cox, Lynn Highley, and David Hafernick. *Archaeological and Historical Investigations at the Site of the New Bexar County Justice Center in Downtown San Antonio, Texas.* San Antonio: Center for Archaeological Research, University of Texas at San Antonio, in press.

Fox, Daniel E. *The Lithic Artifacts of Indians at Spanish Colonial Missions, San Antonio, Texas.* San Antonio: Center for Archaeological Research, University of Texas at San Antonio, 1979.

_____, John Clark, and Dan Scurlock. *Archaeological Investigations at San Fernando Cathedral: A Preliminary Report.* Austin: Office of the State Archeologist, 1977.

Gammel, H.P.N., comp. *The Laws of Texas, 1822-1897.* 10 vols. Austin: Gammel Book Co., 1898.

García, Fray Bartolomé. *Manual para administrar los santos sacramentos de penitencia, eucaristía, extrema unción, y matrimonio.* Mexico, D.F., 1760.

García, Mario T. *Desert Immigrants: The Mexicans of El Paso, 1880-1920.* New Haven: Yale University Press, 1981.

Garrett, [Julia] Kathryn. "The First Newspaper of Texas: *Gaceta de Texas.*" *Southwestern Historical Quarterly* 40, no. 3 (January 1937).

_____. "*Gaceta de Texas:* Translation of First Number." *Southwestern Historical Quarterly* 42, no. 1 (July 1938).

_____. *Green Flag over Texas: A Story of the Last Years of Spain in Texas.* 1939; reprint, Austin: Pemberton Press, 1969.

Garrison, George Pierce. *Texas: A Contest of Civilizations.* Boston: Houghton Mifflin Co., 1906.

Gerhard, Peter. *The North Frontier of New Spain.* Princeton, N.J.: Princeton University Press, 1982.

Gibson, Charles. *The Aztecs under Spanish Rule: A History of the Indians of the Valley of Mexico, 1519-1810.* Stanford, Calif.: Stanford University Press, 1964.

_____. *Spain in America.* New York: Harper & Row, 1966.

Glick, Thomas F. *The Old World Background of the Irrigation System of San Antonio, Texas.* El Paso: Texas Western Press, 1972.

Gómez Canedo, Lino. *Primeras exploraciones y poblamiento de Texas, 1686-1694.* Monterrey: Instituto Tecnológico y de Estudios Superiores de Monterrey, 1968.

Gómez-Quiñones, Juan. "Toward a Perspective on Chicano History." *Aztlán* 2, no. 2 (Fall 1971).

González, Jovita. "Social Life in Cameron, Starr, and Zapata Counties." M.A. thesis, University of Texas at Austin, 1930.

_____. "Tales and Songs of the Texas-Mexicans." In *Proceedings of the Texas Folklore Society,* no. 8 (1930). Edited by J. Frank Dobie.

Graham, Don. "J. Frank Dobie: A Reappraisal." *Southwestern Historical Quarterly* 92, no. 1 (July 1988).

Griffith, William J. "The Spanish Occupation of the Hasinai Country, 1690-1737." Ph.D. diss., University of California, 1942.

Griswold del Castillo, Richard. "Tejanos and California Chicanos: Regional Variations in Mexican American History." *Mexican Studies/Estudios Mexicanos* 1, no. 1 (Winter 1985).

Guice, C. Norman. "Trade Goods for Texas: An Incident in the History of the Jeffersonian Embargo." *Southwestern Historical Quarterly* 60, no. 4 (April 1957).

Guzmán, José R. "Francisco Javier Mina en las islas de Galveston y Soto la Marina." [Mexico, Archivo General de la Nación] *Boletín* 4 (1966).

Habig, Marion A. *The Alamo Chain of Missions: A History of San Antonio's Five Old Missions.* Chicago: Franciscan Herald Press, 1968.

_____. *The Alamo Mission: San Antonio de Valero, 1718-1793.* Chicago: Franciscan Herald Press, 1977.

_____. "Mission San José y San Miguel de Aguayo, 1720-1824." *Southwestern Historical Quarterly* 71, no. 4 (April 1968).

_____. *San Antonio's Mission San José, State and National Historic Site, 1720-1968.* San Antonio: Naylor Co., 1968.

Hackett, Charles Wilson. "The Marquis de San Miguel de Aguayo and His Recovery of Texas from the French, 1719-1723." *Southwestern Historical Quarterly* 49, no. 2 (October 1945).

_____. "Policy of the Spanish Crown Regarding French Encroachments from Louisiana, 1721-1762." In *New Spain and the Anglo-American West: Historical Contributions Presented to Herbert Eugene Bolton,* edited by Charles W. Hackett, et al., vol. 1, pp. 107-45. 2 vols. Los Angeles, 1932.

_____. "Visitador Rivera's Criticism of Aguayo's Work in Texas." *Hispanic American Historical Review* 16, no. 2 (May 1936).

_____, ed. *Pichardo's Treatise on the Limits of Louisiana and Texas.* 4 vols. Austin: University of Texas Press, 1931-1946.

Haggard, J[uan]. Villasana. "The Counter-Revolution of Béxar, 1811." *Southwestern Historical Quarterly* 42, no. 2 (October 1939).

_____. "The House of Barr and Davenport." *Southwestern Historical Quarterly* 49, no. 1 (July 1945).

_____. "The Neutral Ground between Louisiana and Texas, 1806-1821." Ph.D. diss., University of Texas at Austin, 1942.

_____. "The Neutral Ground between Louisiana and Texas, 1806-1821." *Louisiana Historical Quarterly* 28, no. 4 (October 1945).

Hall, Thomas D. *Social Change in the Southwest, 1350-1850.* Lawrence: University Press of Kansas, 1989.

Hallenbeck, Cleve. *Spanish Missions of the Old Southwest.* Garden City, N.Y., 1926.

Hanke, Lewis. *The Spanish Struggle for Justice in the Conquest of America.* Boston: Little, Brown, 1949.

Harrison, James Christopher. "The Failure of Spain in East Texas: The Occupation and Abandonment of Nacogdoches, 1779-1821." Ph.D. diss., University of Nebraska, 1980.

Hatcher, Mattie Austin. "Conditions in Texas Affecting the Colonization Problem, 1795-1801." *Southwestern Historical Quarterly* 25, no. 2 (October 1921).

———. "Joaquín de Arredondo's Report of the Battle of the Medina, August 18, 1813." *Quarterly of the Texas State Historical Association* 11, no. 3 (January 1908).

———. *The Opening of Texas to Foreign Settlement, 1801-1821.* Austin: University of Texas, 1927.

———, ed. and trans. "The Expedition of Don Domingo Terán de los Rios into Texas, 1691-1692." *Preliminary Studies of the Texas Catholic Historical Society* 2, no. 1 (January 1932).

———, trans. "Texas in 1820." *Southwestern Historical Quarterly* 23, no. 1 (July 1919).

Henderson, Harry McCorry. "The Magee-Gutierrez Expedition." *Southwestern Historical Quarterly* 55, no. 1 (July 1951).

Hester, Thomas R. *Digging into South Texas Prehistory.* San Antonio: Corona Publishing Co., 1980.

———, and T.C. Hill. "An Initial Study of a Prehistoric Ceramic Tradition in Southern Texas." *Plains Anthropologist* 16 (1971).

Heusinger, Edward W. *Early Explorations and Mission Establishments in Texas.* San Antonio: Naylor Co., 1936.

Hinojosa, Gilberto M. *A Borderlands Town in Transition: Laredo, 1755-1870.* College Station: Texas A&M University Press, 1983.

Hoffman, Fritz Leo. "The First Three Years of the Administration of Juan María, Barón de Ripperdá, Governor of Texas, 1770-1773." M.A. thesis, University of Texas at Austin, 1930.

———, ed. and trans. *Diary of the Alarcón Expedition into Texas, 1718-1719, by Francisco de Céliz.* Los Angeles: Quivira Society, 1935.

———. "The Mezquía Diary of the Alarcón Expedition into Texas, 1718." *Southwestern Historical Quarterly* 41, no. 4 (April 1938).

Holmes, Jack D.L. "The Marqués de Casa Calvo, Nicolás de Finiels, and the 1805 Spanish Expedition through East Texas and Louisiana." *Southwestern Historical Quarterly* 69, no. 3 (January 1966).

Holmes, William H. "The Acequias of San Antonio." M.A. thesis, St. Mary's University, San Antonio, 1962.

Howren, Alleine. "Causes and Origin of the Decree of April 6, 1830." *Southwestern Historical Quarterly* 16, no. 4 (April 1913).

Hunnicutt, Helen M., ed. and trans. "Election of Alcaldes in San Fernando, 1750." *Southwestern Historical Quarterly* 54, no. 3 (January 1951).

Jackson, Jack. "Father José María de Jesús Puelles and the Maps of Pichardo's Document 74." *Southwestern Historical Quarterly* 91, no. 3 (January 1988).

_____. *Los Mesteños: Spanish Ranching in Texas, 1721-1821*. College Station: Texas A&M University Press, 1986.

Jarrett, Rie. *Gutiérrez de Lara, Mexican Texan: The Story of a Creole Hero*. Austin: Creole Texana, 1949.

Jiménez, Judith M. "Joaquín Arredondo, Loyalist Officer in New Spain, 1810-1821." Ph.D. diss., University of Michigan, 1933.

John, Elizabeth A.H. "Nurturing the Peace: Spanish and Comanche Cooperation in the Early Nineteenth Century." *New Mexico Historical Review* 59, no. 4 (October 1984).

_____. *Storms Brewed in Other Men's Worlds: The Confrontation of Indians, Spanish, and French in the Southwest, 1540-1795*. College Station: Texas A&M University Press, 1975; Lincoln: University of Nebraska Press, 1981.

_____, ed., and John Wheat, trans. *Views from the Apache Frontier: Report on the Northern Provinces of New Spain by José Cortés, Lieutenant in the Royal Corps of Engineers, 1799*. Norman: University of Oklahoma Press, 1989.

Jones, Oakah L. *Los Paisanos: Spanish Settlers on the Northern Frontier of New Spain*. Norman: University of Oklahoma Press, 1979.

Kennedy, William. *Texas: The Rise, Progress, and Prospects of the Republic of Texas*. 1841; reprint, Fort Worth: Molyneaux Craftsman, 1925.

King, Nyal C. "Captain Antonio Gil Y'Barbo: Founder of Modern Nacogdoches, 1729-1809." M.A. thesis, Stephen F. Austin State University, 1949.

Kinnard, Lawrence, ed. and trans. *The Frontiers of New Spain: Nicolás de Lafora's Description, 1766-1768*. Berkeley: Quivira Society, 1958.

Kress, M.K., ed. and trans. "Diary of a Visit of Inspection of the Texas Missions Made by Fray Gaspar José de Solís in the Years 1767-1768." *Southwestern Historical Quarterly* 35, no. 1 (July 1931).

Laquest, Katherine W. "A Social History of the Spaniards in Nacogdoches." M.A. thesis, Baylor University, 1941.

Leal, Carmela, ed. and comp. *Residents of Texas, 1782-1836*. 3 vols. San Antonio: University of Texas Institute of Texan Cultures at San Antonio, 1984.

Leutenegger, Benedict, ed. and trans. *Guidelines for a Texas Mission: Instructions for the Missionary of Mission Concepción in San Antonio, ca. 1760*. San Antonio: Old Spanish Missions Historical Research Library at San José Mission, 1976.

_____. *Inventory of the Mission San Antonio de Valero, 1772*. Austin: Texas Historical Commission, 1977.

_____. *Letters and Memorials of the Father Presidente Fray Benito Fernández de Santa Ana, 1736-1754: Documents on the Missions of Texas from the Archives of the College of Querétaro*. San Antonio: Old Spanish Missions Historical Research Library at Our Lady of the Lake University, 1981.

_____. "New Documents on Father José Mariano Reyes." *Southwestern Historical Quarterly* 71, no. 4 (April 1968).

_____. "Report on the San Antonio Missions in 1792." *Southwestern Historical Quarterly* 77, no. 4 (April 1974).

_____, and Marion A. Habig, eds. and trans. Fr. Gerónimo de Mendieta's History: *An Introduction to the Antecedents of the Spanish Missions in Texas*. San Antonio: Old Spanish Missions Historical Research Library at San José Mission, 1978.

_____. *Journal of a Texas Missionary, 1767-1802: The Diario Histórico of Fr. Cosme Lozano Narvais, pen name of Fr. Mariano Antonio de Vasconcelos*. San Antonio: Old Spanish Missions Historical Research Library at San José Mission, 1977.

_____. *Letters and Memorials of Fray Mariano Francisco de los Dolores y Viana, 1737-1762: Documents on the Missions of Texas from the Archives of the College of Querétaro*. San Antonio: Old Spanish Missions Historical Research Library at Our Lady of the Lake University, 1985.

_____. *Management of the Missions of Texas: Fr. José Oliva's Views concerning the Problem of Temporalities in 1788*. San Antonio: Old Spanish Historical Research Library at San José Mission, 1977.

_____. "Memorial of Father Benito Fernández concerning the Canary Islanders, 1741." *Southwestern Historical Quarterly* 82, no. 3 (January 1979).

_____. *The San José Papers: The Primary Sources for History of Mission San José y San Miguel de Aguayo from Its Founding in 1720 to the Present*. 2 vols. San Antonio: Old Spanish Missions Historical Research Library at San José Mission, 1978.

_____. *The Texas Missions of the College of Zacatecas in 1749-1750: Report of Fr. Ignacio Antonio Ciprián, 1749, and Memorial of the College to the King, 1750*. San Antonio: Old Spanish Missions Historical Research Library at San José Mission, 1979.

_____. *The Zacatecan Missionaries in Texas, 1716-1834: Excerpts from the Libros de los Decretos of the Missionary College of Zacatecas, 1707-1828*. Austin: Texas Historical Survey Committee, Office of the State Archeologist, 1973.

Limón, José. "El Primer Congreso Mexicanista de 1911: A Precursor to Contemporary Chicanismo." *Aztlán* 5, nos. 1-2 (Spring-Fall 1974).

Loomis, Noel M., and Abraham P. Nasatir. *Pedro Vial and the Roads to Santa Fe*. Norman: University of Oklahoma Press, 1967.

Lynch, Margaret A. "Colonial Texas as a Frontier Problem." Ph.D. diss., Boston College, 1935.

McCaleb, Walter F. "The First Period of the Gutiérrez-Magee Expedition." *Quarterly of the Texas State Historical Association* 4, no. 3 (January 1901).

_____. "Some Obscure Points in the Mission Period." *Quarterly of the Texas State Historical Association* 1, no. 3 (January 1898).

_____. *The Spanish Missions of Texas*. San Antonio: Naylor Co. 1954.

McCloskey, Michael B. *The Formative Years of the Missionary College of Santa Cruz de Querétaro, 1683-1733*. Washington, D.C.: Academy of Franciscan History, 1955.

_____. "Fray Isidro Félix de Espinosa, Companion and Biographer of Margil." *The Americas* 7, no. 3 (January 1951).

McCollum, Dudley Foster. "Spanish Texas." Ph.D. diss., New York University, 1931.

McCorkle, James L., Jr. "Los Adaes and the Borderlands Origins of East Texas." *East Texas Historical Association* 22, no. 2 (Fall 1984).

McGill, Margaret. "The Administration of Carlos Franquis de Lugo, Governor of Texas, 1736-1737." M.A. thesis, University of Texas at Austin, 1928.

MacLachlan, Colin M., and Jaime E. Rodríguez O. *The Forging of the Cosmic Race: A Reinterpretation of Colonial Mexico*. Los Angeles: University of California Press, 1980.

McLean, Malcolm, ed. *Papers concerning Robertson's Colony in Texas*. Vol. 1. Fort Worth: Texas Christian University Press, 1974.

MacMillan, Esther. "The Cabildo and the People, 1731-1784." In *San Antonio in the Eighteenth Century*. Edited by the San Antonio Bicentennial Heritage Committee. San Antonio: Clarke Printing Co., 1976.

McReynolds, James M. "Family Life in a Borderland Community: Nacogdoches, Texas, 1779-1861." Ph.D. diss., Texas Tech University, 1978.

_____. "Mexican Nacogdoches." In *Nacogdoches: Wilderness Outpost to Modern City, 1779-1979*. Edited by Archie McDonald. Nacogdoches: privately printed, 1979.

McWilliams, Carey. *North from Mexico: The Spanish Speaking People of the United States*. New York: Greenwood Press, 1968.

Madsen, William. *The Mexican-Americans of South Texas*. New York: Holt, Rinehart, and Winston, 1964.

Magnaghi, Russell M., ed. and trans. "Texas as Seen by Governor Winthuysen, 1741-1744." *Southwestern Historical Quarterly* 88, no. 2 (October 1984).

Mecham, J. Lloyd. *Francisco de Ibarra and Nueva Viscaya*. Durham, N.C.: Duke University Press, 1962.

Meinig, D.W. *Southwest: Three Peoples in Geographical Change, 1600-1970*. New York: Oxford University Press, 1971.

Meyer, Michael C. *Water in the Hispanic Southwest: A Social and Legal History, 1550-1850*. Tucson: University of Arizona Press, 1984.

Miller, E.T. "The Connection of Peñalosa with the La Salle Expedition." *Quarterly of the Texas State Historical Association* 5, no. 2 (October 1901).

Milligan, James Clark. "José Bernardo Gutiérrez de Lara, Mexican Frontiersman, 1811-1841." Ph.D. diss., Texas Tech University, 1975.

Montejano, David. *Anglos and Mexicans in the Making of Texas, 1836-1986*. Austin: University of Texas Press, 1987.

Moore, Mary L., and Delmar L. Beene., eds. and trans. "The Interior Provinces of New Spain. The Report of Hugo O'Conór. January 30, 1776." *Arizona and the West* 13, no. 3 (Autumn 1971).

Moorhead, Max L. *The Presidio: Bastion of the Spanish Borderlands.* Norman: University of Oklahoma Press, 1975.

Morey, Elizabeth May. "Attitude of the Citizens of San Fernando toward Independence Movements in New Spain, 1811-1813." M.A. thesis, University of Texas at Austin, 1930.

Murphy, Henrietta. "Spanish Presidial Administration as Exemplified by the Inspection of Pedro de Rivera, 1724-1728." Ph.D. diss., University of Texas at Austin, 1938.

Murphy, Retta. "The Journey of Pedro de Rivera, 1724-1728." *Southwestern Historical Quarterly* 41, no. 2 (October 1937).

Murray, Paul V. "Venerable Antonio Margil de Jesús, O.F.M., Friar of the Winged Feet." *The Americas* 7, no. 3 (January 1951).

Myers, Sandra [L.]. *The Ranch in Spanish Texas, 1691-1800.* El Paso: Texas Western Press, 1969.

_____. "The Spanish Cattle Kingdoms in the Province of Texas." *Texana* 4, no. 3 (Fall 1966).

Nathan, Paul D., trans., and Lesley Byrd Simpson, ed. *The San Sabá Papers: A Documentary Account of the Founding and Destruction of San Sabá Mission.* San Francisco: John Howell Books, 1959.

Navarro García, Luis. *Don José de Gálvez y la Comandancia General del las Provincias Internas del Norte de Nueva Españas.* Seville: Escuela de Estudios Hispano-Americanos, 1964.

_____. "La gobernación y comandancia general de las provincias internas del norte de Nueva España. Estudio institucional." *Revista de historia del derecho Ricardo Levene* (Buenos Aires) 14 (1963).

Nelson, Al B. "Juan de Ugalde and Picax-Ande Ins-Tinsle, 1787-1788." *Southwestern Historical Quarterly* 43, no. 4 (April 1940).

Newcomb, James P., ed. *Memoirs by Antonio Menchaca.* San Antonio: Yanaguana Society, 1937.

Newcomb, W.W., Jr. *The Indians of Texas from Prehistoric to Modern Times.* Austin: University of Texas Press, 1961.

Nixon, Pat Ireland. *A Century of Medicine in San Antonio.* San Antonio, 1936.

_____. *The Medical Story of Early Texas, 1528-1853.* San Antonio, 1946.

Oberste, William Herman. *History of Refugio Mission.* Refugio, Tex.: Refugio Timely Remarks, 1942.

_____. *The Restless Friar: Venerable Fray Antonio Margil de Jesús, Missionary to the Americas, Apostle of Texas.* Austin: Von Boeckmann-Jones Co., 1970.

O'Connor, Kathryn Stoner. *The Presidio La Bahía del Espíritu Santo de Zuñiga, 1721-1846.* Austin: Von Boeckmann-Jones Co., 1966.

O'Donnell, Walter J. "La Salle's Occupation of Texas." *Preliminary Studies of the Texas Catholic Historical Society* 3, no. 2 (April 1936). Also published in *Mid-America* 18 (April 1936).

O'Rourke, Thomas P. *The Franciscan Missions in Texas, 1690-1793.* Washington, D.C.: Washington Monotype Composition Co., 1927.

Paredes, Américo. *"With His Pistol in His Hand": A Border Ballad and Its Hero.* Austin: University of Texas Press, 1958.

Partin, James G. "A History of Nacogdoches and Nacogdoches County, Texas, to 1877." M.A. thesis, University of Texas at Austin, 1968.

Perales, Alonso. *El méxico-americano y la política del sur de Tejas.* San Antonio, 1931.

_____. *En defensa de mi raza.* 2 vols. San Antonio: Artes Gráficas, 1936.

Persons, Billie. "Secular Life in the San Antonio Missions." *Southwestern Historical Quarterly* 62, no. 1 (July 1958).

Phares, Ross. *Cavalier in the Wilderness: The Story of the Explorer and Trader Louis Juchereau de St. Denis.* Baton Rouge: Louisiana State University Press, 1952.

Portillo, Esteban L. *Apuntes para la historia antigua de Coahuila y Texas.* Saltillo: Biblioteca de la Universidad Autónoma de Coahuila, 1886.

Powell, Lydia O. "A Study of the Influence on Changes in Sixteenth, Seventeenth and Eighteenth Century Spanish Cartography of Texas." M.A. thesis, St. Mary's University, San Antonio, 1985.

Powell, Philip Wayne. *Soldiers, Indians, and Silver: North America's First Frontier War.* Berkeley: University of California Press, 1952.

Poyo, Gerald E., and Gilberto M. Hinojosa. "Spanish Texas and Borderlands Historiography in Transition: Implications for United States History." *Journal of American History* 75, no. 2 (September 1988).

Price, Catherine. "The Comanches' Threat to Texas and New Mexico in the Eighteenth Century and the Development of Spanish Indian Policy." *Journal of the West* 24, no. 2 (April 1985).

Ramsdell, Charles. "Espíritu Santo: An Early Texas Cattle Ranch." *Texas Geographic Magazine* 13 (January 1949).

Rendón Lozano, Rubén. *Viva Tejas: The Story of the Tejanos, the Mexican-Born Patriots of the Texas Revolution.* San Antonio: Southern Literary Institute, 1936.

Reps, John W. *Cities of the American West: A History of Frontier Urban Planning.* Princeton, N.J.: Princeton University Press, 1979.

_____. *Planning in Frontier America.* Princeton, N.J.: Princeton University Press, 1969.

Ricard, Robert. *The Spiritual Conquest of Mexico.* Berkeley: University of California Press, 1966.

Rios, Eduardo Enrique. *Life of Fray Antonio Margil, O.F.M.* Translated and revised by Benedict Leutenegger. Washington, D.C.: Academy of American Franciscan History, 1959.

Romano-V, Octavio. "The Anthropology and Sociology of the Mexican-Americans." In *Voices: Readings from "El Grito."* Edited by Octavio Romano-V. Berkeley: Quinto Sol Publications, 1971.

Rubel, Arthur J. *Across the Tracks: Mexican-Americans in a Texas City.* Austin: University of Texas Press, 1966.

Rueckings, F.H., Jr. "Ceremonies of the Coahuiltecan Indians of Southern Texas and Northeastern Mexico." *Texas Journal of Science* 6, no. 3 (1954).

_____. "The Economic System of the Coahuiltecan Indians of Southern Texas and Northeastern Mexico." *Texas Journal of Science* 5, no. 4 (1954).

San Antonio Bicentennial Heritage Committee, ed. *San Antonio in the Eighteenth Century.* San Antonio: Clarke Printing Co., 1976.

Sánchez, José María. "A Trip to Texas in 1828." Translated and edited by Carlos E. Castañeda. *Southwestern Historical Quarterly* 29, no. 4 (April 1926).

_____. *Viaje a Texas en 1828-1829.* Mexico, D.F., 1939.

Santos, Richard. "Proposed View of San Antonio de Valero." *Texana* 3, no. 3 (Fall 1965).

_____. "The Quartel de San Antonio de Béxar." *Texana* 5, no. 3 (Fall 1967).

_____, ed. and trans. *The Aguayo Expedition into Texas, 1721: An Annotated Translation of the Five Versions of the Diary Kept by Br. Juan Antonio de la Peña.* Austin: Jenkins Publishing Co., 1981.

Saragoza, Alex. "The Significance of Recent Chicano-related Historical Writings: An Appraisal." *Ethnic Affairs* 1, no. 1 (Fall 1987).

Schmitt, Edmond J.P. "Who Was Juchereau de Saint Denis?" *Quarterly of the Texas State Historical Association* 1, no. 3 (January 1898).

Schuetz, Mardith Keithly. *Excavation of a Section of the Acequia Madre in Bexar County, Texas, and Archaeological Investigations at Mission San José in April, 1968.* Austin: Texas Historical Survey Committee, 1968.

_____. *The History and Archaeology of Mission San Juan Capistrano, San Antonio, Texas, Vol. I: Historical Documentation and Description of Structures.* Austin: State Building Commission, 1968.

_____. *The History and Archaeology of Mission San Juan Capistrano, San Antonio, Texas, Vol. II: Description of the Artifacts and Ethno-History of the Coahuiltecan Indians.* Austin: State Building Commission, 1969.

_____. "Indians in the San Antonio Area." In *San Antonio in the Eighteenth Century.* Edited by the San Antonio Bicentennial Heritage Committee. San Antonio: Clarke Printing Co., 1976.

_____. "The Indians of the San Antonio Missions, 1718-1821." Ph.D. diss., University of Texas at Austin, 1980.

_____. "Professional Artisans in the Hispanic Southwest: The Churches of San Antonio, Texas." *The Americas* 40, no. 1 (July 1983).

Schwartz, Ted. *The Forgotten Battlefield of the First Texas Revolution: The Battle of Medina, August 18, 1813*. Edited by Robert H. Thonhoff. Austin: Eakin Press, 1985.

Seed, Patricia. "Social Dimensions of Race: Mexico City, 1753." *Hispanic American Historical Review* 62 (November 1982).

Shelby, Charmion Clair. "Efforts to Finance the Aguayo Expedition: A Study of Frontier Financial Administration in New Spain." *Hispanic American Historical Review* 25, no. 1 (February 1945).

_____. "St. Denis's Second Expedition to the Rio Grande, 1716-1719." *Southwestern Historical Quarterly* 27, no. 3 (January 1924).

_____, ed. and trans. "St. Denis's Declaration concerning Texas in 1717." *Southwestern Historical Quarterly* 26, no. 3 (July 1923).

Sibley, Marilyn McAdams. *Lone Stars and State Gazettes: Texas Newspapers before the Civil War*. College Station: Texas A&M University Press, 1983.

_____. *Travelers in Texas, 1761-1860*. Austin: University of Texas Press, 1967.

Simpson, Lesley Byrd. *The Encomienda in New Spain: The Beginnings of Spanish Mexico*. Berkeley: University of California Press, 1950.

_____, and Paul D. Nathan, eds. and trans. *The San Sabá Papers: A Documentary Account of the Founding and Destruction of San Sabá Mission*. San Francisco, 1959.

Spears, Louis. "Galveston Island, 1816-1821: Focal Point for the Contest for Texas." M.A. thesis, University of Texas at El Paso, 1973.

Spell, Lota M. "The First Text Book Used in Texas." *Southwestern Historical Quarterly* 29, no. 4 (April 1926).

_____. *Pioneer Printer: Samuel Bangs in Mexico and Texas*. Austin: University of Texas Press, 1963.

_____, ed. and trans. "The Grant and First Survey of San Fernando de Béxar." *Southwestern Historical Quarterly* 66, no. 1 (July 1962).

Spicer, Edward H. *Cycles of Conquest: The Impact of Spain, Mexico, and the United States on the Indians of the Southwest, 1533-1960*. Tucson: University of Arizona Press, 1962.

Starnes, Gary B. "Juan de Ugalde and the Coahuila-Texas Frontier." *Texana* 10, no. 2 (1972).

Steck, Francis Borgia. "Forerunners of Captain De León's Expedition to Texas, 1670-1675." *Southwestern Historical Quarterly* 36, no. 1 (July 1932).

Stenberg, Richard. "The Western Boundary of Louisiana, 1762-1803." *Southwestern Historical Quarterly* 35, no. 2 (October 1931).

Stern, Peter Alan. "Social Marginality and Acculturation on the Northern Frontier of New Spain." Ph.D. diss., University of California, Berkeley, 1984.

Stovenour, Robert E. "A History of San Antonio under Spanish Rule." M.A. thesis, Southern Methodist University, 1965.

Taylor, Paul S. *An American-Mexican Frontier: Nueces County, Texas.* Chapel Hill: University of North Carolina Press, 1934.

Taylor, Virginia H., ed. and trans. "Calendar of the Letters of Antonio Martínez, Last Spanish Governor of Texas, 1817-1822." *Southwestern Historical Quarterly* 61, no. 1 (July 1957); 61, no. 2 (October 1957).

_____. *The Letters of Antonio Martínez, Last Spanish Governor of Texas, 1817-1822.* Austin: Texas State Library, 1957.

Thomas, Alfred B., ed. and trans. *Teodoro de Croix and the Northern Frontier of New Spain, 1776-1783.* Norman: University of Oklahoma Press, 1941.

Thonhoff, Robert H. "The First Ranch in Texas." *West Texas Historical Association Year Book* 40 (October 1964).

_____. *The Texas Connection with the American Revolution.* Burnet, Tex.: Eakin Press, 1981.

Tijerina, Andrew Anthony. "Tejanos and Texas: The Native Mexicans of Texas, 1820-1850." Ph.D. diss., University of Texas at Austin, 1977.

"Titulo de gobernador e instrucciones a Don Martín de Alarcón para su expedición a Texas." [Mexico, Archivo General de la Nación] *Boletín* 6, no. 4 (1935).

Tjarks, Alicia V. "Comparative Demographic Analysis of Texas, 1777-1793." *Southwestern Historical Quarterly* 77, no. 3 (January 1974).

_____. "Evolución urbana de Texas durante el siglo XVIII." *Revista de Indias* (1973-1974).

_____. "Política y sociedad en Texas a fines del siglo XVIII (1770-1790)." Ph.D. diss., University of Madrid, n.d.

Tous, Gabriel, ed. and trans. "The Espinosa-Olivares-Aguirre Expedition of 1709." *Preliminary Studies of the Texas Catholic Historical Society* 1, no. 3 (March 1930).

_____. "Ramón's Expedition: Espinosa's Diary of 1716." *Mid-America* 12, no. 4 (April 1930).

Vaca, Nick C. "The Mexican-American in the Social Sciences 1917-1920." *El Grito* 8 (Fall 1970).

Vigness, David M. "Don Hugo O'Conór and New Spain's Northeastern Frontier, 1764-1766." *Journal of the West* 6, no. 1 (January 1967).

_____. *The Revolutionary Decades: The Saga of Texas, 1810-1836.* Austin: Steck-Vaughn Co., 1965.

_____, and Ernest Wallace, comps. *Documents of Texas History.* Austin: Steck Co., 1960.

Walker, Henry P., ed. "William McLane's Narrative of the Magee-Gutiérrez Expedition, 1812-1813." *Southwestern Historical Quarterly* 66, no. 2 (October 1962); 66, no. 3 (January 1963); 66, no. 4 (April 1963).

Walters, Paul H[ugh]. "The Secularization of the La Bahía Missions." *Southwestern Historical Quarterly* 54, no. 3 (January 1951).

———. "Survey of the History of La Bahía del Espíritu Santo, 1721-1821." M.A. thesis, University of Texas at Austin, 1944.

Warren, Harris Gaylord. "Documents Relating to George Graham's Proposals to Jean Lafitte for the Occupation of the Texas Coast." *Louisiana Historical Quarterly* 21, no. 1 (January 1938).

———. "Documents Relating to the Establishment of Privateers at Galveston, 1816-1817." *Louisiana Historical Quarterly* 21, no. 4 (October 1938).

———. "The Origin of General Mina's Invasion of Mexico." *Southwestern Historical Quarterly* 42, no. 1 (July 1938).

———. *The Sword Was Their Passport.* Baton Rouge: Louisiana State University Press, 1943.

Weber, David J. *The Mexican Frontier, 1821-1846: The American Southwest under Mexico.* Albuquerque: University of New Mexico Press, 1982.

———, and Roger W. Lotchin. "The New Chicano History: Two Perspectives." *History Teacher* 16, no. 2 (February 1983).

Weber, David J., ed., and Conchita Hassell Winn, trans. *Troubles in Texas, 1832: A Tejano Viewpoint from San Antonio.* Dallas: DeGolyer Library, Southern Methodist University, 1983.

Weddle, Robert S. *San Juan Bautista: Gateway to Spanish Texas.* Austin: University of Texas Press, 1968.

———. "San Juan Bautista: Mother of Texas Missions." *Southwestern Historical Quarterly* 71, no. 4 (April 1968).

———. "The San Sabá Mission: Approach to the Great Plains." *Great Plains Journal* 4 (Spring 1965).

———. *The San Sabá Mission: Spanish Pivot in Texas.* Austin: University of Texas Press, 1964.

———. *Spanish Sea: The Gulf of Mexico in North American Discovery, 1500-1685.* College Station: Texas A&M University Press, 1985.

———. *Wilderness Manhunt: The Spanish Search for La Salle.* Austin: University of Texas Press, 1973

———, and Robert H. Thonhoff. *Drama and Conflict: The Texas Saga of 1776.* Austin: Madrona Press, 1976.

Weeks, O. Douglas. "The Texas-Mexican and Politics in South Texas." *American Political Science Review* 24, no. 3 (August 1930).

West, Elizabeth Howard, ed. and trans. "Bonilla's Compendium of the History of Texas, 1772. An Annotated Translation." *Quarterly of the Texas State Historical Association* 8, no. 1 (July 1904).

_____. "De León's Expedition of 1689. An Annotated Translation." *Quarterly of the Texas State Historical Association* 8, no. 3 (January 1905).

_____. "Diary of José Bernardo Gutiérrez de Lara, 1811-1812." *American Historical Review* 34, no. 1 (October 1928); 34, no. 2 (January 1929).

Wharton, Clarence R. *The Jurisdiction of the Alcalde Courts in Texas prior to the Revolution*. n.p., 1921.

White, Theodore L. "The Marqués de Rubí's Inspection of the Eastern Presidios on the Northern Frontier of New Spain." Ph.D. diss., University of Texas at Austin, 1951.

Wilson, Maurine T. "Philip Nolan and His Activities in Texas." M.A. thesis, University of Texas at Austin, 1932.

_____, and Jack Jackson. *Philip Nolan and Texas: Expeditions to the Unknown Land, 1791-1801*. Waco: Texian Press, 1987.

Woodman, David, Jr. *Guide to Texas Emigrants*. Boston, 1835; reprint, Waco: Texian Press, 1974.

Yoakum, H. *History of Texas from Its First Settlement in 1685 to Its Annexation to the United States in 1846*. 2 vols. New York: Redfield, 1855; facsimile, Austin: Steck-Vaughn Co., 1939.

INDEX

www.ingramcontent.com/pod-product-compliance
Ingram Content Group UK Ltd.
Pitfield, Milton Keynes, MK11 3LW, UK
UKHW031842110225
454967UK00001B/38